A Hobbit Journey

DISCOVERING
the ENCHANTMENT *of*
J. R. R. TOLKIEN'S
MIDDLE-EARTH

MATTHEW DICKERSON

BrazosPress

a division of Baker Publishing Group
Grand Rapids, Michigan

© 2012 by Matthew Dickerson

Published by Brazos Press
a division of Baker Publishing Group
P.O. Box 6287, Grand Rapids, MI 49516-6287
www.brazospress.com

Printed in the United States of America

Library of Congress Cataloging-in-Publication Data
Dickerson, Matthew T., 1963–
    A Hobbit journey : discovering the enchantment of J.R.R. Tolkien's Middle-earth
Matthew Dickerson.
        p.   cm.
    Rev. ed. of : Following Gandalf, 2003.
    Includes bibliographical references.
    ISBN 978-1-58743-300-9
    1. Tolkien, J. R. R. (John Ronald Reuel), 1892–1973. Lord of the rings. 2. Epic litera-
ture, English—History and criticism. 3. Fantasy fiction, English—History and criticism.
4. Free will and determinism in literature. 5. Middle Earth (Imaginary place). 6. Battles in
literature. 7. Courage in literature. 8. Ethics in literature. I. Dickerson, Matthew T., 1963–
Following Gandalf. II. Title.
    PR6039.O32L633345 2012
    823'.912—dc23   2012010627

Unless otherwise indicated, Scripture quotations are from the Douay-Rheims Catholic Bible.

Scripture quotations labeled JB are from THE JERUSALEM BIBLE, copyright © 1966 by Darton, Longman & Todd, Ltd. and Doubleday, a division of Random House, Inc. Reprinted by permission.

Scripture quotations labeled NIV are from the Holy Bible, New International Version®. NIV®. Copyright © 1973, 1978, 1984, 2011 by Biblica, Inc.™ Used by permission of Zondervan. All rights reserved worldwide. www.zondervan.com

The internet addresses, email addresses, and phone numbers in this book are accurate at the time of publication. They are provided as a resource. Baker Publishing Group does not endorse them or vouch for their content or permanence.

12   13   14   15   16   17   18   7   6   5   4   3   2   1

To my wife, Deborah, and my sons, Thomas, Mark, and
Peter, who allowed me to read *The Hobbit*, *The Lord
of the Rings* (including some of the appendixes!), and
even *The Silmarillion* as part of family read-aloud.

Contents

Contents

Contents

Acknowledgments

I am grateful to Tom Shippey, who remains at the forefront of Tolkien scholarship, for his many years of indispensible scholarly work that is at once profoundly insightful and very enjoyable to read, and also for his personal encouragement (and occasional suggestions) over the past few years; to several other scholars and writers who, through talks and essays and especially personal conversations, have contributed to my understanding, including Jonathan Evans, Christopher Vaccaro, Charles Taliaferro, Michael Drout, David Bratman, Colin Duriez, Peter Kreeft, Thomas Howard, Sandra Miesel, and Paul Kerry; to literary colleagues at Middlebury College for many other stimulating conversations about Tolkien and related literary topics, especially Professors Kathy Skubikowski, John Elder, and Dan Brayton; to many years of Middlebury College students who have taken my Tolkien classes and made the effort to write insightful papers and engage in class discussions; to numerous readers as well as critics of *Following Gandalf* for their comments; to the late Professor Marion Singleton (of Dartmouth College), to whom I am greatly indebted for her teaching on writing, and literature, and writing about literature, and for investing in me as a person; and finally to my good friend David O'Hara for his friendship over the years, not only for the frequent discussions about philosophy, myth, and literature, but even more for the numerous times when we went fishing instead of discussing philosophy, myth, or literature.

Matthew Dickerson, September 2011

References and Conventions

Citations to works by J. R. R. Tolkien are given parenthetically in the text, using the conventions and abbreviations described here and below. Citations from *The Lord of the Rings* are from the Houghton Mifflin second edition. Because of the many different editions and typesettings of this three-volume work (with different page numberings), references are by volume number and chapter number (rather than by page number), in uppercase and lowercase Roman numerals respectively. Thus the reference "III/iv" refers to volume 3, chapter 4 of *The Lord of the Rings*, a chapter titled "The Siege of Gondor" found in *The Return of the King*. Except where noted, Scripture citations come from the Douay-Rheims Catholic edition commonly in use during the lifetime of Tolkien. All other works (authors other than Tolkien) are cited using endnotes, with a list of sources at the end of the book.

Abbreviations for Works by J. R. R. Tolkien

"Fairy"	"On Fairy-Stories." In *The Monsters and the Critics, and Other Essays*. Edited by Christopher Tolkien. Boston: Houghton Mifflin, 1984.
Foreword	Foreword to *The Lord of the Rings*. 2nd ed. Boston: Houghton Mifflin, 1966.
Hobbit	*The Annotated Hobbit*. Revised and expanded ed., annotated by Douglas A. Anderson. Boston: Houghton Mifflin, 1994.

"Homecoming" "The Homecoming of Beorhtnoth Beorhthelm's Son."
In *The Tolkien Reader*. New York: Ballantine, 1966.

Letters *The Letters of J. R. R. Tolkien*. Selected and edited by
Humphrey Carpenter, with the assistance of Christopher
Tolkien. Boston: Houghton Mifflin, 1981.

"Monsters" "Beowulf: The Monsters and the Critics." In *The Monsters
and the Critics, and Other Essays*. Edited by Christopher
Tolkien. Boston: Houghton Mifflin, 1984.

Morgoth *Morgoth's Ring: The Later Silmarillion, Part One*. Vol. 10
of The History of Middle-Earth. Edited by Christopher
Tolkien. Boston: Houghton Mifflin, 1993.

"Niggle" "Leaf by Niggle." In *Tree and Leaf*, including the poem
"Mythopoeia," with an introduction by Christopher
Tolkien. Boston: Houghton Mifflin, 1989.

Prologue Prologue to *The Lord of the Rings*. 2nd ed. Boston:
Houghton Mifflin, 1966.

Silm *The Silmarillion*. 1st American ed. Boston: Houghton
Mifflin, 1977.

Treason *The Treason of Isengard: The History of the Lord of the
Rings, Part Two*. Edited by Christopher Tolkien. London:
Unwin Hyman, 1989.

A Note on Capitalization

There does not seem to be any standard and consistently used convention for the capitalization of races. My preferred convention is
to capitalize a race (Dwarf, Hobbit, Elf, etc.) only when it is used
to refer to the race as a whole, or to characteristics of that race,
and to leave the word lowercased when referring to any number
of individuals of that race (for example, "the hobbits Merry and
Pippin" or "the hobbits of the Shire"). This convention, however,
is not universally used in Tolkien scholarship, and there are places
in the text where a distinction is difficult to make. For this reason,
I leave lowercased all the following race names: dwarf/dwarves, elf/
elves, goblin/goblins, hobbit/hobbits, orc/orcs, troll/trolls, wizard/
wizards. Of these, only *hobbit* is a linguistic creation of Tolkien.
Though his conception of elves, goblins, trolls, and even dwarves is

unique, these names appear in other earlier literature and Tolkien borrowed something from previous conceptions. As for orcs, they belong to the same race as goblins, and so do not constitute a new race (even if Tolkien's concept of them matured from *The Hobbit* to *The Lord of the Rings*). Likewise, hobbits belong to the race of men and so do not constitute a new race. Only the Ents—though the word *ent* itself, like the word *orc*, can be traced to Old English and Old Norse—are a race entirely of Tolkien's creation. For that reason, and to keep consistent with Tolkien's own usage, Ent/Ents will remain capitalized, along with Entwives and Entings.

Introduction

"Middle-earth," by the way, is not a name of a never-
never land without relation to the world we live in.

J. R. R. Tolkien

Finding Meaning in Fantasy

In October 1958, three years after J. R. R. Tolkien's long labors writing and revising *The Lord of the Rings* had reached fruition with its third and final volume at last in print,[1] the author wrote a long and interesting letter to a fan named Rhona Beare. Miss Beare had posed a series of questions about the languages, history, and cultures of Middle-earth. In his response, Tolkien makes what for some readers may seem a very curious claim: Middle-earth, he explains, is *our own world*, and the tales told in *The Lord of the Rings* are in some sense connected to our own history.

Now Tolkien acknowledges in this letter that the geology of Middle-earth doesn't match in details with the geology of our world. As he tells Miss Beare, he considered trying to make these details fit with greater verisimilitude. Before he thought of attempting this, however, the story had already progressed too far. It would have taken too much time and too much work to rewrite his story in order to make Middle-earth more closely tied physically to our world. Despite these geological dissimilarities, however, Tolkien goes on to explain, "I have, I suppose, constructed an imaginary *time*, but

1

kept my feet on my own mother-earth for *place*." And, dismissing the idea put forth by many reviewers that Middle-earth was some other planet, he adds, in clarification of his point, "Middle-earth is . . . a modernization . . . of an old word for the inhabited world of Men" (*Letters*, 283). What we might say, then, is that Tolkien's great *legendarium*—the corpus of all his stories, legends, and histories of Middle-earth, which many readers and scholars alike consider the preeminent work of *otherworldly* literature—was not about another world at all, but about our world.

Where Is Middle-earth?

This assertion, that Middle-earth is closely connected to our own world and that its stories are indeed a part of our own history, appears frequently in Tolkien's letters. In a letter written in 1955 to help his publisher Houghton Mifflin with publicity, he explains:

> "Middle-earth," by the way, is not a name of a never-never land without relation to the world we live in. . . . It is just a use of Middle English *middel-erde* (or *erthe*), altered from Old English *Middan-geard*: the name for the inhabited lands of Men "between the seas." And though I have not attempted to relate the shape of the mountains and land-masses to what geologists may say or surmise about the nearer past, imaginatively this "history" is supposed to take place in the period of the actual Old World of this planet. (*Letters*, 220)

In a letter to the publishers Allen & Unwin written later in the same year, Tolkien is even more specific, relating the Shire explicitly to England. He claims that the Shire is *not* based on some place near Oxford (as had been suggested), but rather that it "is in fact more or less a Warwickshire village of about the period of the Diamond Jubilee" (*Letters*, 230).[2] Again, a year later, he writes (apparently for his own satisfaction and not as an actual letter to anyone) a rather long response to a W. H. Auden review of *The Return of the King*. In this essay he notes, "I am historically minded. Middle-earth is not an imaginary world. . . . The theatre of my tale is this earth, the one in which we now live, but the historical period is imaginary" (*Letters*, 239). Several paragraphs later he repeats the same point: "Mine is not an 'imaginary' world, but an imaginary historical moment on 'Middle-earth'—which is our habitation" (*Letters*, 244).

These letters are quite clear and direct, and require little comment. It is worth citing one more because of the context, which for Tolkien was not funny at all, although in hindsight it does have a certain humor. In a 1956 letter to Rayner Unwin, Tolkien responds to the decision of a Dutch translator to change the place names in *The Lord of the Rings* in order to make them sound more Dutch. Tolkien objects "*in principle* . . . as strongly as is possible to the 'translation' of the *nomenclature* at all (even by a competent person)" (*Letters*, 249–50). The reason he gives for this strong reaction is very interesting.

> "The Shire" is based on rural England and not any other country in the world—least perhaps of any in Europe on Holland, which is topographically wholly dissimilar. (In fact so different is it, that in spite of the affinity of its language, and in many respects of its idiom, which should ease some part of the translator's labour, its *toponymy* is specially unsuitable for the purpose.) The toponymy of *The Shire*, to take the first list, is a "parody" of that of rural England, in much the same sense as are its inhabitants; they go together and are meant to. After all the book is English, and by an Englishman, and presumably even those who wish its narrative and dialogue turned into an idiom that they understand, will not ask of a translator that he should deliberately attempt to destroy the local colour. (*Letters*, 250)

Tolkien's critique of the translator is strong, bordering on scathing. He seems to be questioning not only the translator's competence but even his motives, suggesting that the translator was *deliberately* attempting to destroy the sense of the Englishness of the hobbits and the Shire. The point of citing the passage, though, is the reasoning behind Tolkien's critique: that the Shire was meant to portray rural England and its people.

At this point it is fair to ask just what Tolkien might mean in suggesting that Middle-earth is really our own world. It is certainly not our world geographically or geologically. Not exactly anyway, though neither is it without some relationship. The Shire, like the England it represents, lies in the northwestern part of the great continent of Middle-earth and has a landscape and climate similar to that of England; the coastal kingdom of Gondor sits far to the south and east, past a range of mountains, in geographic relation to the Shire very much like ancient Rome (on the southern end of the Alps) sat in distant relation to ancient Briton.[3] Still, as Tolkien notes above, the geologic dissimilarities are difficult to ignore, not the least of which is that the Shire is not an island.

Neither does Tolkien's history of Middle-earth correspond in detail with the actual history of Europe (or any other place on earth). He certainly did not intend his books to be read literally as history of our world. Indeed, *The Lord of the Rings* can't even be said to take place in any one particular period of our history—not in the sense that a "realistic" historical novel would. Rohan, at the end of the Third Age of Middle-earth, is certainly inspired by Anglo-Saxon England during the second half of the first millennium AD. And I believe that Gondor is in some way drawn from the late Roman Empire. If we define "Old World" broadly enough, these two Middle-earth kingdoms thus might be seen as belonging to the same "Old World of this planet" as Tolkien noted. But the Shire, coexisting with these two kingdoms at the end of the Third Age, is drawn from late nineteenth-century England; to Tolkien it was not in any sense the "Old World" but rather was very close to his modern day. Thus the *time* in which Tolkien's stories are set really is imaginary.

If we suggest a cultural and especially a literary connection between Middle-earth and our world, then the relation is much closer. For example, both the language and literature of the land of Rohan in Middle-earth are heavily drawn from the Old English language and literature of Anglo-Saxon England (as we will explore later in this book). And, at a deeper level, which has been pointed out so carefully and insightfully by Tom Shippey in both *The Road to Middle-earth* and *J. R. R. Tolkien: Author of the Century*, so much of Tolkien's Middle-earth world was drawn from names, words, hints of words, and stories found in the medieval literature of the north, including Icelandic and Finnish literary sources as well as Old English ones.

But perhaps the deepest connection that exists between Tolkien's Middle-earth and this world of men in which we live—the most profound way in which he kept his feet on his own mother-earth, and in which Middle-earth is *not* without relation to the world we live in—is philosophical. Tolkien's Middle-earth *legendarium* incarnates a particular philosophy or worldview. It is based on implicit answers to certain questions. What is the meaning of life? What constitutes a good life? How should we act? What is true? How do we know what is true?

Of course the works rarely *preach* that philosophy in any direct way. They are not didactic. Yet Tolkien's philosophy permeates his works like the flavor of a stew permeates all its ingredients. Indeed, this is true not only of Tolkien's works but of all literature: a work of literature always reflects the philosophy of its author. As philosopher Peter Kreeft has noted, "All literature incarnates some philosophy."[4] Kreeft wrote this in a book that was explicitly about the philosophy of Tolkien—or the "worldview behind *The Lord of the Rings*," as he describes it in the subtitle. And quoting C. S. Lewis, he argues earlier that fantastic literature may be particularly good at bringing philosophies to life: "The value of the myth is that it takes all the things we know and restores to them the rich significance which had been hidden by 'the veil of familiarity.' . . . By putting bread, gold, horse, apple, or the very roads into a myth, we do not retreat from reality: we rediscover it. As long as the story lingers in our mind, the real things are more themselves."[5]

Which brings us back to the connection between Tolkien's created world and the world we live in. The most profound ideas that permeate Tolkien's world of Middle-earth are drawn from, and are applicable to, our world. The important truths of Middle-earth, Tolkien believed, are also the important truths of our world. Or to explore this from another angle, Tolkien's *fictional* characters are in some important way *real* people, or are drawn from real human nature. They live out or encounter the profoundest of human experiences and emotions, choices and challenges. When we read Tolkien's books, we look in a mirror. What we see in Tolkien's characters is ourselves. What we see in his world is our world. It is not a never-never land.

This is especially true of hobbits, despite their diminutive size. And that leads me to a central point of this book.

The Making of Books

The author of Ecclesiastes knew of what he spoke when he wrote, "Of making many books there is no end" (12:12 NIV).[6] It is rather stunning to think that he wrote those words well over two millennia ago, before the existence of the printing press, the big box bookstore, or the online superstore. Yet to say that the words of Ecclesiastes are just as true today as when they were written would be a grave understatement.

The writing of many books is certainly evident in the field of Tolkien studies and more broadly in the popular culture surrounding Tolkien's works. Concerning Tolkien's friend and fellow fantasy writer C. S. Lewis, who for some time was also Tolkien's fellow scholar at Oxford, Alan Jacobs laments in his book *The Narnian*, "Long ago the writers of books and articles concerning 'What C. S. Lewis Thought About X' ran out of subjects and began to write books and articles concerning 'What C. S. Lewis *Would* Have Thought About X if He Had Lived Long Enough to See It.'"[7] The situation might not be expected to be quite as bad in Tolkien's case because he did not write and publish nearly as much nonfiction as did Lewis, and the little he did publish was not about philosophy and theology but was almost exclusively in his academic fields of philology and Old English language and literature. Unfortunately, for precisely that same reason,[8] and perhaps also because Tolkien's fantasy novels have sold more copies and reached an even broader audience than those of his friend, the situation with Tolkien studies might actually be worse.

Certainly I bear some guilt in the proliferation of books, though hopefully not with respect to the specific critique leveled by Jacobs. This book, which is an expanded and updated edition of my 2003 title, *Following Gandalf: Epic Battles and Moral Victory in "The Lord of the Rings,"* is now the fourth I have authored or coauthored exploring Tolkien's writing, and I have contributed essays (or book chapters) about Tolkien's writing to several other books.[9] Nonetheless, I believe there are at least five appealing and important motivations to continue studying and writing about the works of the late Oxford professor, and in particular for investing more time in this book.

The first, and for me the most significant, is in some ways quite selfish: writing about Tolkien means I can continue to read and enjoy *his* writing. *The Hobbit*, *The Lord of the Rings*, and many of the posthumously published tales in his Middle-earth *legendarium* were written as stories and are intended first and foremost to be *enjoyed*. Writing about them in a scholarly way, then, for me always involves returning to the books and entering into them and enjoying them as stories—or, rather, as story: as one continuous tale with many smaller parts, if we follow the thinking of Sam and Frodo in their dialogue on the Stairs of Cirith Ungol at the end of the Third Age of Middle-earth, when they connect their part of the tale to that of Beren, the great hero of the First Age.[10] Not that I need any excuse to return to these great works of literature. But I will take the excuse offered. I often find that when I turn to some particular passage to study it and write about it, I once again get caught up in the narrative and end up reading many pages (or chapters) beyond what I "need" to read. This is both the delight of the venture and—when I need to be "productive" or meet some deadline—the danger. It is also a delight and danger I hope to share, and in that way it is not selfish at all. I hope that in reading this book my readers will be inspired to return to Tolkien's works and delve into them once again, perhaps with new insights, new questions, or just a deeper appreciation. If I succeed in this, then I consider the book worthwhile, whatever else it does or does not accomplish.

A second motivation, or feature, of Tolkien scholarship that makes the pursuit not only interesting but worthwhile and productive is that Tolkien himself was a scholar—a scholar, in fact, of the very pieces of medieval literature that were important sources and inspirations for his own work and indeed were much the same sort of works that he was writing, though from an earlier era. Although Tolkien published only a small number of essays on Old English language and literature, and one essay on myth and fantasy literature in general, those essays were deeply illuminating and influential, especially "Beowulf: The Monsters and the Critics" and "On Fairy-Stories." One might disagree with Tolkien's observations or conclusions expressed in those essays—and many scholars have—but these essays provide valuable insights into what he was seeking to accomplish in his fiction and how he thought that sort of writing should be approached. In addition to these essays, he also wrote many letters in which he discusses his own works.[11]

Added to these insightful and polished essays and his personal letters, the numerous posthumously published volumes of the histories of Middle-earth (containing what are sometimes less polished earlier versions of important stories), edited by Tolkien's son Christopher, also provide new and fresh ideas about the development of Tolkien's thinking as well as the development of his myths and narratives themselves. And the Raynor Memorial Library at Marquette University houses an extensive collection of early-draft editions of Tolkien's works (mostly unpublished) that scholars and interested parties can mine for further insights—in addition to an extensive collection of secondary scholarship. So we have a more solid ground not just for enjoying Tolkien's works but for trying to understand them in the light of his own ideas.

A third and related motivation, not only for writing about Tolkien in general but specifically for revisiting my previous published work (*Following Gandalf*) in order to revise and update it, is that there continues to be new material to draw on (perhaps prompted by similar motivations that brought about this book). This includes both previously unpublished source material from Tolkien himself and new and perceptive secondary scholarship.[12] In terms of the former, the years since my earlier book's publication have seen the publication of both *The Children of Húrin* (2007), a version of one of the two longest and most important tales from the First Age of Middle-earth, and *The Legend of Sigurd and Gudrun* (2009), Tolkien's retelling of one of the important Norse legends that so inspired him.

Much helpful new secondary scholarship has been recently published. Douglas Anderson, who earlier had done a wonderful job providing insights and information in the annotations of *The Annotated Hobbit* (2002), has since contributed to and edited the volumes *Tales before Tolkien: The Roots of Modern Fantasy* (2005), which presents and comments on important source material for Tolkien, and *Tolkien on Fairy-Stories* (2008), which presents Tolkien's own essay with a scholarly but readable introduction and commentary. Another Tolkien scholar, Michael Drout, who edited the important 2002 contribution *Beowulf and the Critics* (bringing into print a previously unpublished, earlier, longer, and in some ways more readable version of Tolkien's important essay "Beowulf: The Monsters and the Critics"), undertook the daunting task of putting together the seminal and remarkably thorough *J. R. R. Tolkien Encyclopedia: Scholarship and Critical Assessment*, which was published in 2006 and has contributions from many of the world's most respected Tolkien scholars.

Whereas many scholars dealt only briefly in the past with specific aspects of Tolkien's writing, such as its environmental or ecological components, recent works have offered more in-depth and well-deserved scholarly treatment of these aspects of his writing, as evidenced in my 2006 publication *Ents, Elves, and Eriador: The Environmental Vision of J. R. R. Tolkien* coauthored with Jonathan Evans. Still other recent books have brought to light significant new aspects of, or insights into, the importance of Tolkien's relationships with Lewis and the group of writers known as the Inklings. Diana Glyer's 2008 book, *The Company They Keep: C. S. Lewis and J. R. R. Tolkien as Writers in Community*, is particularly notable and thoughtful. Also worthy of mention are several other new and helpful books exploring spiritual and theological aspects of Tolkien's writing, including *The Ring and the Cross: Christianity and "The Lord of the Rings"* (2010, edited by Paul E. Kerry) and a companion volume, *Light beyond All Shadows: Religious Experience in Tolkien's Work* (2011, edited by Paul E. Kerry and Sandra Miesel). These arrived at my house in the final weeks of my work on this book and yet quickly proved insightful enough to find their way into my own writing.

This is only a small sample of the recent books on Tolkien. It would take pages to include several years' worth of journal articles and conference papers. Consider the important creation of the journal *Tolkien Studies*, started by founding editors Drout, Anderson, and Verlyn Flieger in 2004 (the year after *Following Gandalf* was first published). Indeed, the problem is not a lack of material but that there is too much to keep up with.

The fourth and fifth motivations for continued study of Tolkien's writings are closely related to each other. The fourth is that Tolkien's original works continue to yield new insights with each rereading. As philosopher Peter Kreeft wrote more than thirty years ago about *The Silmarillion*, "It is a bottomless well of Wonder. It rewards endless rereading. Like a Great Cow, it gives fresh milk every time: you never milk it dry."[13] The same is true of *The Lord of the Rings* and even *The Hobbit*. Frequent rereadings are continuously rewarding and illuminating. Thus it is also true that there is still much more

9

that can be said about Tolkien and his writing—much that is both interesting and significant. I, at least, continue to learn more about Tolkien and his writing, understand his works better, and have new perceptions worth sharing.

This brings us to the fifth and final motivation, the one that relates most closely to the start of this introduction: Tolkien's works remain not only enjoyable but also relevant to our times. For me, this is probably the most important reason for publishing what I would otherwise keep as my own private explorations and reflections. The ideas, insights, and inspiration that may be gained from a reading of these works are as relevant to today's issues and culture as they were roughly a century ago when Tolkien first began writing the stories that would become *The Silmarillion*, or three quarters of a century ago when *The Hobbit* was first published, or half a century ago when readers first enjoyed the continuing story of the Great Ring in the three-volume book known as *The Lord of the Rings*.

As one example of the continued relevance of Tolkien's writings, we need look no further than the first chapter of this book, which explores the practices of various persons and races of Middle-earth with regard to the treatment of prisoners. In particular, what do Tolkien's stories suggest regarding the practice of torture and whether it is, or is not, considered justified in times of war? This is not a peripheral question, although it may at first seem like one. The treatment of prisoners turns out to be a significant and recurring theme in Tolkien's works, and it relates directly to many of the most central themes.

The question of torture remains relevant to the world today and will continue to be so as long as there is war. It was brought again to the forefront of our national consciousness not long after the events of 9/11. The US government's treatment of prisoners in Guantanamo Bay has received considerable attention (though perhaps not enough); "water-boarding" became almost a household word. Even as I write this chapter, a former CIA operative has come forward with the claim that he was involved in torturing terror suspects in secret foreign prisons under orders from the US government, and that the techniques of torture were worse than the water-boarding practices of Guantanamo.[14] Whether one agrees with the answers presented by the wise of Middle-earth, it is difficult to argue that the questions are not important. Tolkien's writings have much to say to our present day. As we said earlier, Tolkien's world is *our* world.

Allegory and Applicability

Indeed, the treatment of prisoners during war is only one of many broader issues of social justice that surface in Tolkien's writing. Yet the moment one starts looking for "principles" or "answers" or "applications" in a work of fiction—especially in a work of fantasy—some warning flags ought to go up. Isn't any such effort bound to turn a story into a sermon, or a myth into an allegory? To ask this in another way, isn't there some inherent tension between my first motivation above, the *enjoyment* of a good story as a story, and my fourth and fifth motivations, which relate to the ideas incarnate in a story and the relevance of those ideas? Can one enjoy a story *as story* while simultaneously trying to explore it for relevant applications?

This last question is a big one. It could easily require a book, or many books, to answer. And no answer would satisfy everyone. Nonetheless, a few words about my own approach to this question are in order, if for no other reason than to let potential readers know whether to read this book.[15] Here Tolkien's own reflections on mythopoeic and fantasy literature and on his Middle-earth writings are our best guide. What did Tolkien suggest about how—or even *whether*—one might approach fantasy literature with any sort of scholarly lens? If you take his critical nonfiction writing seriously, does that encourage or discourage a careful study of his fiction and a search for its meaning?

One obvious place to start is with a cautionary note. Tolkien himself is known for disliking allegory and being suspicious of reading meanings *into* a story. In the now famous foreword to the second edition of *The Lord of the Rings*, he writes, "As for any inner meaning or 'message,' it has in the intention of the author none. It is neither allegory nor topical." He then goes on to make an even stronger statement: "I cordially dislike allegory in all its manifestations, and always have done so since I grew old and wary enough to detect its presence." Earlier in the foreword, he also claimed that his "prime motive" was just "the desire of a tale-teller to try his hand at a really long story that would hold the attention of readers, amuse them, delight them, and at times maybe excite them or deeply move them" (Foreword).

Now a statement such as this might discourage some from trying to find any meaning at all in Tolkien's fiction. Certainly we should be dissuaded from trying to reduce *The Lord of the Rings* to any one particular message or lesson, or to a disguised (or ill-disguised) tract on some political, religious, or philosophical topic—or to an allegory. Doing so, as Tolkien argues, would miss the story as story. At the very least, I am inclined to take at face value his statement regarding his prime motive. He certainly succeeded admirably at it. If there are two possible opposite errors, one of which is to look for no meaning at all and the other is to force into the story some meaning that is not there, I think the former error (if it is an error) is the less dangerous of the two. Indeed, in his famous essay on the poem *Beowulf*, Tolkien describes with strong language the error of a certain type of overly analytic analysis.

> The significance of a myth is not easily to be pinned on paper by analytical reasoning. It is at its best when it is presented by a poet who feels rather than makes explicit what his theme portends; who presents it incarnate in the world of history and geography, as [the poet of *Beowulf*] has done. Its defender is thus at a disadvantage: unless he is careful, and speaks in parables, he will kill what he is studying by vivisection, and he will be left with a formal or mechanical allegory, and, what is more, probably with one that will not work. For myth is alive at once and in all its parts, and dies before it can be dissected. ("Monsters," 15)

Note that Tolkien does not say here that we cannot understand the meaning of myths. But he says something close. It is difficult to pin down the significance of a myth, at least analytically. The best way to get across that significance, or to convey some theme, he argues, is not to make it explicit, but to incarnate it in poetry—or in story. It is possible to kill a myth by vivisection in an attempt to analyze it.

And yet, we must ask, how strongly did Tolkien intend his warnings—either in his foreword or in the essay on *Beowulf*—to be taken? Or, rather, in what light were they intended? Even in the above passage, Tolkien does not say that the analysis should not or cannot be done. What he says is that it must be done carefully, with respect to the myth as a whole, and especially without a sort of reductionism that turns it all into some narrow formal allegory. Consider that Tolkien himself writes about the meanings and themes of the great works of literature he loved. His essay "The Homecoming of Beorhtnoth Beorhthelm's Son" is a wonderful example in which he argues carefully about the meaning of three different medieval heroic poems and what he thought the poets were trying to convey in them. The ideas Tolkien finds in these poems clearly bear on what it means to be a leader, a servant, or a hero.

In many other places, as well, Tolkien describes in great detail the underlying truths that can be found in fantasy literature. He speaks also of the importance of fantasy literature being *applicable*. Certainly he believed that the medieval literature he loved, and the fantasy literature he wrote, had meaning. Moreover, and more importantly, he claims that this meaning is not merely subjective. That is, the meaning of the stories is inherent in the stories themselves, not just in the readers' approach to the stories. After all, if the meanings of the stories were merely subjective, and if all possible interpretations of any readers were equally valid, then Tolkien would have had no place to argue *against* some of the particular meanings or allegorical interpretations that were suggested with respect to his own work. Thus Tolkien doesn't argue that one should not suggest meanings in his work but rather that the *particular* meanings suggested by *certain* readers were the *wrong* meanings.

In fact, Tolkien frequently wrote about meaning, truth, and applicability in fantasy literature, including his own. In the foreword cited above, for example, although he rejects a strictly allegorical interpretation of *The Lord of the Rings*, he goes on to write: "I much prefer history, true or feigned, with its varied applicability to the thought and experience of readers. I think that many confuse 'applicability' with 'allegory'; but the one resides in the freedom of the reader, and the other in the purposed domination of the author" (Foreword). Certainly, having individual readers apply ideas or lessons to their own lives, in free and varied ways—subjective ways, we might suggest—is a very different thing from having a scholar present a particular supposedly "correct" interpretation of a piece of writing. But Tolkien's words at least suggest that there is no fundamental disconnect between the feigned history of his fantasy world and the real history of our own world. Readers might be inspired to apply in their own lives those principles seen in the lives of the heroes of Tolkien's tales—principles, for example, of how one ought to treat a prisoner during times of war. And this can lead us to ask what those principles are.

If we move beyond the trilogy's foreword to Tolkien's essays and to some of his personal letters, we find that his words about the possibility and even necessity of fantasy literature containing a reflection of the truths of our world, including philosophical and religious truth, are often clearer and stronger. He goes so far as to concede that even allegorical interpretations of a certain type may be both possible and helpful. In a famous letter, written in 1951 to Milton Waldman, while in one breath he affirms his "dislike" for "conscious and intentional allegory," he goes on to note that "the more 'life' a story has the more readily will it be susceptible of allegorical interpretations: while the better a deliberate allegory is made the more nearly will it be acceptable just as a story" (*Letters*, 145). In other words, it is not when stories are dead that they begin to have specific interpretations but rather when they are really full of life. He then goes on in that letter to suggest what his own work is actually about. And again, in 1955, in a letter to his friend, the great poet W. H. Auden, Tolkien acknowledges the validity of readers interpreting his works while also suggesting that some of the interpretations are wrong.

> What appreciative readers have got out of the work or seen in it has seemed fair enough, even when I do not agree with it. Always excepting, of course, any "interpretations" in the mode of simple allegory: that is, the particular and topical. In a larger sense, it is I suppose impossible to write any "story" that is not allegorical in proportion as it "comes to life"; since each of us is an allegory, embodying in a particular tale and clothed in the garments of time and place, universal truth and everlasting life. (*Letters*, 212)

Tolkien, while denying certain "particular and topical" allegorical interpretations of his work, yet again acknowledges not only that some sort of allegorical interpretation is actually valid but that it is indeed *inevitable* if the story "comes to life" at all. Stories, he claims, embody universal truths. They wrap, in the particulars of the time and place of one tale, principles that are eternally true. That's a powerful statement, and it invites us to ask what those truths are.

Tolkien repeats this sort of discussion several times, adamantly denying narrow allegorical meaning of his works, yet at the same time acknowledging that his works convey important truths—indeed, that they are even *meant* to convey important ideas he believed to be true, and not just true within Middle-earth, but true in our world. Because, to again echo Tolkien's often-repeated claim, Middle-earth *is* our world. In a letter written in 1956—a letter in which, incidentally, he mentions the practice of torture during war—Tolkien comments:

> [*The Lord of the Rings*] is a "fairy-story," but one written—according to the belief I once expressed in an extended essay "On Fairy-stories" that they are the proper audience—for adults. Because I think that fairy story has its own mode of reflecting "truth," different from allegory, or (sustained) satire, or "realism," and in some ways more powerful. But first of all it must succeed just as a tale, excite, please, and even on occasion move, and within its own imagined world be accorded (literary) belief. To succeed in that was my primary object.
>
> But, of course, if one sets out to address "adults" (mentally adult people anyway), they will not be pleased, excited, or moved unless the whole, or the incidents, seem to be about something worth considering, more e.g., than mere danger and escape: there must be some relevance to the "human situation" (of all periods). So something of the teller's own reflections and "values" will inevitably get worked in. (*Letters*, 232–33)

Tolkien again affirms that fantasy stories must succeed as stories. They must be enjoyable and captivating. But Tolkien says more than this here. He speaks of fairy stories as "reflecting truth." He even claims, as he does in the referenced essay, that it is precisely in this task of reflecting truth that fairy tales are "more powerful" than some other forms of story. He also points out that fairy stories must be about something important. They must have ideas worth reflecting on. They must be relevant to our lives. Indeed, I believe it is the very relevance of Tolkien's stories—their lasting relevance—that, as much as any other feature of the tales, has made them as powerful and appealing as they are. One might say that their relevance is as important to their appeal as is their beauty, but I would say instead that their relevance is a significant and inseparable part of their beauty.

And finally, Tolkien also explicitly acknowledges that his own values and beliefs are of necessity "worked in" to the tale. Indeed, he says something even stronger in a letter written in 1958 to a fan. While stating his desire not to "preach" or to express "overtly" what he believes to be theological and religious truth, he nonetheless acknowledges that *The Lord of the Rings* is "merely an imaginative invention, to express, in the only way I can, some of my (dim) apprehensions of the world," and then goes on to say, "I have *deliberately* written a tale, which is built on or out of certain 'religious' ideas, but is *not* an allegory of them (or anything else)" (*Letters*, 283–84, emphasis added). Not only is it natural, then, to ask what those values, beliefs, apprehensions (or understandings), and religious ideas are, but we should also expect to find those ideas incarnate *in the tale*.

We could go on citing passages from Tolkien's letters reinforcing these ideas,[16] but perhaps one more will suffice. He wrote the following to his potential publisher Stanley Unwin in July of 1947, about an early draft of *The Lord of the Rings*, which Unwin had given to his son Rayner to read:

> Do not let Rayner suspect "Allegory." There is a "moral," I suppose, in any tale worth telling. But that is not the same thing. . . . Of course, Allegory and Story converge, meeting somewhere in Truth. . . . You can make the Ring into an allegory of our own time, if you like: an allegory of the inevitable fate that waits for all attempts to defeat evil power by power. But that is only because all power magical or mechanical does always so work. You cannot write a story about an apparently simple magic ring without that bursting in, if you really take the ring seriously, and make things happen that would happen, if such a thing existed. (*Letters*, 121)

Again, Tolkien affirms the presence of truth in his story, though the story is not allegory. He goes on to speak of one specific truth about the nature of evil and the desire for power (mechanical or magical) reflected in his portrayal of the Ring, and he argues that this is an objective and universal truth: *all* power *always* works this way. And he again acknowledges that truths like this cannot help but come into a good story.

Tolkien sums up some of these ideas in a more polished form in his published essay "On Fairy-Stories." In the essay he writes, "Probably every writer making a secondary world, a fantasy, . . . hopes that he is drawing on reality: hopes that the peculiar quality of this secondary world (if not all the details) are derived from Reality or are flowing into it." He goes on, then, just a couple of sentences later to add, "The peculiar quality of the 'joy' in successful Fantasy can thus be explained as a sudden glimpse of the underlying reality or truth" ("Fairy," 64).

This book explores some of those truths that can be glimpsed in Tolkien's very successful works of fantasy literature. They are truths that are as applicable today as when Tolkien lived and wrote. The central question this book addresses is, What can we learn from hobbits and from their vision of the Good Life, and how does that apply to our own present situation? In particular, we will look at the hobbitish pursuit and practice of peace, even in the midst of a world at war. And we will start with the question of what actions war does or does not justify.

1

On Hobbits, the Treatment of Prisoners, and the Ethics of War

> "The Wood-elves have him in prison, but they treat him with such kindness as they can find in their wise hearts."
>
> —Gandalf (speaking about Sméagol)

Since *The Hobbit* was first published in 1937, various estimates for sales of J. R. R. Tolkien's classic work about the adventures of Bilbo Baggins range from a minimum of 35 million copies to as many as 100 million. And these figures do not count sales of *The Lord of the Rings* or *The Silmarillion* or any of Tolkien's other posthumously published works set in Middle-earth. Tom Shippey, in his book *J. R. R. Tolkien: Author of the Century*, sets total sales for the three books in *The Lord of the Rings* at approximately 150 million copies.[1] And that was *before* the phenomenally successful release of Peter Jackson's film adaptation, which gave yet another boost to the sales of books that have remained continuously in print for over half a century. Peter Jackson's two new films about *The Hobbit*, set for release in 2012 and 2013, will only increase Tolkien's legacy.

The films will also increase the worldwide influence of Tolkien's works, which is already astounding. *The Hobbit* has been translated into more than forty languages, and as Shippey has also pointed out, *The Lord of the Rings* has consistently been rated the greatest book of the twentieth century (hence the appropriate title of Shippey's own book).[2] Tolkien's influence includes not only superficial aspects—naming pets, children, restaurants, farms, and inns after characters and places in Middle-earth; going to festivals dressed as hobbits and elves; learning to speak and write in elvish languages and scripts—but also more profound, if rarer, elements. For example, there are some who directly imitate, or are at least consciously inspired by, the agricultural practices of the hobbits. Others seek to model the conservation practices of Ents and elves. Tolkien scholar Jarred Lobdell, after noting that "certainly the forests are the heart of Tolkien's world," goes on to make the connection to modern practices: "If there is one thing more than another that has distinguished the last forty years from the time before, most especially in the United States, it is the growth of a generation that loved trees."[3] Noted nature writer John Elder has made a more personal claim: "I do not take up my hiking stick and follow a trail through the woods without remembering the quests of Frodo and his Fellowship of the Ring."[4]

Tolkien's stories have also provided numerous heroes that we seek to imitate, from Bilbo and Frodo Baggins to Aragorn Elessar Telcontar the Strider, to the elf Legolas, to even the lowly gardener-turned-mayor Samwise Gamgee. Sometimes jokingly—but at other times perhaps seriously—we may even be tempted to ask, WWBD? That is, what would Bilbo do? Or, if we are up for a greater challenge, WWFD: What would Frodo do?

Now at one level, that phrase makes me cringe. The specific context of the discussion doesn't even matter; raising that sort of question about a fictional character risks many dangers. It risks trivializing an important moral or ethical issue about the real world. And it also risks trivializing a work of literature by turning it into a sermon or moral tract.

And yet, at another level—if the person who asks avoids a trite or clichéd response—the question can invite one to a closer pondering of a great work of literature. If we agree with any of Tolkien's own ideas about meaning in fantasy literature, then we are invited to ponder not only the meanings of his own tales but also how those meanings are relevant to our lives. Avoiding the temptation to allegorize, we still may—and indeed must—ask about applicability. Middle-earth is our world.

Consider the question of the ethics of warfare, and in particular the treatment of prisoners during the time of war. I do not know of anybody who would attempt to argue that it is ethically acceptable to torture prisoners (or anybody else) merely for the "pleasure" of torture—although, sadly, some historical figures have practiced torture as a sort of sadistic fun. But is it ethical to torture prisoners in order to gain knowledge?[5] In particular, if a prisoner is suspected of having some knowledge of an impending attack, is it ethically justifiable to use any means possible, including inflicting pain or bodily harm, in order to extract this knowledge? What if the information held by the prisoner could be used to prevent an attack and thus save lives? And what if the prisoner is guilty of some crime?

These are pressing questions that will remain relevant as long as there is war. The torture of prisoners has been a widespread practice throughout history. In the little more than a decade since the terrorist attacks of 9/11, the United States has been embroiled in controversy over the practice of torturing suspected terrorists. Guantanamo Bay, on the island of Cuba, where the United States detains suspected terrorists, became famous worldwide in part because of the treatment and suspected torture of prisoners there, and the term *waterboarding*—which I had never heard prior to the Guantanamo Bay controversy—has entered our national lexicon as a result.

One argument against the torture of prisoners for the sake of gaining information is that we can never be completely sure that the prisoner being tortured actually possesses that information; we may be torturing either an innocent prisoner or at the very least a prisoner incapable of providing the information for which he or she is being tortured. One rejoinder to this objection raises the question, But what if we could be positive beyond a shadow of doubt that the prisoner not only is guilty of some crime (say, of terrorism) but also possesses vital information about *future* crimes? And furthermore, what if the information obtained through the torture of one

21

prisoner might save countless lives? Doesn't the saving of thousands or hundreds or even dozens of innocent lives justify the torture of one guilty prisoner?

As with many important questions and concerns, some underlying principles and even specific explorations relevant to the issue of prisoner torture can be found in Tolkien's *legendarium*, especially in *The Lord of the Rings*.

Principles of Ethics in Warfare

Before looking at the specific question of prisoner torture, it is worth reviewing some broader ethical principles illustrated throughout Tolkien's work. One of the most basic ethical principles practiced by the wise of Middle-earth is that it is never acceptable to defeat an enemy, no matter how cruel that enemy is, by resorting to the cruel practices of the enemy. Evil means will not defeat evil; if you overthrow Sauron by becoming Sauron then you haven't really won a victory.[6]

The principle is probably most clearly seen in the response of the wise to the temptation of the Ring. One of the fundamental examples of this response is the understanding of the wise that they must not use the Ring in order to defeat Sauron. One wise character after another—Gandalf, Elrond, Aragorn, Galadriel, and even Faramir—all refuse the Ring because they understand it will turn them into another Sauron. Galadriel refuses it even as her only hope to save Lothlórien. Gandalf says that *only* the use of the Ring would guarantee a victory over Sauron, yet he refuses the Ring anyway and counsels all others to refuse it also.

That Sauron himself does not understand this—in other words, that this is a principle associated with good rather than with evil—is illustrated in the fact that the hopeless (or "fool's hope") strategy of destroying the Ring actually succeeds. Sauron cannot imagine that his enemy will *not* try to defeat him by using his own weapon against him. That evil cannot comprehend this strategy illustrates that it is a good strategy.

This principle also stands behind many remarks and comments made by the wise. Faramir, when accused by Frodo of being deceitful, replies, "I would not even snare an orc with a falsehood" (IV/v). Frodo, after the hobbits have ousted Saruman's lackeys from the Shire and finally found the wizard himself, refuses to "meet revenge with revenge" (VI/viii), despite all the evil that Saruman has done. This idea is repeated in so many ways, at so many times, and by so many characters in *The Lord of the Rings* that it must be centrally important to the author. One cannot accomplish good ends by the use of evil means; ends do not justify means. Or, put another way, evil means and devices will lead to evil ends.

Stratford Caldecott does an excellent job, in his book *Secret Fire: The Spiritual Vision of J. R. R. Tolkien*, of exploring this aspect of Tolkien's work. He writes, "Yet the real danger is not that the free world might be defeated; it is that we might be corrupted, brutalized and degraded by the conflict itself, and in particular by the means employed to secure victory." Caldecott explains this more fully, summarizing this theme in Tolkien's works and citing one of Tolkien's own letters that compares the wars of the Third Age of Middle-earth to World War II: "Our mistake in the great wars of our own time has been to accept the false idea that the end justifies the means, and that 'if a thing can be done, it must be done.' For, as Tolkien wrote to his son in 1944, the Allies were attempting to defeat Sauron by using the Ring. The penalty would be to breed new Saurons, and to turn Men and Elves into Orcs."[7] This principle, explored in Tolkien's works and explained by Caldecott, could be applied to many practices of war, including of course the practice of torture.

This whole discussion, however, raises the question of whether torture is, inherently, a device of evil. And here I must define what I mean by the word *torture*, since it can have both a narrow and a broad meaning. I mean by torture simply the intentional inflicting of pain, injury, or bodily harm on a prisoner unable to defend himself or herself (as opposed to inflicting bodily harm on an armed opponent in the course of battle). I certainly acknowledge that psychological actions, including the threat of pain, death, or bodily injury, could be equally harmful—or equally *torturous*—and perhaps the same moral principles that are explored below could be examined with respect to psychological torture. Yet psychological harm may be somewhat more difficult to identify than physical harm. Also, with respect to the issue of the threat of harm, it is arguable that such threat holds little coercive value until the inquisitor has proven the willingness to inflict actual harm. In other words, physical and psychological torture tend to go hand in hand, and so we will focus only on the former.

Now it is certainly possible that one could agree with the moral principle suggested above by Caldecott, that war itself does not justify use of the *evil* devices of the enemy (like the One Ring), and yet simultaneously argue that torture itself is not fundamentally evil. By way of illustration, consider the use of swords (or any other physical weapons). Orcs use swords. So do the Southrons who are in service of Sauron and attack Minas Tirith. So also do the men of Minas Tirith, the Riders of Rohan, Aragorn, Gandalf, and even the hobbits (though at the end of the tale Frodo alone completely eschews even the use of the sword). Using a sword to defend Minas Tirith almost certainly does not fall under the category of defeating the enemy by using the enemy's own devices. Does torture fall into the category of the Ring: an evil device or weapon of the enemy that ought not be used under any circumstance, even in trying to defeat the enemy? Or, in Tolkien's moral structure of Middle-earth, is the practice of torture in order to extract important information from a prisoner something more like a sword: something that is not inherently evil and can be used by (and for) good and evil alike?

Torture by the Enemy

One starting point is to look for examples of the treatment of prisoners in Tolkien's creative works and see how the author treats the subject of torture. Given that Tolkien lived through the two world wars, that he fought on foreign soil in the first of these, and his son Christopher served in the British Royal Air Force (RAF) in the second, it is perhaps not surprising that his books would contain some mention of the treatment of prisoners. What might be surprising is just how many examples there are.

Our first observation is that the enemy (Sauron and Saruman in the Third Age of Middle-earth and Morgoth and Sauron in the First Age) and the servants of the enemy (most notably orcs) do torture their prisoners. Specifically, they practice torture in order to gain information from prisoners (though readers are led to believe that they torture prisoners for fun and sport). There are numerous cases of this. One early reference to torture in *The Lord of the Rings* is Gandalf's description at the Council of Elrond of his own treatment at the hands of Saruman. Gandalf was a prisoner in Orthanc, and Saruman was trying to extract from him information about the location of the Ring. As Gandalf recounts it, Saruman gave him an ultimatum: "I gave you the chance of aiding me willingly, and so saving yourself much trouble and pain. The third choice is to stay here, until the end. . . . Until you reveal to me where the One may be found. I may find means to persuade you" (II/ii). It is clear that Saruman is trying to gain information from Gandalf—information that Gandalf does indeed have about the whereabouts of the Ring. Exactly what means or devices Saruman intends to use to "persuade" Gandalf are left to readers' imaginations—piercing cold and solitary confinement are only the first means—but the text makes it clear that Saruman is willing to inflict "trouble and pain" to get the information he wants.

Later in the tale, the orc captors of Pippin and Merry also threaten torture. There are numerous references to inflicting pain on the hobbits, either to "pay" them in retaliation for any resistance or simply for "sport" or "fun." "If I had my way," one of the orcs tells Pippin in the Common Speech, "you'd wish you were dead now. I'd make you squeak, you miserable rat." The reference to squeaking at this point may refer simply to crying out in pain, having nothing to do with revealing knowledge. But later, Grishnákh, the leader of the Lugburz party of orcs, speaks straightforwardly about torturing the hobbits in order to get information from them: "Grishnákh hissed, 'Everything you have, and everything you know, will be got out of you in time: everything! You'll wish there was more that you could tell to satisfy the Questioner, indeed you will: quite soon. We shan't hurry the enquiry. Oh dear no! What do you think you've been kept alive for?'" (III/iii).

When orcs take Frodo prisoner later in the tale, they move beyond the mere threat of torture. Although the actual torture is not described, the results are. It is Sam who finds Frodo in the tower at Cirith Ungol. Even as he comes to rescue his master, he hears the crack of a whip and then sees the orc Snaga standing over Frodo preparing to hit him again. After Sam disposes of Snaga, the narrator

25

describes Frodo's state: "He was naked, lying as if in a swoon on a heap of filthy rags: his arm flung up, shielding his head, and across his side there ran an ugly whip-weal." Even apart from the whip, these are clear signs of Frodo having been tortured. The reasons for the torture are probably many. Snaga speaks of whipping Frodo as "fun." The orcs Snaga and Shagrat also use or threaten harm as a means of getting people—including even other orcs—to obey them. Yet, although these two motives are certainly involved, acquiring information from Frodo that will be useful to the orcs (and to Sauron) is certainly part of the reason for the torture. This is clear from Frodo's account given later to Sam: "Two great brutes came and questioned me, questioned me until I thought I should go mad, standing over me, gloating, fingering their knives. I'll never forget their claws and eyes" (VI/i).

Frodo is part of another, subtler example of something that may be thought of torture—namely, the effects caused by his possession of the Ring. This suggested connection between the torture of prisoners and the Ring's impact on Frodo may seem like a stretch, but Tolkien himself uses torture as a metaphor to describe the situation. In a letter written in 1956, Tolkien responds to a critic who argued that Frodo was a failure because he could not destroy the Ring on Mount Doom. Tolkien defends Frodo by comparing his fate to that of prisoners of war who had been tortured: "It seems sad and strange that, in this evil time when daily people of good will are tortured, 'brainwashed,' and broken, anyone could be so fiercely simpleminded and self righteous [as to condemn Frodo as a failure]" (*Letters*, 253). This was not the first time he'd made that connection. In a draft of another letter written earlier the same year, also discussing the actions of Frodo on Mount Doom, Tolkien comments, "I did not foresee that before the tale was published we should enter a dark age in which the technique of torture and disruption of personality would rival that of Mordor and the Ring and present us with the practical problem of honest men of good will broken down into apostates and traitors" (*Letters*, 233). Tolkien's point seems to be that the Ring has a destructive effect on its bearers comparable to that of torture. The Ring may not have been seeking information from Frodo in the sense that the torturers of the previous examples were seeking information from prisoners, but it was definitely breaking him.

Yet again, seven years later, Tolkien makes the same argument in defense of his hero, though he uses the word *torment* rather than *torture* in this later letter: "I do not myself see that the breaking of [Frodo's] mind and will under demonic pressure after torment was any more a *moral* failure than the breaking of his body would have been—say, by being strangled by Gollum, or crushed by a falling rock." And then, as though to back up his own opinion, Tolkien appeals to the opinions of two of the wise characters within his tale: "That appears to have been the judgement of Gandalf and Aragorn and of all who learned the full story of his journey" (*Letters*, 327). Here, though the reference to "torment" may specifically point only to his treatment at Cirith Ungol, the "demonic pressure" almost certainly refers to the pressure that came from possessing the Ring. In any case, the entire quest taken as a whole was torture to Frodo, and Tolkien considers that torture to be evil.

We could continue, perhaps tediously, to explore additional passages in which the enemy applies the techniques of torture explicitly to gain information from prisoners. Gandalf, in "The Shadow of the Past," suggests to Frodo that Sméagol was tortured by Sauron to get information about the Ring and Bilbo. "All he knew was forced from him," Gandalf later tells the Council of Elrond (II/ii). We learn in appendix A that Thrain, the father of Thorin, was tormented by Sauron in the pits of Dol Guldur. In *The Silmarillion*, Sauron's hunters torment Gorlim in order "to learn the hidings of [Beren's father] Barahir and all his ways" (*Silm*, 163). Later in the same tale, we see that Sauron cruelly slays the companions of Beren and Finrod in a dark pit at Tol-in-Gaurhoth in order to determine their identities. Morgoth likewise tortures Húrin and places a curse on his offspring in an effort to gain information about the location of the hidden kingdom of Gondolin. And there are more examples.

None of these examples alone suffices to show that torture is wrong in Tolkien's world. Tolkien's narration describes orcs and the servants of Sauron and Morgoth as eating and sleeping, for example; the fact that orcs do some activity does not, in and of itself, imply the wrongness of that activity. As noted above, orcs also use swords and weapons of war similar to those used by the heroes. Tolkien does not portray these activities (eating, sleeping, or using a sword in battle) as necessarily wrong. Certainly the tone and adjectives used in some of these passages—the association of torment with cruelty or that the orcs seem to take pleasure in it—provide a stronger hint as to the immorality of torture in Tolkien's world. Likewise, the language Tolkien used in his letters referencing torture also suggests that it is inherently evil, especially his connection of torture to "demonic pressure" (in the later letter) and to Mordor and "a dark age" (in the earlier letters).

Still, we might look for stronger evidence in Tolkien's writing before we claim any moral principle at work in Middle-earth. What about those who oppose Morgoth and Sauron? What are the practices of the wise of Middle-earth, and of those whom the stories put forth as heroic and virtuous?

The Ethics of the Wise

While the servants of the enemy practice torture, at first glance it would appear that the wise of Middle-earth, despite both ample opportunities and pressing needs for information, choose not to torture prisoners. Even in *The Hobbit* when King Thranduil of Mirkwood imprisons Thorin and his company of dwarves—and one could make a case that he does so wrongfully, motivated by both pride and greed—it is never suggested that he tortures them in any way other than the imprisonment itself. He gives them food and drink and orders that they be untied to minimize their discomfort.

But the most telling example of how the heroes treat their prisoners is the treatment of Gollum (or Sméagol) by Gandalf, Aragorn, and the elves. When Gandalf tells Gollum's story to Frodo, he explains, "The Wood-elves have him in prison, but they treat him with such kindness as they can find in their wise hearts" (I/ii). Later, at the Council of Elrond, Aragorn summarizes the same story from his own perspective and repeats this information (while also affirming Gandalf's suspicion that Sméagol had been tortured by Sauron): "He is in prison, but no worse. He had suffered much. There is no doubt that he was tormented, and the fear of Sauron lies black on his heart" (II/ii).

When, also at the Council of Elrond, Legolas shares the bad news of Sméagol's escape, he also makes it clear that the elves had sought to treat him kindly and gently. "Sméagol . . . has escaped . . . not through lack of watchfulness, but perhaps through over-kindliness. . . . Gandalf bade us hope still for his cure, and we had not the heart to keep him ever in dungeons under the earth" (II/ii). Beyond treating Sméagol gently and kindly, two additional aspects of the elves' approach are worth noting. First, one of the motivations for the kind treatment is the hope that Sméagol might be cured. Part of the argument against torture is that the mistreatment of a prisoner would make the cure of that prisoner less likely. And, as we shall explore later in this book, the notion of a cure is a very important one to Tolkien, even for characters like Saruman and Sméagol.

The second noteworthy aspect of the elves' approach to Sméagol is the great lengths to which they go in treating their prisoner kindly. They are willing not only to go to considerable effort but also to take considerable risks. The virtue of treating a prisoner well is worth paying a cost for. It is a principle espoused by Faramir. When his father Denethor chastises him for practicing gentleness (or wanting to appear gentle), telling him "gentleness may be repaid with death," Faramir replies very simply, "So be it" (VI/iv). What a powerful statement! (The scene in Peter Jackson's film showing Faramir and his soldiers brutally kicking and beating the prisoner Gollum is entirely antithetical to the real character of Faramir as described by Tolkien—as were many other aspects of Jackson's unfaithful portrayal of Faramir.)

We even see this principle practiced by Frodo when Sméagol becomes his prisoner. Though earlier in the story Frodo had heard of the treachery of Gollum and had wished him dead, when he actually meets the pitiful creature he is much more merciful. Initially he has Sméagol tied up in the elven rope. But the rope causes Sméagol to writhe and scream in agony (IV/i). When Frodo becomes convinced that simply the touch of this elven rope torments Gollum, he is willing to remove it at great personal risk rather than to act with the injustice or cruelty of tormenting his prisoner.

These examples could be used to make a strong case that the ethic expressed in Tolkien's Middle-earth writings is that the torture of a prisoner, even in times of war, even in order to gain information that could be vital to that war—vital to the saving of countless lives—is wrong. Even the most desperate of circumstances, the possibility of

29

horrific defeat by the forces of Sauron, do not justify desperate actions, such as torture, that would otherwise be understood clearly as evil.

But there is one problem. Gandalf's treatment of Sméagol when he first finds him, and is still trying to get information from him, appears less kind. Even by Gandalf's own words, his treatment of his prisoner borders on something like torment or torture. Moreover, he does this specifically to get needed information. He describes the scene to Frodo: "I endured [Gollum] as long as I could, but the truth was desperately important, and in the end I had to be harsh. I put the fear of fire on him, and wrung the story out of him, bit by bit, together with much snivelling and snarling. He thought he was misunderstood and ill-used" (I/ii). We must consider this troubling passage closely. It is not just that Sméagol thought he was "ill-used"; it is that Gandalf himself describes his treatment as "harsh." Might not the same words used to describe Gandalf's treatment of Sméagol also be used of the practice of water-boarding prisoners at Guantanamo Bay? Except, instead of the fear of fire, the Guantanamo interrogators sought to wring the story from their prisoners by putting in them the fear of water. So we ask, did Gandalf *torture* Gollum? And if so, was that act justified, as Gandalf seeks to justify it, by the fact that "the truth was desperately important"?

Considering the passage closely, and considering also the character of Gandalf, three possible explanations—not necessarily exclusive of one another—come to mind. Since the argument that torture is immoral within the framework of Tolkien's Middle-earth seems elsewhere so strong, for me the most appealing explanation for the above passage is that Gandalf did not actually torture Gollum; he was simply speaking metaphorically when he speaks of wringing the story out of him.

This explanation is not without merit. Consider Gandalf's earlier treatment of Bilbo when he was trying to get the true story of the Ring from the hobbit. Bilbo complains of harsh treatment from the wizard, and of being badgered. Gandalf responds: "I had to badger you. I wanted the truth. It was important" (I/i). Note the similarities. As with Gollum, Gandalf justifies his actions by stating the importance of discovering the truth. Yet Bilbo is clearly annoyed. To use the description of Gollum, Bilbo feels misunderstood and ill-used. Later on, Frodo recounts to Gandalf Bilbo's memory of this: "He told me the true story soon after I came to live here. He said you had pestered him till he told you" (I/ii). Yet despite Gandalf's words to Bilbo, it is difficult to imagine that Gandalf actually *tortured* Bilbo in any sense of the word, however pestered Bilbo might have felt.

An even more vivid scene takes place when Gandalf tries to convince Bilbo to give up the Ring after his "long-expected party," and the hobbit resists. "It will be my turn to get angry soon," the wizard tells the hobbit. "If you say that again, I shall. Then you will see Gandalf the Grey uncloaked." The narrator goes on to describe the scene: "[Gandalf] took a step towards the hobbit, and he seemed to grow tall and menacing; his shadow filled the little room" (I/i). This must have appeared very threatening to Bilbo. Was Gandalf, like the orcs we discussed earlier, implying that he would harm the hobbit if the hobbit did not comply with his command? If so, it would be entirely out of character for Gandalf, who—as we will explore in chapter 7—never tries to *force* others to act a certain way but rather tries to encourage and strengthen people to make their own choices. More likely, Gandalf was simply responding to Bilbo's own threat; the hobbit had, after all, let his hand stray to his sword. Gandalf was also, I think, both angry and afraid. Not afraid for himself but afraid for his friend Bilbo. He cared deeply about the hobbit—which is why we cannot imagine the wizard torturing Bilbo in any way. What if he treated Gollum in much the same way he treated Bilbo? Gollum, being much more given over to evil, might well perceive that behavior in a darker light, more akin to torture.

This view is, as I said, an appealing possibility for the reader who believes that torture is wrong and yet wants to admire Gandalf. Ends do not justify means; there is no *end*—we can well imagine Gandalf arguing, not even saving Middle-earth from Sauron—that would justify the *means* of torturing a sentient being. Unfortunately, this view of Gandalf is hard to reconcile with the words, "I put the fear of fire on him, and wrung the story out of him"—Gandalf's own words, not Gollum's.

The Complexities of Narratives, and of Life

There is, however, yet another answer. It neither affirms nor contradicts the above possibility but simply *explains* the scene from a developing narrative need rather than justifying or condemning it from a moral viewpoint. Keep in mind the history of Tolkien's development of *The Hobbit* and *The Lord of the Rings*. In the first edition of *The Hobbit*, published in 1937, the entire riddle contest between Bilbo and Gollum plays out somewhat differently. The riddles are the same, but the ending is not. In the first edition, when Bilbo (by sheer luck) wins the contest, Gollum simply lets him keep the ring as a reward or gift. The two then part amicably. It is as though the first published edition of the story was the version that Bilbo first tells the dwarves in order to justify his own claim on the Ring.

Of course, as Tolkien began to develop the concept of the One Ring while he wrote *The Lord of the Rings*, and he learned that Bilbo's ring was indeed Sauron's Ring of Power, this ending to the riddle game would no longer do. Tolkien needed to portray the Ring as much more powerful, more evil, and more addicting than he had portrayed it in the first edition of *The Hobbit*. It was not merely something that was possessed *by* its owner but something that possessed its owner. It would *never* be given away—at least not by one like Gollum, who was already by nature greedy and murderous. So even as Tolkien created a new edition of *The Hobbit* with this new ending to the riddle game, and explained away the first edition's account as Bilbo's story told to the dwarves rather than the true story, he also began to develop his concept of the Ring's power. In his prepublication drafts of *The Lord of the Rings*, he slowly changes and adapts the dialogue between Gandalf and Frodo in which the wizard presents to the young hobbit the history of the Ring. In an unpublished version somewhere between the first draft and the eventual published draft, Gandalf recounts to Frodo his interaction with Gollum as follows:

> What I have told you is what Gollum was willing to tell—though not, of course, in the way I have reported it. Gollum is a liar, and you have to sift through his words. . . . I fancy he had made up his mind what to say, if necessary, so that the stranger would accept the Ring without suspicion, and think the gift natural. . . . There was no need to tell the lie, of course, when he found the Ring had gone; but he had told that lie to himself so many times in the darkness, trying to forget Deagol, that it slipped out, whenever he spoke of the Ring. He

repeated it to me, but I laughed at him. He then told me more or less the true story, but with a lot of snivelling and snarling. He thought he was misunderstood and ill-treated. (*Treason*, 26)

The changes from this earlier draft are interesting. Note what is present in this earlier version and what is not. Gollum is still a liar and does not immediately give the true story. He still snivels and snarls. When he does give the true story, he still feels misunderstood and ill-treated. But the resemblance ends there. In the earlier draft, Gandalf does not put the fear of fire into him. He does not wring the story out of him. He simply laughs at Gollum, and that's all it takes for Gollum to come out with the true story. All hint of torture that appears in the later, final version is absent in this earlier version.

Unfortunately, this version would not work; it simply does not convey the complete corruptive and enslaving power of the Ring. In order to get across the nature of the Ring—both its power and its evil—Tolkien was required to do more with this scene; he had to show just how difficult it would have been for Gandalf to get the truth from Gollum. And thus, I believe, he eventually moves to the final version: the version where Gandalf must be harsh, must use the fear of fire, must wring the story out of Gollum. Tolkien must do this to convince the reader just how much power the Ring wields over its bearers. Without such a description at the start, not only does the scene at the Crack of Doom lose its power, but much of the entire narrative regarding the struggles of Frodo loses its power. I don't think Tolkien wrote that description of Gandalf and Gollum in order to justify the torture of a criminal, no matter how guilty that prisoner is (and Gandalf makes it clear that Gollum is indeed guilty and deserving of death). Rather, the scene is there to convey the power of the Ring.

And yet that scene did make it into the book. Gandalf did, by all appearances and by his own admission and use of the words "fear" and "wring," do something to Gollum: something probably best described as torture, either physical or psychological—probably both. Desperate for knowledge, the wizard's treatment of his prisoner was *not* gentle. The description is there for narrative reasons as the author wrestled with a difficult concept and required the reader to understand the power of the One Ring. Yet even if Tolkien was not considering the moral implications of this action at the time he revised the scene, even if the scene arose for primarily narrative considerations—to convey the power of the One Ring—that does not mean that the author did not eventually ponder the morality of Gandalf's actions.

Sometime around March 1960, Tolkien wrote a typescript manuscript titled "Orcs." It is, as the title suggests, an essay on the nature of the orcs, and was eventually published (posthumously) in the volume *Morgoth's Ring* in the section "Myths Transformed." Like many of the pieces in the volume, according to Tolkien's son Christopher, this essay had in the mind of the author some authority as a "finished piece," possibly for inclusion in a published volume of *The Silmarillion* (*Morgoth*, 415). In this essay, Tolkien explores the issue of the treatment of prisoners.

> But even before this wickedness of Morgoth was suspected the Wise in the Elder Days taught always that the Orcs were not "made" by Melkor, and therefore were not in their origin evil. They might have become irredeemable (at least by Elves and Men), but they remained within the Law. That is, that though of necessity, being the fingers of the hand of Morgoth, they must be fought with the utmost severity, they must not be dealt with in their own terms of cruelty and treachery. Captives must not be tormented, not even to discover information for the defence of the homes of Elves and Men. If any Orcs surrendered and asked for mercy, they must be granted it, even at a cost.[8] This was the teaching of the Wise, though in the horror of the War it was not always heeded. (*Morgoth*, 419)

This, then, is the third explanation for Gandalf's description of his treatment of Gollum. He did, indeed, torture Gollum at some level, although probably in a way not nearly as violent or awful as the way we imagine Sauron and the orcs torturing their prisoners; he did not use whips or other devices of torture, nor did he scar Gollum, but he may well have caused Gollum some physical pain and certainly willingly caused him some psychological distress. He did so in desperation. *And he did so wrongly.* His torture of Gollum was, in Tolkien's fabric of Middle-earth, an immoral act.

That, at least, is what the essay above makes clear. Tolkien was addressing the exact moral issue of this chapter. And he states a clear, strong, and straightforward conclusion: "Captives must not be tormented, not even to discover information for the defence of the homes of Elves and Men." He goes on to lay out the very principle we see illustrated in the elves' treatment of Sméagol, and later in Frodo's treatment of him: they treat him with gentleness and mercy, even at personal risk or personal cost. Yet Tolkien also recognizes that beings of free will, even beings as good and wise as Gandalf, will sometimes fail morally. Gandalf passed the moral test of refusing the Ring, and refusing power, greatly though he felt the need for power.

But at least once, in pursuit of knowledge, Gandalf failed the moral test. In the objective moral framework that defines what is right and wrong in Middle-earth, it is wrong to torture a prisoner under any circumstances for any purpose. It really is an instance of becoming the very enemy you are trying to defeat. And that, of course, is a moral lesson that applies to any age in which there is war.

2

Epic Battles

So began the battle that none had expected; and
it was called the Battle of Five Armies, and it was
very terrible.

—*The Hobbit*

For some readers of this book—particularly those whose view of
Tolkien's writings have been more influenced by Peter Jackson's
film adaptations than by Tolkien's literary works themselves—there
might seem to be a certain irony in the previous chapter. I have
presented at least a starting point for a case that Tolkien's heroes
model the virtue of gentleness (among many other virtues). This is
especially true of his great hobbit hero Frodo, but it applies also to
his human heroes Aragorn and Faramir, and to other wise figures
such as Galadriel and the wizard Gandalf. Even in the midst of war,
the virtue of gentleness—a virtue that seems inherently antithetical
to war itself—should still be practiced, and indeed is practiced by
Tolkien's heroes.

In particular, war does not justify the torture of prisoners. Not
even the most desperate of circumstances and needs brought on
by war are sufficient to justify the torture of a prisoner. Tolkien

not only modeled this principle in his heroic characters but was explicit about it in at least one posthumously published passage on the nature of orcs. There are virtues and ethical principles that should be practiced even at great personal cost, even at the cost of military defeat.

The reason this might seem ironic is that Tolkien is known, to many fans of *The Lord of the Rings*, for his epic battle scenes. If he really wanted to model the virtues of gentleness and peace, why would he write so much about war? Might it not be more effective to promote such virtues *outside* the context of war than to present so much war and violence, and then suggest that one still needs to be virtuous? Put another way, scenes and dialogues suggesting a strong ethic against the torture of enemy prisoners may be completely lost when they immediately precede or follow other scenes in which heroes are portrayed running spears, swords, and arrows through their enemies in the midst of battle. To some, Tolkien seems even to glorify violence. This certainly seems unhelpful if an author wants to promote peace.

What does one say to such a criticism? Battles do hold a significant place in the tales of Middle-earth. *The Hobbit* culminates in the Battle of Five Armies, in which many fortunes and futures are made (or lost). Nearly all of *The Lord of the Rings* focuses on a single war, moving (or so it seems) from one battle to another: the skirmishes at Weathertop, Moria, and Amon Hen; the Battle of Helm's Deep; the skirmish in Ithilien between Faramir's men and the Southrons; the Siege of Minas Tirith and the Battle of the Pelennor Fields; and the battle on the Morannon in front of the Black Gate of Mordor. The same can be said for *The Silmarillion*, in which the battles are given lofty elvish names, such as Dagor Agloreb, Dagor Bragollach, Dagor-nuin-Giliath, and Nirnaeth Arneodiad. Just the cinematic trailer to Jackson's film version of *The Two Towers*, with the violent battle scenes depicted there, might be enough to convince some that Tolkien glorifies violence. The officially licensed video games with graphic and gory depictions of orcs spilling blood (and having their blood spilled) were inevitable.

In light of this, it is instructive to explore how exactly Tolkien portrays war. How does he describe battle scenes? What images does he use? What narrative devices? What voices?

The Battle of Five Armies

As the first major battle in either *The Hobbit* or *The Lord of the Rings*, the Battle of Five Armies is an appropriate place to begin our exploration of Tolkien and war. From the perspective of Middle-earth's history (if not also from the perspective of the narrative), it is the second most important event in *The Hobbit*, behind only Bilbo's finding of the Ring. Does this battle read like a description of a video game? Or like something altogether different?

As the battle approaches—in a chapter appropriately titled "The Clouds Burst"—the pace of the narrative increases toward its climax. Finally we read, "So began the battle that none had expected; and it was called the Battle of Five Armies, and it was very terrible" (*Hobbit*, 339). Except that the battle did not begin quite yet. Or at least the narrative account of the battle did not begin. Four and a half more paragraphs ensue that give an overview of the situation leading up to the battle from an omniscient narrative voice. This overview describes the historical setting for the battle, the geography of the battle site, and, most important, the work of Gandalf in bringing together the elves, men, and dwarves, who give up their enmity toward one another and unite to fight a common enemy. One thing we do get from this opening line, however, is the first adjective Tolkien uses to describe battle: *terrible*.

Then comes the actual description of fighting: "A few brave men were strung before them to make a feint of resistance, and many there fell before the rest drew back and fled to either side" (*Hobbit*, 340). At this point the battle begins in earnest, and as it does, *The Hobbit* takes an interesting turn in its narrative voice; Tolkien temporarily abandons the omniscient view and begins to describe the battle from the very limited viewpoint of Bilbo, the hobbit: "It was a terrible battle. The most dreadful of all Bilbo's experiences, and the one which at the time he hated most—which is to say it was the one he was most proud of, and most fond of recalling long afterwards, although he was quite unimportant in it" (*Hobbit*, 341). Again we see the same word, *terrible*, as the descriptive adjective for battle. One cannot help but see in this depiction something of Tolkien's own World War I experience of fighting in battle in 1916 as an infantryman. He viewed the war from the trenches, unable ever to see the big picture or understand how his actions fit into the broader perspective of the war as a whole, or even into that particular battle. Tolkien lost two of his closest friends and then contracted trench fever.

But the main point I wish to make is that this approach—the switch from an omniscient overview to Bilbo's perspective—personalizes the battle while adding distance to it. That is, the focus of Tolkien's narrative at this stage, rather than focusing on the details of the fighting, shifts to the feelings of one individual involved. In this case, moreover, the individual is one who is "quite unimportant" from a military or strategic viewpoint, who doesn't really understand what is happening and is invisible to the rest of the combatants. This helps connect the battle with the reader, who would likely feel much the same in a battle of that scope, while adding spatial distance to the narrative, as of one watching the events from afar. Tolkien adds even more distance to the battle—this time temporal distance—by describing it in the way that this unimportant character Bilbo remembers it "long afterwards" rather than the way he views it at the moment. A conclusion one might draw is that Tolkien is more concerned with those involved in the battle than with the battle itself. (We will return to this point later.)

The battle continues from there, but it is described in broad brushstrokes, once more from a high and distant perspective, with hours flashing past in just a few sentences. We get this in such simple statements as, "Day drew on" (*Hobbit*, 343). As for description of the fighting itself—swords whacking off body parts, spears plunging into enemies, or any of the sort of visual detail we might expect in a modern video game—there is almost none. In over twenty paragraphs that narrate the battle, there are only a handful of descriptions that might be called graphic: "The rocks were stained black with goblin blood" (*Hobbit*, 341). "Many of their own wolves were turning on them and rending the dead and the wounded" (*Hobbit*, 342). "Thorin wielded his axe with mighty strokes" (*Hobbit*, 343). "Once again the goblins were stricken in the valley; and they were piled in heaps till Dale was dark and hideous with their corpses" (*Hobbit*, 343–44). Note that even these descriptions are broad and general; only the third of these four even mentions a specific person. If the reader imaginatively fills in the missing detail, the broad brushstrokes painted by the author make it clear that it would not be pleasant detail. It is a gruesome and negative picture of war: bloodstained rocks, betrayal, and dead bodies.

That's about all the detailed graphic description of the violence of the fighting we are given. The narrative then returns again to Bilbo.

> On all this Bilbo looked with misery. . . .
> "Misery me!" [thought Bilbo.] "I have heard songs of many battles, and I have always understood that defeat may be glorious. It seems very uncomfortable, not to say distressing. I wish I was well out of it." (*Hobbit*, 344–45)

As we know, of course, the battle does not end in defeat for Bilbo but in victory. Tolkien, however, avoids describing the victory because his narrator is knocked unconscious before the battle ends: "'The Eagles!' cried Bilbo once more, but at that moment a stone hurtling from above smote heavily on his helm, and he fell with a crash and knew no more" (*Hobbit*, 345). This is significant. If one wanted to glorify war, then victory would be the ideal moment to do so. Yet Tolkien doesn't even let us experience victory with the victors. It is not until well later, after the battle is over and victory won, that Bilbo awakens.

> When Bilbo came to himself, he was literally by himself. He was lying on the flat stones of Ravenhill, and no one was near. A cloudless day, but cold, was broad above him. He was shaking, and as chilled as stone, but his head burned with fire. . . .
> "Victory after all, I suppose!" he said, feeling his aching head. "Well, it seems a very gloomy business." (*Hobbit*, 346)

Between these two passages, Tolkien is quite explicit. Battle is neither glorious in defeat (contrary to what Bilbo had always thought) nor even glorious in victory. Rather, it is miserable, "uncomfortable," "distressing," and overall "a very gloomy business." Indeed, it would be difficult to look at the scene to which Bilbo awoke and call it victory. Many good elves, men, and dwarves lie dead, and many others mortally wounded. In short, there is little glory in it—not in Tolkien's narrative description, anyway.

The Black Gate and the Skirmish with Southrons

If we move from *The Hobbit* to *The Lord of the Rings*, the three biggest battles are (in chronological order) the Battle of Helm's Deep, the Siege of Minas Tirith (also called the Siege of Gondor, which culminates in the Battle of the Pelennor Fields), and the battle in front of the Black Gate. We will start with the last of these and move backward.

Interestingly enough, Tolkien describes the battle in front of the Black Gate in a way so closely parallel to the Battle of Five Armies in *The Hobbit* that I can only imagine the parallel is intentional—in the same way that the two stories also open with parallel passages of parties, although one is "unexpected" and one "long-expected," and both end with the homecoming of hobbits to the Shire after a long time away. Both are the final major battles in their respective books, both involve several different armies coming together to fight a common foe, both involve a single hobbit (as an unimportant character), and both end with the unexpected coming of the eagles presaging an unlooked-for hope and victory. Both battles also involved Gandalf as a critical agent in bringing the allied forces together to fight the common enemy.

The battle in front of the Black Gate begins with the armies of Mordor sweeping down upon Aragorn's army as Sauron springs his trap. Four paragraphs describe Aragorn's quick ordering of his troops as the enemy rushes toward them from all sides. Then, as with the Battle of Five Armies in *The Hobbit*, the narrative suddenly switches from a distant omniscient view to the perspective of an unimportant hobbit.

> Pippin had bowed crushed with horror when he heard Gandalf reject the terms and doom Frodo to the torment of the Tower; but he had mastered himself, and now he stood beside Beregond in the front rank of Gondor with Imrahil's men. For it seemed best to him to die soon and leave the bitter story of his life, since all was in ruin.
>
> "I wish Merry was here," he heard himself saying, and quick thoughts raced through his mind, even as he watched the enemy come charging to the assault. . . .
>
> He drew his sword and looked at it, and the intertwining shapes of red and gold; and the flowing characters of Númenor glinted like fire upon the blade. "This was made for just such an hour," he

thought. "If only I could smite that foul Messenger with it, then almost I should draw level with Old Merry. Well I'll smite some of the beastly brood before the end. I wish I could see cool sunlight and green grass again!"

Then even as he thought these things the first assault crashed into them. . . .

"So it ends as I guessed it would," his thought said, even as it fluttered away; and it laughed a little within him ere it fled, almost gay it seemed to be casting off at last all doubt and care and fear. (V/x)

As noted, this narrative switch in perspectives occurs the moment the battle begins. The focus turns to the thoughts and feelings of the *character* rather than the graphic details of the *battle*. The words used to describe Pippin's thoughts on this battle are similar to those used of Bilbo's perspective on the earlier battle: *horror, doom, bitterness*, and *ruin*. There are, however, two contrasts between the scenes. First, though this battle is even more significant to the peoples of Middle-earth than the battle at the end of *The Hobbit*—and involves considerably larger and more powerful armies—it is described with far fewer words. Once the preliminary bargaining and diplomacy are over, and Gandalf has rejected the terms of Sauron's emissary, barely over one page (eight paragraphs) is given to the actual description of this important battle, all of which comes from Pippin's perspective. Then Pippin (like Bilbo) is knocked unconscious.

A second difference is that the reader gets somewhat more of the hobbit's thoughts and feelings at the moment (rather than retrospectively), which is surprising since there is less overall narrative devoted this battle than is devoted to the Battle of Five Armies. In particular, not only is the narrator concerned with Pippin's role and position as the battle begins, but he tells us just what is going through the hobbit's mind during those first few moments. Certainly some of his thoughts are directed toward the present instant: the horrors he is about to face and what he hopes to accomplish against his foes. But much of his thought is turned toward things having little to do with battle: first toward his friend Merry, and then toward "cool sunlight and green grass." These are the things—friends, sunlight, grass—that are really important in the tale; this, and not war and battles, is the stuff of life, the stuff that counts. And thus this, even in the midst of a battle scene, is what Tolkien's narrative brings us back to.

These are not the only two instances where Tolkien uses a hobbit to give us a perspective on the wars of men. Nowhere is that hobbitish view more stark than the view we get from Sam of the skirmish fought between Faramir's men and the Southron forces passing through Ithilien. Most of the battle is described only as faint sounds heard by Sam, with one comment of narration from Damrod, one of Faramir's men who is guarding Sam and Frodo. There is only one actual paragraph with any visual description of the battle itself, again only as seen by Sam in glimpses through the trees. The description ends with one of the enemy soldier's falling dead almost at Sam's feet. And then we have Sam's summary, which is very telling: "It was Sam's first view of a battle of Men against Men, and he did not like it much. He was glad that he could not see the dead face. He wondered what the man's name was and where he came from; and if he was really evil of heart, or what lies or threats had led him on the long march from his home; and if he would not really rather have stayed there in peace" (IV/iv). Here Tolkien not only personalizes those on "our side," as we might call the free peoples of Middle-earth, but he also personalizes one of the enemy soldiers. The young Southron has a name, a heart, and a history. He may be evil, or he may not be. He may, Sam realizes, even have a desire for peace; he may be as much a victim of Sauron's threats and lies as the folk of Gondor. Even the long march this enemy soldier followed to this battle is one that took him from a home, much as Sam himself had arrived at that same spot on a long march taking him away from his own home. In short, the fallen figure has a face, and Tolkien lets us know he has a face even though we cannot see it. It is a dead face that Sam is glad he cannot see, and that comment alone strengthens the sense of the humanity of this foe: a humanity he shares with Sam, and with the soldiers of Faramir who killed him. One cannot construe this as a glorious image of war.

The Rohirrim and the Anglo-Saxons

Working backward through the story, we turn next to a lengthy discussion about the Siege of Minas Tirith, the longest and most involved battle in this war. It would take considerable time to examine that entire battle, as the siege along with the Battle of the Pelennor Fields spans three chapters of *The Return of the King*. But one observation first needs to be made of the battle as a whole. Though the siege and battle last for many days, none of the narration takes place on the battlefield until the very end when the Rohirrim, led by King Théoden, arrive, and even then the reader sees only a little of the battle before it sweeps past. Next, the reader experiences the battle but only dimly through the eyes of the uncomprehending hobbit Merry. Up to that point, what little description of the battle Tolkien does provide is given from the perspective of those on top of the walls—Pippin and Beregond—looking out at the distant battleground and trying to guess what is happening. In other words, there is little description of the warfare. Rather, the real narrative action takes place within the city and focuses on how the characters respond to the siege: what they feel, what they think, what they say. The battle Tolkien describes in most detail is the battle against despair, and especially the ability of Gandalf and the Prince of Dol Amroth to bring hope to those who have lost it.

When the narrative finally switches from the spectators within the walls of Minas Tirith to the fighting outside the walls, the one scene Tolkien chooses to emphasize is the battle between Éowyn and the Nazgûl, and the subsequent death of King Théoden: a microcosm, but an important one, within the Battle of the Pelennor Fields. This fight is described with a very different narrative voice than the previous two battles I have commented on.

> But lo! Suddenly in the midst of the glory of the king his golden shield was dimmed. The new morning was blotted from the sky. Dark fell about him. Horses reared and screamed. Men cast from the saddle and lay groveling on the ground.
> "To me! To me!" cried Théoden. "Up Eorlingas! Fear no darkness!" But Snowmane wild with terror stood up on high, fighting with the air, and then with a great scream he crashed upon his side: a black dart had pierced him. The king fell beneath him.
> A great shadow descended like a falling cloud. And behold! It was a winged creature: if bird, then greater than all other birds, and it was naked, and neither quill nor feather did it bear, and its vast pinions were as webs of hide between horned fingers; and it stank. . . . Upon it sat a shape, black-mantled, huge and threatening. A crown

of steel he bore, but between rim and robe naught was there to see, save only a deadly gleam of eyes: the Lord of the Nazgûl. To the air he had returned, summoning his steed ere the darkness failed, and now he was come again, bringing ruin, turning hope to despair, and victory to death. A great black mace he wielded.

But Théoden was not utterly forsaken. The knights of his house lay slain about him, or else mastered by the madness of their steeds were borne far away. Yet one stood there still: Dernhelm the young, faithful beyond fear; and he wept, for he had loved his lord as a father. . . .

And so he died, and knew not that Éowyn lay near him. And those who stood by wept, crying: "Théoden King! Théoden King!" (V/vi)

In this battle, after Théoden is struck down, his niece Éowyn (initially in the guise of a male soldier named Dernhelm) faces the Lord of the Nazgûl in combat. And with the aid of Merry, she defeats him, though in the process both she and Merry are grievously wounded. As mentioned, it is a scene very different from the majority of Tolkien's battles. Unlike many other battles, in which the reader is given very little graphic description of the fighting, this battle is described in great detail: the "swift stroke" of Éowyn's "steel-blade," the fall of the Nazgûl-Lord's mace, each word spoken between the combatants, even the shivering of shield and breaking of bone. Why the difference? Why the sudden level of detail?

One thing to be considered here is that Éowyn is not facing a foe of flesh and bones. Unlike with the Southron who falls dead at Sam's feet, we are not intended to feel any sympathy for Éowyn's foe. The Nazgûl whom she destroys is not a mortal or physical being but a spiritual foe: a wraith. The Nazgûl has no blood to be shed. Thus, though the battle between the two takes place in the physical world with physical weapons, Tolkien may be giving us a glimpse of the deeper nature of reality. There is both a physical part of reality and a spiritual part of reality. Since the eye cannot see the spiritual plane, Tolkien visualizes it in the physical realm. We might well conclude that since the only foe we see close up on the Pelennor Fields is a wraith, the real enemy that must be faced in Middle-earth is a spiritual enemy. No battle against a physical foe is depicted with such detail.

There are also at least two other important reasons for the narrative voice and style of description that Tolkien uses in this scene, neither of which have the purpose of glorifying war—or the *effect* of glorifying war when read in their context. The first reason lies in understanding who Théoden and Éowyn are, and more generally who the Rohirrim are. Tolkien models the people of Rohan directly after the Anglo-Saxon people.[1] The language of Rohan is Old English (Anglo-Saxon). The word *Riddermark*, for example, comes from *Ridenna-mearc*; *ridan* is Old English for "to ride," *ridda* for "rider," and *mearc* for "border" or "marches"; hence, *Ridenna-mearc* for "riders of the border." *Meduseld* means "mead hall." Likewise, names of many people in Rohan are often just Anglo-Saxon words. *Théoden* is simply Old English for "prince" or "lord." The poetry of Rohan takes the same verse form in meter and alliteration as that of Old English poetry. (Those familiar with Old English poetry should consider the poem sung by Éomer after Théoden's death: "Mourn not overmuch! Mighty was the fallen" [V/vi].)

Even the speech patterns of the Rohirrim are modeled after Old English heroic verse. Consider the "welcome" given to Gandalf, Aragorn, Gimli, and Legolas by the guards at the gates of Edoras (the palace of King Théoden).

> "None are welcome here in days of war but our own folk, and those that come from Mundburg in the land of Gondor. Who are you that come heedless over the plain thus strangely clad, riding horses like to our own horses? Long have we kept guard here, and we have watched you from afar. Never have we seen other riders so strange, nor any horse more proud than is one of these that bear you. He is one of the Mearas, unless our eyes are cheated by some spell. Say, are you not a wizard, some spy from Saruman, or phantoms of his craft? Speak now and be swift!" (III/vi)

This speech is borrowed almost directly from the welcome given to Beowulf and his warriors by the beach-guards when they arrive at Heorot to visit Hrothgar in the Old English poem *Beowulf*. The Dane's coastguard speak thus:

> "What are you, bearers of armor, dressed in mail-coats, who thus have come bringing a tall ship over the sea-road, over the water to this place? Lo, for a long time I have been guard of the coast, held watch by the sea so that no foe with a force of ships might work harm on the Danes' land: never have shield-bearers more openly undertaken

to come ashore here; nor did you know for sure of a word of leave from our warriors, consent from my kinsmen. I have never seen a mightier warrior on earth than is one of you, a man in battle-dress. That is no retainer made to seem good by his weapons—unless his appearance belies him, his unequalled form. Now I must learn your lineage before you go any farther from here, spies on the Danes' land. Now you far-dwellers, sea-voyagers, hear what I think: you must straightway say where you have come from."[2]

No one who is deeply familiar with *Beowulf* could miss the similarities:

Tolkien	Beowulf
who are you that come over the plain	what are you that come over the sea-road
long have we kept guard here	long have we kept guard here
I have never seen a horse more proud	I have never seen a warrior mightier than is one of you
some spy from Saruman	spies in the Dane's land
speak now and be swift	speak now and be swift

About the only significant difference is that in the former case the arriving party has come by horse, and in the latter case by ship.

So why is this connection important? What does it matter that the Rohirrim are Tolkien's Anglo-Saxons who found their way into Middle-earth? Part of the answer is simply the narrative richness imparted in the tale. If the Rohirrim have Anglo-Saxon names and Anglo-Saxon speech patterns and sing the poetry of Old English heroic verse, then in a scene that focuses on the death of their great king, it makes sense for the narrative voice—in addition to the voices of the characters themselves—to complete the richness by using the idiom of Old English heroic verse. That is what Tolkien, a professional scholar of Anglo-Saxon language and literature, has done. Tolkien's description begins with a phrase similar to that at the start of *Beowulf*: "Lo!" or "But, Lo!" It continues in a manner consistent with Old English narrative style—namely, that really important actions are described three times with three slightly different images: "Shield was dimmed. Morning was blotted. Dark fell."

But the language and literature of the Anglo-Saxons (and thus of the Rohirrim) come out of an early Germanic culture, in which war was glorified; or, if not war, then at least the *warrior*—whether in death or in victory. A chieftain became a chieftain because of his prowess in battle, and when he died he was buried with his weapons and with those of his vanquished opponents. The great heroes at the start of *Beowulf* are praised for their military victories and brave deeds, and especially for conquering other peoples and making them pay tribute. In short, we see this scene sometimes through the eyes of the Rohirrim (Théoden, Éowyn, and later Éomer) and sometimes through the eyes of Merry. When seen through the eyes of the Rohirrim, we do get a glimpse of this glorification of the life and death of a warrior that would have characterized the society of Rohan. "I go to my fathers," Théoden says. "And even in their mighty company I shall not now be ashamed" (V/vi).

The hobbit Merry, however, provides us another perspective on this battle, much as the hobbits Bilbo, Pippin, and Sam did for the battles already discussed. Or, rather, Tolkien—while giving us the narrative richness of Anglo-Saxon verse—provides us, through Merry, another perspective that is less glorious. Indeed one might say that the hobbits, when present at a battle, bring realism to our understanding of war. War, as seen through their eyes, is as close as we can come in the book to war as seen through the author's eyes. Even in a society that glorifies the warrior, such as that of the Rohirrim, Tolkien uses the hobbits to give us a clearer picture of what war is really about; the hobbits deglorify it when others have glorified it. At the Pelennor Fields, when seen through Merry's eyes, there is no glory but only sorrow, dread, and blind, sick horror (V/vi). And it is through Merry's eyes, not those of the Rohirrim, that the narrator gives us our final glimpse of this battle: Théoden is dead, Éowyn unconscious, and Éomer gone. The outcome is not glory but death, and tears, and sorrow.

So Fair, So Desperate

Without diminishing the importance of the narrative richness of Tolkien's depiction of the people of Rohan, I believe there is a second and more significant reason that this scene is described as it is, why Tolkien's narrative gives it a certain glory. We must look at each of the three characters involved: Théoden, Merry, and Éowyn.

Consider, first, King Théoden. Just days before this battle begins, he is "a man so bent with age that he seemed almost a dwarf" (III/vi). If he were bent with age because his body really was old and decrepit, then the reader would have no reason to be dismayed. But Théoden is only deceived into thinking himself too old and frail to do anything. In reality, there is still considerable strength left in his bones and muscles. As the visitors to his hall notice, "his eyes still burned with a bright light," and "bent though he was, he was still tall" (III/vi). What has happened to him? The most obvious thing is that he has listened to the lies of his supposed counselor Gríma, son of Gálmód (whom all save Théoden have aptly named "the Wormtongue"), who is passing on the lies of Saruman. Gríma's rhetoric is that "those who truly love [Théoden] would spare his failing years" (III/vi). Thus Théoden has come to believe himself old and frail, and his people weak, and has been convinced that his only hope is to withdraw into a defensive cocoon and let the world's problems pass over him and his country. Gandalf later tells him, "And ever Wormtongue's whispering was in your ears, poisoning your thought, chilling your heart, weakening your limbs, while others watched and could do nothing, for your will was in his keeping" (III/vi). And because of that deception—that falling under the spell of Saruman—Théoden is unwilling to fight in the battle against Sauron or to lend the aid of his people to the desperate need of his neighbors in Gondor.

We must also note that in addition to the illness brought about by this deceit, there is yet a subtler decline of the nobility of the House of Eorl, one that perhaps has gone back many generations. Théoden himself later describes this condition: "Long have we tended our beasts and our fields, built our houses, wrought our tools, or ridden away to help in the wars of Minas Tirith. And that we called the life of Men, the way of the world. We cared little for what lay beyond the borders of our land. Songs we have that tell of these things, but we are forgetting them, teaching them only to children, as a careless custom" (III/viii). In short, the kings of Rohan have ceased to believe in the wisdom of the old stories passed on from generation to generation; they have forgotten how broad and wonderful and mysterious is the wide world around them. This fall is evident in the dark tales and words they speak of Galadriel, calling her a "sorceress" and "net-weaver"—as Gimli says, speaking evil of "that which is fair beyond the reach" of their thoughts (III/ii). It is equally evident in that they no longer have any knowledge of, belief in, or concern for the Ents of Fangorn Forest, which is on the very border of Rohan.

When Gandalf comes to Théoden's Golden Hall, however, a healing begins for both of these ills. The deceit of Saruman, being the more recent, is the more quickly and easily cured. By breaking this spell—in part by silencing Wormtongue—Gandalf helps Théoden see that there is still strength in his bones, still strength in his people, and still hope if they can "stand unconquered a little while."

> "It is not so dark here," said Théoden.
>
> "No," said Gandalf. "Nor does age lie so heavily on your shoulders as some would have you think. Cast aside your prop!"
>
> From the king's hand the black staff fell clattering on the stones. He drew himself up, slowly, as a man that is stiff from long bending over some dull toil. Now tall and straight he stood, and his eyes were blue as he looked into the opening sky. (III/vi)

In a very real sense, Théoden has been healed; Gandalf has set him free from the chains of deceit that bound him to inaction. As the imagery suggests, he moves from darkness to light; he has been blind and now he sees.

With this healing accomplished, Théoden's eyes are also opened to the decline that has come with the loss of the old wisdom and the shrinking of his world. A few days later, Gandalf—aided by the appearance of the Ents—spurs this process, reopening Théoden's eyes.

> "Is it so long since you listened to tales by the fireside? There are children in your land who, out of the twisted threads of story, could pick the answer to your question. You have seen Ents, O King, Ents out of Fangorn Forest, which in your tongue you call the Entwood. Did you think that the name was given only in idle fancy? Nay, Théoden, it is otherwise: to them you are but the passing tale; all the years from Eorl the Young to Théoden the Old are of little count to them; and all the deeds of your house but a small matter. . . . You should be glad, Théoden King. . . . For not only the little life of Men is now endangered, but the life also of those things which you have deemed

50

the matter of legend. You are not without allies, even if you know them not." (III/viii)

What happens here, fundamentally, is that Gandalf restores Théoden's perspective (his sight). When the world of the House of Eorl grew too small, then it was only natural that the kings of Rohan considered themselves larger and more important than they really were. They had become selfish, forgetting that their own needs and problems were but a small part of Middle-earth, in both time and space. As the contact with the Ents reminds Théoden, however, their lives are but a small matter in the broad sweep of time, and their kingdom is just one of many kingdoms in danger from Sauron. Yet, in realizing this, Théoden also realizes that he is not alone; he has allies even if he knows them not. And this gives him both the motivation to begin to fight for a bigger cause and the hope that this larger battle may be won.

And so the real glory of the scene at the Battle of Pelennor Fields is not the glory of a physical battle, whether of victory or defeat, but the glory of those who choose to use whatever strength they have to resist evil. "You may say this to Théoden son of Thengel," says Aragorn, "open war lies before him, with Sauron or against him" (III/ii). If Théoden does not choose to fight against Sauron, he will be serving him. He must choose. And he does. Thus, though he falls slain in the physical battle, he is victorious in the moral battle to *choose well.*

The stories of Merry and Éowyn are also important in understanding this scene. Merry is the easier of the two to understand. In addition to providing the hobbitish perspective we explored earlier, there is something personal about his individual story that is worth exploring. Merry is terrified of battle in general, and terrified of the Black Rider in particular. He has no love whatsoever of war. He is a hobbit, and although he is (or is to become) more adventurous and more noble than most of the other folk of the Shire, he does not long for battle or see it as glorious. For Meriadoc Brandybuck, the victory comes in overcoming his fear in order to come to the rescue of Éowyn, even if it means doing so in the most *in*glorious fashion of crawling on his belly and stabbing the Nazgûl from behind: "She should not die, so fair, so desperate! At least she should not die alone, unaided." And the glory of the scene is also his love for a king who had become like a father: "'King's man! King's man!' his heart cried within him. 'You must stay by him. As a father you shall be to me, you said.'" The glory is the awakening of the "slow-kindled courage of his race" (V/vi). It is his sheer choice to move and act, despite the terror that could have paralyzed him. It is his will not to give in to despair. That this choice is made in the context of a battle, and involves a sword, is not the critical aspect of the heroism (or glory), for we see the same glory in each step taken by Sam and Frodo across the plains of Mordor. Indeed, the battle itself is very inglorious.

By contrast, Éowyn's character is far more complex. We do see in this scene a certain glory in the love that she holds for her uncle: she is "faithful beyond fear," loving Théoden "as a father." And as with Merry, we see a glory in her courage, "so fair, so desperate." But Tolkien is working something else in her character. Like her uncle Théoden, Éowyn needs to find healing, but it is a different type of healing. While her uncle is so afraid of death that he has become shameful, she is so afraid of shame that she seeks death. As Gandalf later indicates to Éomer, Éowyn's brother: "She, born in the body of a maid, had a spirit and courage at least the match of yours. Yet she was doomed to wait on an old man, whom she loved as a father, and watch him falling into a mean dishonoured dotage; and her part seemed to her more ignoble than that of the staff he leaned on" (IV/viii). And so, in her despair, seeing nothing left in life, Éowyn seeks glory in death, and in particular, glory through death *in battle* (an Anglo-Saxon ideal). But unlike Théoden, whose healing has already come, who is willing to die, and who finds death though he does not seek it, Éowyn is denied the very death she seeks. In sparing her from death, Tolkien gives his reader the opportunity to see the healing she later finds. It is by the author's grace that Éowyn does not die but is able to learn that the type of glory she sought earlier is not the answer.

To understand this healing, we must understand the illness. Éowyn's illness is twofold. The first part is observed by both Aragorn and Éomer. She loves Aragorn, but he does not return her love: "Few other griefs amid the ill chances of this world have more bitterness and shame for a man's heart than to behold the love of a lady so fair and brave that cannot be returned" (IV/viii). The second part of her illness is described by Gandalf: she suffers the shame of watching the king she loved as a father falling into "mean dishonoured dotage; and her part seemed to her more ignoble than that of the staff he leaned on." And yet the two illnesses are really one. As Aragorn observes, she doesn't so much love him as "only a shadow and a thought: a hope of glory and great deeds, and lands far from the fields of Rohan" (IV/viii). Her "illness"—if *illness* is even the right word—is a desire for glory. In other words, if what we earlier observed about the Rohirrim and their Anglo-Saxon love of the warrior's glory is true, then Éowyn is simply the manifestation of her people's weakness, exaggerated to an extreme by the taunting of Wormtongue perhaps, but still true to the character of her people. And so, while her bravery and loyalty embody the best traits of the Rohirrim, her longing for glory in battle—which Tolkien illustrates so vividly in that battle scene—shows their weakness. In this subtle presentation of both the strengths and weakness of a "real" character in a "real" world we see the skill of Tolkien as a writer.

Éowyn's physical healing, from the wound inflicted by the Nazgûl, comes at the hands of Aragorn. Her spiritual healing, however, is administered by the steward Faramir in the Houses of Healing at Minas Tirith.

"I wished to be loved by another," she answered. "But I desire no man's pity."

"That I know," he said. "You desired to have the love of the Lord Aragorn. Because he was high and puissant, and you wished to have renown and glory and to be lifted far above the mean things that crawl on the earth. And as a great captain may to a young soldier he seemed to you admirable. For so he is, a lord among men, the greatest that now is. But when he gave you only understanding and pity, then you desired to have nothing, unless a brave death in battle. Look at me, Éowyn!"

And Éowyn looked at Faramir long and steadily; and Faramir said: "Do not scorn pity that is the gift of a gentle heart, Éowyn! But I do not offer you my pity. For you are a lady high and valiant and have yourself won renown that shall not be forgotten; and you are a lady beautiful, I deem, beyond even the words of the Elven-tongue to tell. And I love you. Once I pitied your sorrow. But now, were you sorrowless, without fear or any lack, were you the blissful Queen of Gondor, still I would love you. Éowyn, do you not love me?"

Then the heart of Éowyn changed, or else at least she understood it. And suddenly her winter passed, and the sun shone on her. (VI/v)

The healing seems instant here, but it really takes place over several days. It is only completed at this moment, as we see through Éowyn's response: "I will be a shieldmaiden no longer, nor vie with the great Riders, nor take joy only in the songs of slaying. I will be a healer, and love all things that grow and are not barren" (VI/v). Éowyn is willing to give up her pursuit of glory, especially the glory of the warrior: the glory of "slaying," the glory of the "shieldmaiden" and the "great Riders." And so, through the Rohirrim in general and through the battle of Éowyn with the Nazgûl in particular, Tolkien gives us a view of a culture that really does glorify war and battle, and the life of a warrior. But through Éowyn's illness he also shows us what such pursuits and values ultimately lead to, while through her healing he shows us the good that results when such pursuits are renounced.

Hope and Healing

One other note is in order regarding Éowyn. In her story, one might be tempted to see a male chauvinist attitude: that a woman's healing comes by finding the love of a man, giving up the world at large, and settling down to the supposedly more feminine pursuits of home and kitchen. Several chapters could be written on Éowyn alone, but this would represent quite a divergence from the main subject of this book. I will limit myself to a few brief comments. Tolkien's professional world as an Oxford professor was unquestionably a male world, and certainly there is a male romantic image in the way he portrays women in general, and in particular in his portrayal of Éowyn finding healing through the love of a man. But to simplify it further would miss most of what we can learn from this scene. Among other things, it is remarkable that Tolkien gives voice to this very concern. That is, he gives voice to Éowyn as a woman living in a man's world: "All your words are but to say: you are a woman, and your part is in the house. But when the men have died in battle and honour, you have leave to be burned in the house, for the men will need it no more. But I am of the House of Eorl and not a serving-woman. I can ride and wield blade, and I do not fear either pain or death" (V/ii). Éowyn's argument here is in response to Aragorn when he reminds her of her duty to her people. If Tolkien thought there was no virtue in this argument, then why would he include her words in his narrative? At the very least, if Tolkien thought her argument was fundamentally flawed, then he could have put a reply in Aragorn's mouth; surely Aragorn understands duty and responsi-bility. Yet Aragorn shows only sympathy and understanding, asking her what it is that she does fear. Including this passage, without any rebuttal, gives credence to Éowyn's argument. Even more respect and understanding is given to Éowyn's position through the wisdom and gentleness of Aragorn.

Probably the most important aspect of the depiction of Éowyn and especially of her healing, however, lies in the commonality between her and Faramir. Faramir, a man, is as much opposed to battle as Éowyn later becomes. Not only does Tolkien's female character commit herself to "be a healer" and to "love all things that grow and are not barren," but Faramir himself is also com-mitted to the same goals. "Let us cross the River," he says, "and in happier days let us dwell in fair Ithilien and there make a garden. All things will grow with joy there" (VI/v). To say that in Tolkien's narrative Éowyn ought to give up battle *only* because she is a woman would miss the depth of the author's portrayal of both Éowyn and Faramir and the extent to which the author's narrative really does deglorify war.

In fact, the great desire of Sam and Frodo, and even of Merry and Pippin, is to give up their swords, return to the Shire, and take up peaceful pursuits such as gardening. In short, Tolkien does not portray it as solely a womanly virtue to abandon the glories of the battlefield and to turn instead to the house and garden and the pur-suit of peace, but as a manly virtue as well.

Sandra Miesel, in her excellent essay "Life-Giving Ladies: Women in the Writings of J. R. R. Tolkien," acknowledges that "Tolkien idealized women" with a "positive—even too positive—attitude that weaves through all his works."[3] This is a much more accurate criticism than that Tolkien's women are either useless, merely ornamental, or altogether negative. But regarding the cause of Éowyn's unhappiness and Tolkien's portrayal of it, Miesel notes both simply and insightfully that Éowyn "fastens on Aragorn as the answer to her bitter lot but mistakes the hero for the man and is rebuffed. Tolkien is sympathetic to the frustration of this steely lily flower but rejects her notion that men's work is the only kind worth doing." And with respect to Éowyn's healing, or newfound happiness, Miesel concludes, with equal insight, "Éowyn outgrows her hero-worshipping crush for genuine love. She and her husband . . . will rule a deserted region as prince and princess. The lily finally gets to bloom in a real garden where both courage and nurturing skills count."[4]

The "Contest" at Helm's Deep

Though the Battle of Helm's Deep involves considerably smaller armies than either the Siege of Minas Tirith or the battle in front of the Black Gate, and though it lasts only one night, an entire chapter of *The Lord of the Rings* is devoted to this battle, and it seems to take on an importance even beyond that. (This one chapter dominates Peter Jackson's film version of *The Two Towers*.) This battle is somewhat different from the others we have explored. Helm's Deep is described in the present, by characters who are physically present, rather than with the spatial and temporal distance characteristic of the narrative descriptions of other battles. Of greater significance, it is the one important battle at which no hobbit is present!

Some might argue that the evidence of Tolkien's glorification of war may be found in this battle, in the contest between Legolas and Gimli as to who would kill the most orcs. That such a sport is made of war and killing is certainly disturbing. Why, then, does Tolkien include it? Before seeking to answer this, we should make two important observations. Though the battle, including some hand-to-hand fighting, is described in a very concrete present, here too there is little graphic description of violence. A large majority of the narrative is devoted to dialogue among the defenders during moments of respite, especially to the current state of their hope or despair. We get only occasional glimpses of the defenses at some particular strategic moment.

More specifically, with respect to the contest, even though the narrator recounts some of the dialogue wherein Gimli and Legolas boast to each other of their current scores, we witness very few of the actual tallies. We are with Gimli for numbers one, two, and twenty-one of the forty-two orcs he slays, and that is all. And little picture do we get even of these three: "An axe swung and swept back. Two Orcs fell headless. The rest fled." As for Legolas, we see only number thirty-nine (of forty-one), and that from a distance: "The foremost fell with Legolas' last arrow in his throat, but the rest sprang over him" (III/vii). It is also important to note that it is Gimli who initiates the contest, when he boasts of his first two slain orcs. And Gimli, though he is noble for a dwarf and grows to be wiser than most others of his race, is yet a dwarf and not the symbol of wisdom in Tolkien's tales. That is, he represents the values of his people, not the values of the author.

What does Tolkien accomplish in the chapter "Helm's Deep," and why would he include not only the battle itself but also the subplot of the contest between Gimli and Legolas? The text suggests a number of reasons why Tolkien includes this material, none of which are for the glorification of killing. It is here at the Battle of Helm's Deep that Aragorn keeps the word he gave to Éomer when the two first met.

> "When your quest is achieved," [spoke Éomer,] "or is proved vain, return with the horses over the Entwade to Meduseld, the high house in Edoras where Théoden now sits. Thus you shall prove to him that I have not misjudged. In this I place myself, and maybe my very life, in the keeping of your good faith. Do not fail."
>
> "I will not," said Aragorn. (III/ii)

In giving his aid to Aragorn, Éomer places his life in Aragorn's hands. Aragorn repays that trust and more; he also honors Éomer's plea for help: "Return with what speed you may, and let our swords hereafter shine together!" (III/ii). This is why it is important not only that they meet again but that they draw swords together. Aragorn is meeting the real need of the people of Rohan, which is for military aid against the threat of Saruman. Furthermore, he is doing so at great personal risk, not only to his own life but also to all his dreams and plans. Certainly such self-sacrificial giving on Aragorn's part is worthy of praise. Indeed, it is in Rohan that Aragorn's great nobility begins to show visibly, when he first meets Éomer: "Gimli and Legolas looked at their companion in amazement, for they had not seen him in this mood before. . . . In his living face they caught a brief vision of the power and majesty of the kings of stone" (III/ii). It is seen again at the battle: "So great a power and royalty was revealed in Aragorn, as he stood there alone above the ruined gates before the host of his enemies, that many of the wild men paused" (III/vii). And as the future king of Gondor risks his life for the people of Rohan, he earns the allegiance of Rohan's future king. When it comes to "The Last Debate" of the Captains of the West, deciding whether to ride against Mordor and challenge the Black Gates themselves, Éomer admits, "I have little knowledge of these deep matters." But he goes on to add, very poignantly, "but I need it not. This I know, and it is enough, that as my friend Aragorn succoured me and my people, so I will aid him when he calls. I will go" (V/ix).

What we see here is more than mere allegiance; it is a deep bond of friendship that is forged at Helm's Deep. In fact, three friendships are either forged or solidified at the battle. In addition to that of Aragorn and Éomer, the second is that of Gimli and Éomer, for Gimli also risks his life in the battle several times to help Éomer and the people of Rohan. When he saves the life of Éomer—interestingly enough, by tallying his first two orc heads—and Éomer thanks him for it, we should recall the harsh words spoken between the two at their first meeting, and how close they had come to deadly blows just a few days earlier. Though little more is said of their friendship as the book continues, it becomes clear that there is something significant to it. Not only is Gimli at Éomer's side when the Battle of Helm's Deep is over, but when the entire War of the Ring is finally finished, the dwarf returns to Rohan and makes his permanent home at the Glittering Caves of Aglarond, as Éomer's neighbor.

It is also here in the context of war that we see the blossoming of the friendship between Gimli the dwarf and Legolas the elf and the real care they have for each other. This too is greatly significant, considering not only the animosity between their races, which traces back through countless generations to the very First Age of Middle-earth, but also the tension between the two individuals at the start of the Quest—recall that Gloin, the father of Gimli, had been imprisoned by Thranduil, the father of Legolas, which Gimli alludes to at the Council of Elrond. Even after they had passed through Moria, there was enough tension between the two that Legolas grumbled, "A plague on Dwarves and their stiff necks!" (II/vi). By the time the Battle of Helm's Deep is over, however, it seems that Legolas's greatest concern is the well-being of his friend Gimli. He is certainly more concerned for Gimli than for their contest: "I do not grudge you the game, so glad am I to see you on your legs!" (III/viii). It is shortly after the battle that the two make their famous agreement: Gimli will visit Fangorn with Legolas if Legolas will return with Gimli to Aglarond, epitomizing a friendship between elf and dwarf that may be unique in the entire history of Middle-earth.

The point here is that one may glorify the friendship that is born in the context of war, and see the goodness in that friendship, without glorifying the violence out of which that good came. Many friendships have been born in times of hardship, and there are few hardships greater than those experienced in the Battle of Helm's Deep that night—or the type of battle in which Tolkien himself fought, was wounded, and lost two of his close friends. Put another way, it is said that there is no greater love than to lay down your life for a friend, and it is in war that the opportunity to do so is most apparent.

In a similar vein, we must also realize what a great burden such an evil night is on those involved, even the strongest-willed among them. It is a night that Aragorn describes as "a night as long as years" (III/vii). This burden can probably be fully understood only by those who have suffered it themselves. Such a contest as Gimli and Legolas have, however grim it may be, acts to lighten the heavy load and may even be necessary to the survival of those forced to endure war as soldiers. That such a contest is required of Legolas and Gimli serves to show the horror of war, not its glory.

War, the Individual, and Fellowship

In looking at what Tolkien does *not* do in his depiction of war—he does not glorify war or violence—we have also seen some positive things that he does accomplish. We have begun to notice, in the battle of Éowyn and the Nazgûl, that something is happening at the unseen or spiritual level that is as significant as what goes on in the seen physical world. We have also discovered that the individuals involved in the great battles of Middle-earth are more important than the military outcomes. Tolkien reveals to his readers what the participants of battle think, feel, and value. We see that green grass and friendship are far more valuable than glory. In focusing on the individual character rather than on the physical details of the battle, Tolkien places value on the individual life—whether that of a hobbit, a dwarf, an elf, a man, or even one of Sauron's slaves.

This is not to say, however, that Tolkien was an "individualist"— not in the way that word might be understood in the late twentieth or early twenty-first century. Though an individual life is of greater importance than the military outcome of a battle, this does not mean that the individual is more important than society. On the contrary, time and again throughout the books the main characters subjugate their own desires for the good of the community to which they belong. When the elves of Lothlórien single out Gimli the dwarf to be blindfolded before entering their kingdom, Aragorn insists that the entire Fellowship, including himself, be blindfolded; the unity of the Fellowship as a whole is more important than Aragorn's (or any other member's) own individual pride and comfort. Aragorn, when he chooses to pursue the orcs in hopes of rescuing the two hobbits at the start of *The Two Towers*, is putting aside the longing of his own heart to go to Minas Tirith. Their contest at Helm's Deep aside, we get the strong impression that Gimli's welfare is more important to Legolas than his own.

The same can often be said of all the members of the Fellowship. Even Boromir, at the end of *The Fellowship of the Ring*, gives up his own pursuit of glory in an attempt to save Merry and Pippin. Gandalf, though he may have been the most important foe of Sauron, sacrifices his life to save the others. By contrast, in the few instances when we are given a close-up view of the orcs, we see the exact opposite: the individual orcs—Uglúk, Grishnákh, Shagrat, Gorbag— usually put themselves and their own goals above the good of the community. Looking at the relationship between the individual and community from a different perspective, when Gandalf goes to Rohan and rescues Théoden, he does not simply restore an individual king but an entire kingdom. Likewise, when he comes to Minas Tirith, he does not merely bring help to Denethor and Faramir; he brings hope to all those on top of the walls of Minas Tirith who are fighting the battle.

In fact, this observation is consistent with the other observations we have made so far, and it ought to be seen as central to the conclusion of the chapter. If the individual, as an individual, really *were* the most important thing, then pursuit of personal glory in battle would make sense. But pursuit of glory in war is not what Tolkien espouses. Galadriel does not tell the members of the Company that hope remains as long as each individual is strong and brave, but rather that "hope remains while *all the Company* is true" (II/vii, emphasis added). In other words, their commitment to one another and to community is more important than their individual strength. The nine who set out on the Quest from Rivendell, in contrast to the Nazgûl, are not *nine individuals* but *one Fellowship*. The choice of title of the first book of the trilogy tells us something about Tolkien's view of community!

3

Frodo and the Wisdom
of the Wise

"You have grown, Halfling. Yes, you have grown very
much. You are wise, and cruel. You have robbed my
revenge of sweetness, and now I must go hence in
bitterness, in debt to your mercy."

—Saruman (to Frodo)

In 2005, Tolkien scholar Tom Shippey delivered a paper titled "'A
Fund of Wise Sayings': Proverbiality in Tolkien."[1] Shippey notes that
The Lord of the Rings contains more than seventy proverbs, many
of which are of Tolkien's own creation, though others are drawn or
adapted from surviving Old English proverbs. The central point of
the article is that Tolkien highly valued the surviving literary genre of
proverbs. At their core, proverbs are simply wise sayings, though the
most memorable Old English proverbs also have a surprising poetic
or literary quality. As Shippey notes, not only can they be funny and
grim at the same time, but "they have an absolutely obvious, trite,
banal meaning on the surface, but another one, often a harsh or
unwelcome one, buried underneath."[2]

Not surprisingly, Tolkien appreciated proverbs not only for their literary quality and their insights into Old English language and culture but also for the wisdom they contain. As Shippey notes, Tolkien conveys his own wisdom through the proverbs in his stories; these proverbs give us insight into Tolkien's own worldview (and not just the cultures of his characters) and into the philosophy that undergirds his writing. In Shippey's words, "Because these sayings are shared out among different characters, who nevertheless agree with each other, it seems to me also that this is meant to be not just illuminating, but actually true: the proverbial core . . . expresses in very condensed form what might be seen . . . [as his work's] 'ideological' core."[3]

What Shippey reveals about proverbs in particular is also certainly true more generally about all of the wisdom of the wise of Middle-earth. Tolkien portrays certain of his characters as wise, and the words (and actions) of these characters provide great insight into the philosophical foundations of Tolkien's writings. We might say that the wise of Middle-earth incarnate Tolkien's own wisdom.

Indeed, the wisdom of proverbs noted by Shippey and the wisdom of the wise are closely related. One of the interesting points of Shippey's article—though not its central argument—is that we can recognize the wisdom of characters through their knowledge of proverbs. Those who are wise know the old proverbs and the wisdom they contain. And those who lack wisdom are shown to be foolish in that they don't know or don't believe old proverbs, or else they use pseudo-proverbs that either don't actually say anything or that say something false.[4]

This chapter explores Tolkien's portrayal of war, and the philosophical principles behind that portrayal, through the wisdom of the wise of Middle-earth. What do the wise say and do with respect to war? The goal in asking this—indeed, the goal of this entire book—is to understand J. R. R. Tolkien's writing. We are not looking for those characters whose thoughts are most like our own. We may find we agree with Tolkien's wisdom. We may find we disagree with it. There are plenty of critics who dislike Tolkien precisely because they disagree with what he puts forth as wisdom. Our goal is not to argue that Tolkien is wiser than his critics, or conversely that he is less wise, but simply to find out what he thinks is wise. To do that honestly, we want to look at those characters whom Tolkien most clearly portrays as wise, especially in *The Hobbit* and *The Lord of the Rings*.

Spotting Wisdom in Middle-earth

Wisdom, simply defined, is the ability to make good decisions and judgments. It is the ability to discern between various choices of action. A part of wisdom *may* come from knowledge, and those who are wise certainly learn from experience and know the value of knowledge. Yet wisdom is distinct from knowledge. There are some who have considerable knowledge and yet leave the path of wisdom, as do both Saruman and Denethor. Others, by contrast, lack worldly knowledge and yet still act wisely at the most important times. Bilbo, when he left on his voyage "There and Back Again," had far less knowledge of the world than did any of the dwarves. He could not hoot like an owl any more than he could fly like a bat. He knew little about trolls or dragons (though he learned much about the latter). When he started the journey, he had no idea where in Middle-earth his destination, the Lonely Mountain, even was. Yet in the end, he proved not only resourceful but also wise in some important matters.

Fortunately, there is very little doubt about which central characters Tolkien portrays as wise. I have taught college courses on Tolkien's works for over twenty years and have given numerous talks on his writing at colleges, universities, libraries, and other study centers around the United States and in Canada and Europe. I have often asked my classes and audiences to identify whom they consider to be the wise of Middle-earth. The answers are consistent. Gandalf is always at or near the top of the list, along with Aragorn. Faramir is usually near the top also (though his brother, Boromir, is not). Those who have watched only the Peter Jackson films and have not read the books might not mention Elrond or Galadriel as being among the wise, but readers of the books will almost always list these two elven powers. Treebeard, Glorfindel, and Tom Bombadil are also likely to be named, though perhaps a little farther down the list. Neither Bill Ferny nor Ted Sandyman have ever been named. The judgment about the hobbit Samwise Gamgee may be a little more mixed; he seems to have some share of provincial foolishness but also a mix of wisdom that grows over the course of his journeys through his contacts with Aragorn, Elrond, Gandalf, Galadriel, and Faramir. But readers, almost universally, realize that the hobbit Frodo has grown into great wisdom by the end of *The Lord of the Rings*. Indeed, Frodo's wisdom very much echoes that of Gandalf, and is recognized even by the wizard Saruman, though Saruman is so fallen in his own wisdom that he sadly takes as cruelty the mercy grown out of Frodo's wisdom.

So how do readers know what to think? Why are their lists of wise characters so consistent? Sometimes Tolkien communicates very directly, telling the reader outright that a particular character is wise. Elrond is one example. In *The Silmarillion* we read: "Elrond abode in Imladris, and he gathered there many elves, and other folk of wisdom and power from among all the kindreds of Middle-earth. . . . And the house of Elrond was . . . a treasury of good counsel and wise lore" (*Silm*, 297–98). In addition to telling us that Elrond gathers wise people around him, without discrimination based on race, and that his "house" is full of wisdom, Tolkien goes on to affirm Elrond's own wisdom in which he acts to preserve history, lore, and beauty. *The Hobbit* also tells of Elrond's wisdom when it introduces him: "He was as noble and as fair in face as an elf-lord, as strong as a warrior, as wise as a wizard, as venerable as a king of dwarves, and as kind as summer" (*Hobbit*, 94). The narrator is explicit about the depth and breadth of Elrond's wisdom and later goes on to tell about the wisdom of the advice given by Elrond and how helpful it is to the dwarves and hobbit (*Hobbit*, 95–100).

In other places, however, wisdom is communicated less directly— though still in a way that should make it clear to the reader that a particular character is wise (or, conversely, foolish). The use of proverbs, for example, as has been carefully argued by Shippey and noted above, is one such clue. The wisdom of one character may also be affirmed by another character who has previously been revealed as wise. There are many other clues as well.

The Wisdom of Gandalf

The wisdom of Gandalf, also known as Mithrandir, the Grey Pilgrim, is especially clear. Some of the most powerful and revealing

dialogues in *The Lord of the Rings* involve Gandalf and Denethor, and the Steward of Gondor. Denethor is a great man, both
powerful and proud. The blood of ancient Númenor still runs
in his veins, the narrator tells us. Through the eyes of Pippin,
however—or rather, through some intuitive sixth sense possessed
by the hobbit—readers see how much greater Gandalf's wisdom
is than that of the steward Denethor: "Denethor looked indeed
much more like a great wizard than Gandalf did, more kingly,
beautiful, and powerful; and older. Yet by a sense other than
sight Pippin perceived that Gandalf had the greater power and
the deeper wisdom, and a majesty that was veiled" (V/i). This is
a wonderful device Tolkien uses here, simultaneously emphasizing the similarities and the differences between these two figures,
both of whom are stewards. Denethor may be the only man in
Middle-earth, other than Aragorn, whose knowledge of history,
and of the Rings, and of current events, comes close to that of the
wizards. He has studied the ancient scrolls of lore that probably
nobody else alive has read except Gandalf and perhaps Aragorn.
And yet Pippin perceives that Gandalf has not only greater power
but deeper wisdom as well. Tolkien's use of the verb *perceived*
indicates that Pippin's assessment is true and corresponds with
the reality of the situation.

Even without such occasional direct references to his wisdom, we
see Gandalf's wisdom in the respect given him by others. In "The Last
Debate," Aragorn charges the other captains: "Let none now reject
the counsels of Gandalf. . . . But for him all would long ago have
been lost" (V/ix). Likewise, Galadriel—the eldest and noblest of the
elves still remaining in Middle-earth—thinks so highly of Gandalf
that she argued for him to be the head of the White Council, which
she herself summoned (II/vii). When her husband, Celeborn, questions Gandalf's wisdom after his fall in Moria, Galadriel defends
the wizard.

> "And if it were possible, one would say that at the last Gandalf fell
> from wisdom into folly, going needlessly into the net of Moria,"
> [said Celeborn].
> "He would be rash indeed that said that thing," said Galadriel
> gravely. "Needless were none of the deeds of Gandalf in life." (II/vii)

It is interesting to note that even Celeborn, when questioning the Company's decision to enter Moria, acknowledges Gandalf's long record of wisdom and finds it nearly (though not quite) impossible to question. And Galadriel chides her own husband as "rash indeed" when he does question it. Her reply, in many ways, is the ultimate testimony to Gandalf's wisdom: none of his deeds were vain or meaningless.

Galadriel's statement leads to a broader point: we may judge the wisdom of many types of choices by the fruit that they bear. (I speak here of *strategic* choices rather than *moral* choices. As I will later discuss, there is a moral good in being willing to do what is right even when the outcome of such moral choices may be undesirable or unpleasant.) Thus Gandalf's wisdom may also be seen in his insistence on allowing the young hobbits Merry and Pippin to join the Fellowship. Without them, the Ents might never have been roused, nor the Nazgûl-Lord slain by Éowyn, nor Faramir rescued from the pyre. Foremost, therefore, we see Gandalf's wisdom in the final outcome of the War of the Ring itself. In "The Council of Elrond" and, later, in "The Last Debate," the gathered leaders choose to follow Gandalf's strategies—initially sending a small fellowship into Mordor with a quest to destroy the Ring, and later sending a large army to the Black Gate to distract Sauron from the real task of Sam and Frodo—even though those strategies seem foolish and desperate to many: "'Despair, or folly?' said Gandalf. 'It is not despair, for despair is only for those who see the end beyond all doubt. We do not. It is wisdom to recognize necessity, when all other courses have been weighed, though as folly it may appear to those who cling to false hope. Well, let folly be our cloak, a veil before the eyes of the Enemy!'" (II/ii). Looking only at Gandalf's advice, and not at the outcome, we might not be in a position to judge *his* wisdom save by our *own* preconceived notion of what is wise. If we don't read to the end of the book, we could join the voice of the elf Erestor (to whom Gandalf is responding in the passage above): "That is the path of despair. Of folly I would say, if the long wisdom of Elrond did not forbid me" (II/ii). Denethor also calls Gandalf's plan little more than "a fool's hope" (V/iv). Even Gandalf, in "The Last Debate," leaves open the question of whether his strategy is "wisdom or folly" (V/ix). But the outcome of the trilogy leaves no doubt: it is Gandalf's strategy that eventually results in the victory. As we read in "Of the Rings of Power and the Third Age," the fifth part of *The Silmarillion*, "Now all these things were achieved for the most part by the counsel and vigilance of Mithrandir, and in the last few days he was revealed as a lord of great reverence, and clad in white he rode into battle" (*Silm*, 304). And Treebeard tells Gandalf toward the end of the trilogy, "You have proved mightiest, and all your labours have gone well" (VI/vi). He might equally have said, "You have proved wisest."

At this point, it is an interesting aside to ask just where Gandalf's wisdom comes from. There are a few hints in the narrative, and we will return to these later in this chapter. But a more direct answer is suggested in a personal letter Tolkien wrote in 1954. In this letter, Tolkien describes the nature of Gandalf in particular and of the wizards in general.

> There are naturally no precise modern terms to say what he was. I wd. venture to say that he was an *incarnate* "angel." . . . That is, with the other *Istari*, wizards, "those who know," an emissary from the Lords of the West, sent to Middle-earth, as the great crisis of Sauron loomed on the horizon. By "incarnate" I mean they were embodied in physical bodies capable of pain, and weariness, and of afflicting the spirit with physical fear, and of being "killed," though supported by the angelic spirit they might endure long, and only show slowly the wearing of care and labour.
>
> Why they should take such form is bound up with the "mythology" of the "angelic" Powers of the world of this fable. At this point in the fabulous history the purpose was precisely to limit and hinder their exhibition of "power" on the physical plane, and so that they should do what they were primarily sent for: train, advise, instruct, arouse the hearts and minds of those threatened by Sauron to a resistance with their own strengths; and not just to do the job for them. (*Letters*, 202)

In other words, Gandalf is sent to Middle-earth to provide *wisdom*, not to provide "power on the physical plane" or what one might call "military might." In fact, his natural "angelic" powers were intentionally limited in order to *hinder* their exhibition. Thus, the purpose of the Istari is not so much to *act*, but rather to *know* and to *teach*.[5] Gandalf was sent for training, advising, instructing, arousing. And this, as mentioned in the previous chapter, is precisely what we see Gandalf doing throughout the book. He first rouses Théoden, and later, in the Siege of Gondor, he walks the walls of Minas Tirith, along with the Prince of Dol Amroth, encouraging the hearts of the defenders so that they do not lose strength and hope. As for his function of instructing and training, what is that other than passing wisdom on to others?

This "angelic" nature may also be what Pippin was perceiving, with some sense other than sight, as veiled majesty. Yet the reference to veiled majesty is probably even deeper than simply the angelic nature of the Istari; Saruman is also one of the Istari, and shares that same nature, and yet is fallen from that majesty, while Gandalf's majesty has increased since his return from death. In any case, Gandalf's wisdom is greater and deeper than Denethor's, and though it is coupled with considerable knowledge, it goes beyond knowledge. It is Gandalf who first recognizes Bilbo's ring as the One Ring, even though the ring-lore of Saruman is much greater.

Military Might and True Hope

So, accepting Gandalf as one of the wise, what does he say with respect to war, and battle, and arms? And what of Frodo, whom Gandalf trained? Or Faramir, whose father blamed him for being the pupil of Gandalf? What words does Tolkien put in the mouths of the wise?

When speaking to Denethor about his own role in Middle-earth, Gandalf says: "I will say this: the rule of no realm is mine, neither of Gondor nor any other, great or small. But all worthy things that are in peril as the world now stands, those are my care. And for my part, I shall not wholly fail of my task, though Gondor should perish, if anything passes through this night that can still grow fair or bear fruit and flower again in days to come" (V/i). Gandalf makes this comment in the context of war, as he sits in the fortress of Minas Tirith at the onset of a terrible siege. As with the earlier battle at Helm's Deep, when he speaks these words it is unknown if anything in Minas Tirith will survive the next few days. Several of Gandalf's deepest values are revealed. Consider that for one who glorifies war, or who glorifies the warrior, the greatest thing is victory; we build monuments to the victors, not to the vanquished. But Gandalf values something more than victory, at least if victory is defined in a military sense. Anything that can grow fair, or bear fruit or flower, has worth. It is these things, not the glory of war, that the wizard cares deeply about. War may be a necessity in order to protect "worthy things that are in peril as the world now stands," but it should never be the goal.

We see also that the wizard is not interested in rule, or authority, or command. We learn also that he has a "care," or "task." More to the point of this discussion, it also appears that battle itself is not what most concerns him—certainly not any glory associated with battle. Indeed, it is rare that Gandalf ever takes a direct physical role in battle. He is not present at the siege of Helm's Deep; he appears only at the end of the battle, when he leads into the fray Erkenbrand and his host of a thousand foot soldiers (changed in the film to Éomer and his host of a thousand mounted Rohirrim). Even then, we don't witness Gandalf fight but are left with the impression that his primary task was to bring Erkenbrand to Théoden's aid. Nor is Gandalf present on the Pelennor Fields when that battle is won, though earlier in the siege he does use his might to rescue Faramir on more than one occasion. In particular, though Gandalf lends his wisdom to the battle of Minas Tirith and works tirelessly to bring hope to those fighting, and at a few rare times uses his power, the success of his task is not dependent on military victory.

Later, in "The Last Debate," Gandalf tells the gathered captains, "Victory cannot be achieved by arms, whether you sit here to endure siege after siege, or march out to be overwhelmed beyond the River" (V/ix). That is a very telling statement. Certainly Gandalf hopes for victory in the war against Sauron, and he works hard to accomplish it. Yet he does not see the physical victory of armies involved in a battle as the key to overall victory in the war. This could be viewed simply from a strategic viewpoint: the destruction of the Ring is the key to victory, and everything else is ultimately insignificant. Certainly this is true. Yet Gandalf's comment could—and, I believe, should—also be understood at a much deeper level.

There comes a point in *The Silmarillion* when Ulmo, one of the greatest and wisest immortal Powers of Middle-earth, sends a very similar message to Turgon, elven king of the hidden realm of Gondolin: "Love not too well the work of thy hands and the devices of thy heart; and remember that the true hope of the Noldor lieth in the West, and cometh from the Sea" (*Silm*, 240). Despite all of the hidden might of Gondolin—it is the last of the great elven kingdoms of the First Age to fall—its hope ultimately could not rest in its own strength. Morgoth, the enemy, to whom Sauron is merely a vassal, is too powerful for any elven lord. For Turgon, as for the Captains of the West, victory cannot be achieved by arms.

Gandalf, whose sword was forged in Gondolin years earlier for those very wars, understands this. When trust is placed in human strength, then the glorification of the warrior is natural. But Gandalf and Ulmo warn against trusting in strength in arms. Unlike the world wars of our twentieth century, for example, where the outcome was dependent on military might and military strategy, *The Lord of the Rings* was crafted by Tolkien in such a way that the outcome is *not* ultimately dependent on such things. For all of the glory given to those who lost or risked their lives in battle at the Field of Cormallen, the highest honor is given to Frodo and Sam, who do not fight in any physical battle at all.

One other reason Gandalf might eschew the glorification of war is the great value he places on life. One of the most significant dialogues in all of *The Lord of the Rings* takes place near the beginning of the first book, when Gandalf is explaining to Frodo some of the history of the Ring. When Frodo laments that Bilbo, the elves, and Gandalf all chose to let Gollum live, Gandalf replies: "Many that live deserve death. And some that die deserve life. Can you give it to them? Then do not be too eager to deal out death in judgement. For even the very wise cannot see all ends" (I/iii). With all of their editing of hundreds of pages of writing down to a few hours of screenplay, the screenwriters for Peter Jackson's film version of *The Fellowship of the Ring* left this speech almost completely intact, word for word (though they moved the dialogue out of Bag End and into Moria). It is a significant comment, and it gets at the heart of why Tolkien does not glorify war. People die in war. War is won by killing the enemy. And lives, even enemy lives, have value. "And for me," Gandalf says, "I pity even [Sauron's] slaves" (I/iii).

Faramir

Though there are many other voices of wisdom within Tolkien's story, that of Faramir, son of Denethor, is particularly worth exploring, in part because of the marked contrast between Faramir and both his father, Denethor, and his brother, Boromir. From our first meeting with Faramir, we catch in his speech and actions a glimpse of his wisdom, or at least his desire for such: "Even so," he tells Frodo and Sam, explaining his questioning of them despite the pressing matters of war, "I spare a brief time, in order to judge justly in a hard matter" (IV/v).

Faramir is interesting for several reasons. First, he is one of the few characters—along with Elrond and Gandalf—who makes any allusion to a divine authority.

> Before they ate, Faramir and all his men turned and faced west in a moment of silence. Faramir signed to Frodo and Sam that they should do likewise.
>
> "So we always do," he said, as they sat down: "we look towards Númenor that was, and beyond to Elvenhome that is, and to that which is beyond Elvenhome and will ever be." (IV/v)

Even if one has not read *The Silmarillion* and thus does not recognize "that which is beyond Elvenhome and will ever be" as Eru Ilúvatar, the divine and self-existent Creator in Tolkien's mythology, it is still hard *not* to understand this action as a sort of prayer. Whatever the reader thinks of prayer, in Tolkien's world it is a mark of humility and wisdom to acknowledge one's dependence on something beyond oneself—as Gandalf and Elrond often do—and such an acknowledgment is at the heart of prayer.

A second interesting aspect of Faramir's character is that he is portrayed as a "pupil" of the wizard Gandalf (though, in fact, the two had met on only a few occasions). Denethor chides his son Faramir: "Your bearing is lowly in my presence, yet it is long now since you turned from your own way at my counsel. See, you have spoken skilfully, as ever; but I, have I not seen your eye fixed on Mithrandir, seeking whether you said well or too much? He has long had your heart in his keeping." And a little while later he adds more bluntly, "Boromir was loyal to me and no wizard's pupil"

(V/iv). As Denethor recognizes, with some jealousy, Faramir looks more to the wizard for wisdom and guidance than he does to his own father. Given what we have already seen of Gandalf's wisdom, we must assume that for Faramir to fix his eyes on the wizard is a sign of his own wisdom, whatever his father might say. Indeed, we see much of Gandalf in Denethor's younger son; the fact that Faramir could learn so much wisdom from the wizard in a short time is remarkable and shows that he really is among the wise of Middle-earth.

A third item to note about Faramir's character is the contrast between him and his brother, Boromir, and even between him and his father, Denethor. For example, though "prayer" is an important custom to Faramir and his men, we see no hint that Boromir or Denethor adhere to this custom. Whereas Faramir has a very good understanding of his father and brother—of their strengths as well as their weaknesses—and can appreciate them for who they are, there is little indication that Denethor has much understanding of his younger son. In describing Denethor to Pippin, Gandalf makes reference to this difference between the sons: "[Denethor] is not as other men of this time, Pippin, and whatever be his descent from father to son, by some chance the blood of Westernesse runs nearly true in him; as it does in his other son, Faramir, and yet did not in Boromir whom he loved best" (V/i). That Faramir is more like Denethor than is Boromir makes it more interesting that Denethor would love Boromir better. As we later learn, however, Faramir is like Denethor only with respect to having inherited more truly the blood of Númenor and the possibility of real nobility; we also learn that this nobility fails in Denethor, who becomes like "the heathen kings, under the domination of the Dark Lord" (V/vii), while it does not fail in Faramir. At any rate, this tension within the family makes for some of the most powerful and moving dialogue within *The Lord of the Rings*—and one of the most tragic subplots. But the point for the reader, with respect to this chapter, is that Faramir is portrayed by Tolkien as the wiser of the two brothers, and thus his voice is the one we should look to for the values Tolkien is putting forth in his work.

One of the first glimpses we get of war through Faramir's eyes is his comment to Frodo: "I do not slay man or beast needlessly, and not gladly even when it is needed" (IV/v). In other words, Faramir takes no pleasure and finds no glory in war. A short time later, he shares this view more explicitly: "War must be, while we defend our lives against a destroyer who would devour all; but I do not love the bright sword for its sharpness, nor the arrow for its swiftness, nor the warrior for his glory. I love only that which they defend: the city of the Men of Númenor; and I would have her loved for her memory, her ancientry, her beauty, and her present wisdom. Not feared, save as men may fear the dignity of a man, old and wise" (IV/v). As we later see, Faramir is a very valiant warrior. He is not only strong but brave as well: the first in attack and the last to retreat. Yet he takes no pride in this. He loves his city and his country and is willing to die to defend the lives of his people, but he sees no glory in the work of the warrior. For all his valor and might in battle, he would rather wield the hoe of a gardener than the sharp sword or swift arrow of the soldier. This may be seen most clearly in Faramir's indictment of the state of Gondor: "We . . . can scarce claim any longer the title High. We . . . now love war and valour as things good in themselves, both a sport and an end; and . . . we esteem a warrior . . . above men of other crafts" (IV/v). Faramir sees the love of war, the practice of war as a sport, and the esteeming of the warrior not as signs of the current glory of Gondor but rather as signs of its fall. It would be hard to imagine a much clearer statement from a valiant warrior such as Faramir that war is not to be glorified.

Now consider Boromir's character in contrast to the wisdom portrayed by Faramir. It would be an injustice to say that Boromir kills gladly or needlessly, and yet he does see war and battle as opportunities for personal glory and, in particular, as the chief place where glory is to be earned. Our first glimpse of Denethor's elder son is at the Council of Elrond. In pleading with the council to use the Ring against Sauron, Boromir says: "Valour needs first strength, and then a weapon. Let the Ring be your weapon, if it has such power as you say. Take it and go forth to victory!" (II/ii). His speech, though not explicitly in opposition to the words of Faramir, is nonetheless filled with talk of strength, weapons, power, and victory. We see the folly of Boromir's desire reach its fullest expression when he seeks to take the Ring from Frodo.

"It is a gift, I say; a gift to the foes of Mordor. It is mad not to use it, to use the power of the Enemy against him. The fearless, the ruthless, these alone will achieve victory. What could not a warrior do in this hour, a great leader? What could not Aragorn do? Or if he refuses, why not Boromir? The Ring would give me power of Command. How I would drive the hosts of Mordor, and all men would flock to my banner!"

Boromir strode up and down, speaking ever more loudly. Almost he seemed to have forgotten Frodo, while his talk dwelt on walls and weapons, and the mustering of men; and he drew plans for great alliances and glorious victories to be. (II/x)

For Boromir, what matters is military victory. If one needs to be ruthless to achieve it, then one should be ruthless. He equates being a "great leader" with being a warrior. As the last line tells us, he does see glory in victory. Indeed, he sees a glory in the battle itself: "the power of Command," the driving of the hosts of Mordor, the flocking of men to his banner. In short, he seems to thrive on the promise of war and all that comes with it, from the "great alliances" to the "glorious victories." He is, without doubt, the lesser of the two brothers.

Now we may excuse Boromir in this last instance and say merely that he is under the spell of the Ring at this time and might not otherwise have spoken in such a way. Yet these words do reveal his character. Faramir loves his brother, Boromir, and in many ways respects him, but he also understands his weaknesses. "If [Isildur's Bane, the Ring] were a thing that gave advantage in battle," Faramir says, "I can well believe that Boromir, the proud and fearless, often rash, ever anxious for the victory of Minas Tirith (and his own glory therein), might desire such a thing and be allured by it" (IV/v). And if through the outcome of all of Gandalf's efforts Tolkien offers the final judgment of his wisdom, then through the outcome of Boromir's action—his own death and the breaking of the Fellowship—we are offered the judgment of the worldview that glorifies war.

The Wisdom of the Bagginses

And this brings us, finally, to the wisdom of two hobbits, Bilbo Baggins and his nephew and adopted son, Frodo Baggins. When we first meet Bilbo, at the start of *The Hobbit*, the word *wise* does not jump to mind. Tom Shippey, in *J. R. R. Tolkien: Author of the Century*, offers what might be the best summary of the Bilbo Baggins who begins the journey toward the Lonely Mountain: "Bilbo is something of a snob: not a terrible one, for he is prepared to offer a pipe to passing strangers, but certainly liable to draw a line between 'his sort' and other sorts." Shippey also notes something important about Bilbo's use of words: "It is obvious that much of what Bilbo says is socially coded to mean its opposite."[6] For Tolkien, careful and truthful use of words and language is always a sign of wisdom, while the opposite is a sign of foolishness. Bilbo is something of a fool. But he is not a complete fool. Not yet. There are still seeds of wisdom within him, and some healthy but latent hobbit values and virtues, but they are being stifled.

It is Gandalf who comes along and rescues Bilbo from falling completely into foolishness. Bilbo is, to conclude Shippey's thoughts, in grave danger of becoming like his cousins, the Sackville-Bagginses: "Gandalf means, however, to turn him back . . . [He means] to move Bilbo from the one side, the snobbish side, to the other."[7] Part of Gandalf's strategy is simply to set Bilbo on a journey with Thorin and the dwarves. He seems to do this both for the sake of the dwarves and for the sake of the hobbit. In any case, this journey gets Bilbo out of the Shire and exposes him to a wider world; it involves him in something bigger than himself; and it also puts him into "tight places" where he must rely on some latent hobbit wisdom, as when he finds himself all alone under the Misty Mountains after the escape from the goblins. The narrator tells us, "Hobbits are not quite like ordinary people," explaining that "they have a fund of wisdom and wise sayings that men have mostly never heard or have forgotten long ago" (*Hobbit*, 116–17).

Gandalf's success in rescuing Bilbo and turning him from a path of foolishness to one of wisdom can be seen in what Bilbo becomes: a hobbit who is given honor and "grave respect" (II/ii) even in the house of Elrond by the very wisest of Middle-earth. Perhaps the greatest tribute to Bilbo's wisdom can be found in Thorin's dying words: "There is more in you of good than you know, child of the kindly West. Some courage and some wisdom, blended in measure. If more of us valued food and cheer and song above hoarded gold, it would be a merrier world" (*Hobbit*, 348). Thorin not only speaks directly of Bilbo's wisdom but adds the poignant comment that speaks of the wisdom within the hobbit's values—values that, by the end of the book, have broken through the veneer of snobbishness that had threatened to hide and eventually strangle those values

There is one type of wisdom that Bilbo displays toward the end of the story that is particularly relevant to this chapter, and is also commended by Gandalf with a "Well done!" (*Hobbit*, 332). Bilbo has the wisdom to understand that no amount of treasure is worth warring for. This is a wisdom appreciated also by the elven king Thranduil, who, despite having perhaps too much desire for treasure himself, still announces, "Long will I tarry, ere I begin this war for Gold" (*Hobbit*, 338). After all Bilbo went through to earn a portion of the dragon's treasure, he is willing to sacrifice his entire share in order to prevent a war pitting the dwarves against elves and men. However "impossible" the situation had become, war, he thought, was not the answer. And so, at great personal risk, he enacts his plan to prevent the war. Bilbo's wisdom is a wisdom that loves peace and pursues it. It is a wisdom that would lead to a merrier world.

Gandalf's ability to teach and train others in this kind of wisdom that seeks peace and eschews war and violence is also seen in Frodo at the end of *The Return of the King*. When, after his return from Mount Doom, Frodo and his three companions prepare to reenter the Shire—not yet aware of the disaster that Saruman has wrought there—to their dismay, Gandalf leaves them. As the wizard goes his way, his parting words are: "I am not coming to the Shire. You must settle its affairs yourselves; that is what you have been trained for. Do you not yet understand? My time is over: it is no longer my task to set things to rights, nor to help folk to do so. And as for you, my dear friends, you will need no help. You are grown up now" (VI/vii). Gandalf is correct about the hobbits not needing his help. His wisdom is proven once again, as we see just how much the hobbits have learned!

Consider that it is Frodo, near the beginning of the story, who laments the fact that nobody killed Gollum. Contrast this with the Frodo at the end of *The Lord of the Rings* who seeks to avoid another battle and prohibits vengeance even on those who had committed so much violence.

"Fight?" said Frodo. "Well I suppose it may come to that. But remember: there is to be no slaying of hobbits, not even if they have gone over to the other side. Really gone over, I mean; not just obeying ruffians' orders because they are frightened. No hobbit has ever killed another on purpose in the Shire, and it is not to begin now. And nobody is to be killed at all, if it can be helped. Keep your tempers and hold your hands to the last possible moment!" (VI/viii)

Frodo's voice here is the voice of mercy. It is the voice that values life: not only friendly hobbit life, but even the life of the enemy, the hobbit that has "really gone over" or the evil "ruffian" men. It is an echo of the voice of Gandalf, who pities even Sauron's slaves. Frodo's voice is also the voice of restraint. As we read later, "Frodo had been in the battle, but he had not drawn sword, and his chief part had been to prevent the hobbits in their wrath at their losses, from slaying those of their enemies who threw down their weapons" (VI/viii). He does not urge the hobbits to seek glory in battle as they regain the land that has been taken from them, but rather his urging is that they refrain as much as possible from fighting: to "hold [their] hands to the last possible moment." This is not cowardice. Frodo acts bravely. Rather, it is the wisdom of Tolkien's wise, and it is not a wisdom that glorifies violence.

The greatest test of Frodo's new wisdom and mercy is given him when he returns to the doorsteps of Bag End and finds his beloved home in shambles and his neighborhood in ruins. For he then comes face-to-face with the one who is most responsible for the evil: Saruman. Unlike some of the hobbits or men, who have been acting in either fear or petty greed, Saruman has acted in unmitigated spite, with a desire to destroy. Yet Frodo shows not only mercy but uncommon wisdom of the type that Tolkien espouses: "It is useless to meet revenge with revenge: it will heal nothing," he says, as he commands the hobbits to spare Saruman's life. Even when Saruman draws a knife and seeks (vainly) to kill him, Frodo's mercy prevails. "Do not kill him even now," he tells the others. "For he has not hurt me. And in any case I do not wish him to be slain in this evil mood" (VI/viii). Frodo not only hopes for Saruman's cure and is wise enough to know that he does not have authority to judge another person, but he is also wise enough to realize that the very "mood" of such attempts at vengeance is "evil." It would harm the avengers as much as the one taken vengeance on. Oddly enough, it is Saruman's words to Frodo that capture the situation: "You have grown very much. You are wise, and cruel." Even Saruman must acknowledge Frodo's wisdom. Sadly, though, in the wizard's fallen state—a state that could well be described as a pitiable self-hatred—he sees Frodo's mercy as cruelty.

For Tolkien, however, mercy is part of peace, and both mercy and peace are central to the wisdom of Tolkien's wise.

4

Military Victory or Moral Victory?

"Gentleness may be repaid with death."
—Denethor

"So be it."
—Faramir

Boromir, son of Denethor, has his virtues. Ultimately, however, he is not a model of wisdom. Rather, he is the consummate warrior, who revels in the glory of war. He seems to care about military victory not merely as a means to some other end but as an end in itself. Military victory, to Boromir, is what matters most. And even if the wise of Middle-earth admire Boromir on some grounds—for his courage, his love of his country, or his warrior's willingness to give up his life for others—they disapprove of his values in other ways. If Boromir's values do not correspond to Tolkien's understanding of wisdom, if it is not the military outcome of a battle that matters most, then what does matter?

Much of the rest of this book deals with that question. And our first observation is that in Tolkien's writing, something that might be described as *moral* victory is more important than *military* victory. We see this in several ways. We see it in the way that the wise of Middle-earth treat Gollum, which relates this chapter back to the first chapter of this book. More broadly, we see it in the moral choices that are made in the context of the war. We see it in the costs that the main foes of Sauron are—and are not—willing to pay for victory over Sauron. And, ultimately, we see it in many of the responses to the temptation of the Ring.

Victory, at What Cost?

Consider again the mercy and compassion shown to Gollum by many of the foes of Mordor, including, at one time or another, Gandalf, Aragorn, Faramir, King Thranduil and the wood-elves, Frodo, and even Sam. Though it had become clear that Gollum had done great evil, and is still capable of doing much more evil, these characters still show him mercy on many occasions. One aspect of this is that torture, even under extreme need, would be immoral in Tolkien's Middle-earth. As we saw in the first chapter of this book, Gandalf, in his desperation for knowledge, *may* have treated Gollum cruelly. But if he did so, he did so wrongly.

This discussion goes deeper than the ethic against torture explored in the first chapter, however. The good and wise characters of Middle-earth are committed to treating Gollum with kindness, even though doing so poses great risks and seems to go unappreciated. Given his past acts, Gollum does not deserve kindness. Though Gandalf defends the decision to show mercy to Gollum, he acknowledges that Gollum does instead deserve death: "Deserves it! I daresay he does" (I/ii). Many other good characters also suggest that it would be just to punish Gollum. Before Gandalf speaks these words, Frodo complains that it was a pity that Bilbo did not kill Gollum when he had a chance to do it justly. And at the Council of Elrond, others are bothered by the mercy that Gollum is shown. "He is a small thing, you say, this Gollum?" asks Boromir. "Small, but great in mischief. What became of him? To what doom did you put him?" Even Glóin the dwarf, who has been a prisoner of the elves himself (as told in *The Hobbit*), shows bitterness about the elves' kinder treatment of Gollum, grumbling, "You were less tender to me" (II/ii).

Yet Gollum is shown mercy and compassion, and even "over-kindliness." Why? One reason is Gandalf's foresight that Gollum will play a later role, presumably with a good result, "a part . . . that neither he nor Sauron have foreseen" (II/ii). But most of the others at Elrond's council, even among the wise, don't share that foresight; they foresee just the opposite, that Gollum will do further evil. Aragorn comments: "His malice is great and gives him a strength hardly to be believed in one so lean and withered. He could work much mischief still, if he were free." When he finds out that Gollum has escaped, Aragorn continues: "That is ill news indeed. We shall all rue it bitterly, I fear" (II/ii). When Sam finally has a chance to kill Gollum on Mount Doom, he sees that act not only as "just" but also as "the only safe thing to do." And yet he refrains from hurting him: "Deep in his heart there was something that restrained him" (VI/iii).

So the question remains: Why are the foes of Mordor willing to pay such a price—or at least to take such a risk—in order to help Gollum? The answer is the same as our answer to the question of the first chapter, and we can now begin to see that it is a central theme in Tolkien's books: moral victories are more important to Tolkien's most noble characters than are military victories.

To put it another way, we simply restate the question as an observation: to the foes of Sauron, moral decisions, such as treating a prisoner well, hold greater value than military victory. Showing mercy is the right thing to do. It is right for many reasons. Some of the acts of mercy come from a real concern to help Gollum find his "cure." But whether Gollum is cured or not, showing him mercy is right. Showing mercy is not only a means to an end; mercy is an end in itself.

In *The Hobbit*, Tolkien has Bilbo face a difficult decision at the end of his interaction with Gollum, shortly after the famous riddle game. Bilbo is trying to escape from Gollum's tunnels, and Gollum is guarding the only way out.

> Bilbo almost stopped breathing, and went stiff himself. He was desperate. He must get away, out of this horrible darkness, while he

82

had any strength left. He must fight. He must stab the foul thing, put its eyes out, kill it. It meant to kill him. No, not a fair fight. He was invisible now. Gollum had no sword. Gollum had not actually threatened to kill him, or tried to yet. And he was miserable, alone, lost. A sudden understanding, a pity mixed with horror, welled up in Bilbo's heart: a glimpse of endless unmarked days without light or hope of betterment, hard stone, cold fish, sneaking and whispering. All these thoughts passed in a flash of a second. He trembled. And then quite suddenly in another flash, as if lifted by a new strength and resolve, he leaped. (*Hobbit*, 133)

Though the confrontation is not what we would typically describe as a military battle, it is similar to a battle in that there are two opponents, and the likely outcome is death for one or the other, with the spoils going to the victor. It is an unfair battle, however, because Bilbo has acquired the Ring and is now invisible. Furthermore, Bilbo has a sword, while Gollum is unarmed. Thus, Bilbo has a choice between what appears to be the easy escape route of stabbing Gollum in an unfair fight and the more difficult path of showing mercy to the creature and trying to get past him without killing him. The obvious (and seemingly justifiable) choice is to fight Gollum in the unfair battle. But Bilbo, in a debate that "passed in a flash of a second," chooses instead the values of fairness and pity, even though by that course he takes on himself a much greater risk of defeat.

The hobbits' treatment of the ruffians in the Shire at the end of *The Return of the King* is much the same. Some rightly perceive that the men are dangerous and will harm and kill the hobbits if given the chance. It would seem advantageous, from a strategic standpoint, to attack them first and ask questions later—especially given what the hobbits have already suffered at their hands. But Frodo, as we saw earlier, forbids killing them.

There is an old question, often asked: "What are we willing to fight for?" Every war ever fought raises this question. In *The Lord of the Rings*, we see that the free peoples of Middle-earth are willing to fight Sauron in order to protect their own lives and freedom. When the four hobbits return to the Shire, they find that their people are willing to fight the ruffians—and even to die doing so—in order to regain their freedom. But in a sense, Tolkien has also turned this question around. As much as the question is, "For what causes are we willing to fight (and seek victory)?" an equally important question is, "For what values are we willing to risk defeat?"

The issue of which moral choices Tolkien's heroes make in the context of battle—for what values these people are willing to risk defeat in order to preserve—is illustrated in many ways besides their treatment of Gollum. Aragorn's decision at Parth Galen to pursue Merry and Pippin, rather than to head straight to Gondor, can be seen in this light. There were three choices before Aragorn at the time: following Frodo and Sam to the east in order to aid them, traveling south to Minas Tirith to follow his own heart in hopes of bringing aid to Gondor and taking up his throne, or going west in an effort to rescue the two young hobbits. Of these three choices, the first two are far more advantageous from a strategic viewpoint, at least according to the knowledge Aragorn has at the time. "Boromir has laid it on me to go to Minas Tirith, and my heart desires it," says Aragorn to himself, "but where are the Ring and the Bearer? How shall I find them and save the Quest from disaster?" (III/i). These are the strategic questions. In the war against Sauron, the two young hobbits, Merry and Pippin, would seem to have little strategic importance, while the quest of the Ringbearer and the military might of Minas Tirith are of great import. Yet Aragorn chooses the third of these options, even though it is clear that he believes (wrongly, as it turns out) that by making this choice he has removed himself strategically from the great events of the time: "'I will follow the Orcs,' he said at last. 'I would have guided Frodo to Mordor and gone with him to the end; but if I seek him now in the wilderness, I must abandon the captives to torment and death. My heart speaks clearly at last: the fate of the Bearer is in my hands no longer. The Company has played its part. Yet we that remain cannot forsake our companions while we have strength left'" (III/i). Aragorn's choice, ultimately, is not made for strategic and military reasons but for what might be called moral reasons. He cannot abandon Merry and Pippin to "torment and death"; it would be wrong to forsake them. Even in the midst of the war, it is the clear speaking of Aragorn's heart to which he listens. The moral good is more important than the military good. To understand this is one of the highest marks of wisdom in Tolkien's writing.

Aragorn is not alone in how he chooses nor in what he values most. His choices are echoed by many, if not all, of those whom Tolkien provides as the wise heroes of his work. Once again, Faramir gives us three of the best examples. Early in the conversation after Frodo and Faramir have first met, Frodo realizes that the son of Denethor has been testing him. He feels deceived and suggests that he has been lied to. Faramir responds, "I would not snare even an orc with falsehood" (IV/v). This is a telling statement—and what we see of Faramir through the remainder of the story would suggest that it is true. For this Captain of Minas Tirith, and heir to the Stewardship of Gondor, the value of truth is so important that he would not lie even to an enemy, not even to win a battle. The moral victory of speaking the truth is more important than any military victory that might be won through lies and deceit.

We see a similar principle when Faramir weighs the moral good of Frodo keeping his promise to Gollum to have him as a guide, against the physical harm that might result from that promise should Gollum choose to betray him and guide him into evil (which, in fact, he does). When Frodo asks him, "You would not ask me to break faith with him?" Faramir replies, "No." He goes on to explain why he is tempted to give this advice: "It seems less evil to counsel another man to break troth than to do so oneself, especially if one sees a friend bound unwitting to his own harm." But ultimately he agrees with Frodo that he must keep his word: "But no—if he will go with you, you must now endure him" (IV/vi). Faramir wisely sees the danger ahead for Frodo: that Gollum is not trustworthy and thus Frodo is bound "to his own harm." He rightly predicts the evil that Gollum will seek to do against Frodo and Sam, though he does not know that it will take the form of Shelob's Lair. Yet Faramir also acknowledges that it is a moral evil to knowingly break one's word, to "break faith" or "break troth." Moreover, he recognizes that it is an evil even to "counsel another man to break troth"—though *perhaps* a lesser evil than to actually break troth oneself. And so, when he realizes that Frodo has made a promise to Gollum, both he and Frodo agree that they must stick to the moral good of keeping that promise, even though it brings about a great physical danger. No, he will not counsel Frodo to break faith. In his moral integrity, he will not tell another to do what he himself would not do: to abandon the moral good for the sake of personal safety.

Faramir's integrity and high moral values come even more to
the forefront when he returns to Minas Tirith and faces his father,
Denethor. When Denethor realizes that his son has had a chance to
obtain the Ring of Power and that he has let it go, he is furious. He
chastises his son, telling him that his "gentleness may be repaid with
death," to which Faramir replies, "So be it" (V/iv). The simplicity
of this response is wonderfully powerful. There is nothing else that
needs to be said. Faramir understands clearly the choices his father
has laid before them. Again, he would choose the moral victory of
being gentle, even if it means his own death.

Denethor, by contrast, is of a different mind than his youngest
son. For the Steward of Gondor to be "lordly and generous as a king
of old, gracious, gentle" is fine for times of peace, but all of those
things must be sacrificed in a time of war, in "desperate hours," for
the sake of military victory. He goes so far as wishing, in Faramir's
presence, that Faramir were the one who died and not Boromir: "[Bo-
romir] would have remembered his father's need, and would not have
squandered what fortune gave. He would have brought me a mighty
gift. . . . Would that this thing had come to me!" (V/iv). In Denethor's
defense, we must acknowledge his claim that he would not have used
the Ring. "To use this thing is perilous," he agrees. Unless, of course,
the defeat of Gondor were at stake: "Not used, I say, *unless* at the
uttermost end of need, but set beyond all grasp, save by a victory so
final that what then befell would not trouble us, being dead" (V/iv,
emphasis added). The problem is that even as he speaks these words,
Denethor is already at the point of perceiving this circumstance; in his
mind, the "uttermost end of need" has already arrived. He is willing
to betray moral virtue for the sake of victory—or, rather, for the sake
of avoiding defeat. Unlike Denethor, Faramir is not willing to sacrifice moral good for military victory. Neither is Gandalf. The tale, of
course, ultimately vindicates Faramir and Gandalf and their wisdom.

The Temptation of the Ring: Gandalf and Elrond

That moral victory is more important than military victory for Tolkien's most heroic characters should be understood as one of the chief
concerns (and also one of the most interesting to explore for its own

sake) related to their refusal to use the One Ring. Indeed, we could draw the conclusion that moral victory is the more important victory merely from observing that the wisest and noblest of Middle-earth— Gandalf, Elrond, Galadriel, Aragorn, and Faramir—when given the opportunity to possess the Ring for themselves, all refuse despite their dire need for strength in the fight against Sauron. Their temptations are key scenes in the story and are worth exploring one at a time.

Gandalf is faced with this temptation several times, at different parts of the story. The film version, for example, gives us a memorable shot of the Ring falling to the floor of Bilbo's house when Bilbo departs the Shire after his birthday party. And Gandalf, watching it fall, is unwilling even to touch it long enough to set it on the mantel or return it to the envelope. He leaves it lying where it is on the floor, for he knows how great the temptation would be to keep it and use it, if once he touched it. Later, Frodo explicitly offers the Ring to Gandalf. This time, Tolkien gives us the wizard's reply.

> "Will you not take the Ring?" [pleads Frodo].
>
> "No!" cried Gandalf, springing to his feet. "With that power I should have power too great and terrible. And over me the Ring would gain a power still greater and more deadly." His eyes flashed and his face was lit as by a fire within. "Do not tempt me! For I do not wish to become like the Dark Lord himself. Yet the way of the Ring to my heart is by pity, pity for weakness and the desire of strength to do good. . . . I shall have such need of [strength]. Great perils lie before me." (I/ii)

Note how adamant Gandalf's response is. We see it in the wizard's body: his springing to his feet, the flashing of his eyes, and the light on his face. That his words garner two exclamation points from Tolkien is notable too. He explicitly labels the offer as a "temptation," a word suggesting that the Ring is both something he desires and something he ought not take. *Temptation* is also a word laden with moral implications; refusing temptation might be the very definition of moral victory, while giving in to temptation is the definition of moral defeat.

Elrond, with similar obstinacy, also refuses the Ring—not only for himself but for all those gathered at the council: "Alas, no. We cannot use the Ruling Ring. . . . I fear to take the Ring to hide it. I will not take the Ring to wield it" (II/ii). Much has been made of these passages and others like them, where the refusal is not just for one individual but for all involved. For Elrond, it is not merely that "I" cannot use the Ruling Ring, but that "we" cannot use it. Why does he refuse that power for everyone else?

One idea is that Tolkien viewed all power as essentially corrupting. Tom Shippey astutely points out how thoroughly modern this idea is. "The medieval world had its saints' lives," he writes, "in which the saints used their immense and indeed miraculous power entirely for good purposes; while there is no shortage of evil kings in medieval story, there is rarely any sign that they became evil by becoming kings." He illustrates this a few sentences later with an Old English proverb, the meaning of which, he explains, is that power *reveals* character but does not alter it.[1] Shippey goes on to suggest, however, that in this regard Tolkien (despite his affinities for the medieval) may have been much more modern in his thinking. According to Shippey, Tolkien's experiences with the wars and atrocities of the twentieth century may have made him more sympathetic to the view of Lord Acton: "Power tends to corrupt, and absolute power corrupts absolutely. Great men are almost always bad men."[2] Certainly, Saruman and Denethor appear to have been corrupted by their own power. And Boromir's speech at Amon Hen shows all the dangers of the corruptive lust for power. Regarding the Ring and its temptation, Shippey concludes that any of the kings or powerful heroes of Middle-earth, no matter how good their intentions at the start, if they possessed the Ring, "would come to enjoy having their intentions achieved, the use of power itself, and would end as dictators over others, enslaved to themselves, unable to give up or go back."[3]

And yet ultimately I think that Tolkien did hold to a more medieval view even on this issue. The power of the Ring is fundamentally corruptive, but power itself is not. It is possible, Tolkien's narrative suggests, to be both powerful and good! Though I think Shippey is certainly correct that Tolkien understood more clearly than did the medieval poets he loved that there is *potential* for power to corrupt, he nonetheless also believed in the possibility of saints. What Shippey writes about Tolkien's portrayal of the particular corruptive power of the Ring is fully supported in the text, but Shippey's suggestion that this is true of all power may be the one matter on which

I disagree with him. Consider that Gandalf, Elrond, and Galadriel are three of the most powerful figures in Middle-earth—bearers of the three elven-rings of power, in fact—and none of these three are corrupted by their own power (although they certainly would be corrupted by the power of the Ring). "But do not think that only by singing amid the trees, nor even by the slender arrows of elven-bows," Galadriel tells Frodo, "is this land of Lothlórien maintained and defended against its Enemy" (II/vii). That Galadriel wields such power and yet remains uncorrupted—"There is in her and in this land no evil, unless a man bring it hither himself," Aragorn says of her—is evidence that Tolkien did not hold the view that *all* power is fundamentally corrupting. Other examples beyond the three bearers of the elven-rings of power could also be listed. Aragorn himself is powerful, and becomes a king, and yet nothing suggests that he is ever corrupted by his power. Even in the case of Saruman and Denethor, both of whom are powerful and both of whom seem to become corrupt after growing in power, a stronger case could be made that their ultimate downfall is caused not by their power but by a loss of hope. That loss itself is caused by the deceit of Sauron at work through the *palantíri* (the Seeing Stones), which are controlled by Sauron and thus reveal only what he wants them to reveal.

This distinction between power in general (what we might call "all power") and the particular power of the Ring is such an important one that we will return to it in chapter 6, for it gives insight into not only the nature of the Ring but also the deepest philosophical underpinnings of Tolkien's text. In any case, whatever we may say about power in general, there is no doubt that the One Ring will eventually corrupt any bearer. Throughout the story, Tolkien shows its influence not only on Sméagol, but on Isildur, Bilbo, and Frodo as well. Even some like Boromir, who never actually bear the Ring but only come near it, feel its corrupting influence. The only two bearers who are ever able to give it up freely are Bilbo and Sam, but Sam bears it only a short time, while Bilbo gives it up only after a very long and difficult struggle. We need to consider why the Ring is tempting and how adamant are the refusals of that temptation. What the Ring would have meant to the foes of Mordor is "strength," and particularly "strength to do good" (or so it would seem). Indeed, even Elrond sees it as a real possibility that "one of the Wise should

89

with this Ring overthrow the Lord of Mordor" (II/ii). Gandalf, as the chief agent in the war against Sauron, has need of power for the many perils he faces.

Yet both Gandalf and Elrond refuse. Gandalf guesses, more clearly than any of the others, that using the Ring could actually bring military victory for the foes of Mordor: victory, that is, in the sense of defeating Sauron's armies and overthrowing his power. "War is upon us and all our friends," he tells Aragorn, Gimli, and Legolas shortly after their reunion, "a war in which only the use of the Ring could give us surety of victory" (III/v). And later, in "The Last Debate," he tells the gathered captains that Sauron "is now in great doubt. For if we have found this thing, there are some among us with strength enough to wield it" (V/ix). On the other side, Gandalf also knows that without using the Ring they have only a fool's hope of defeating Sauron's might. He also tells the Captains of the West: "This war then is without final hope, as Denethor perceived. Victory cannot be achieved by arms, whether you sit here to endure siege after siege, or march out to be overwhelmed beyond the River" (V/ix). And a little later he adds: "We have not the Ring. . . . Without it we cannot by force defeat his force" (V/ix). So strong is this understanding that when Gandalf first returns after his fall in Khazad-dûm, he briefly doubts the wisdom of his own choice and wonders about going after the Ring: "He rose and gazed out eastward, shading his eyes, as if he saw things far away that none of them could see. Then he shook his head. 'No,' he said in a soft voice, 'it has gone beyond our reach. Of that at least let us be glad. We can no longer be tempted to use the Ring. We must go down to face a peril near despair, yet that deadly peril is removed'" (III/v).

In short, then, the situation is plain. Use of the Ring, by the right one of Sauron's enemies, would bring *military* victory. Refusal of the Ring leaves them no hope at all of *military* victory—that is, a defeating of Sauron's armies using their own military strength—and only a fool's hope in the overall war: a "peril near despair." They choose the fool's hope. And this choice is central to the entire trilogy. It is one of the choices that characterize the great among Tolkien's characters. They choose the moral victory, the moral good of refusing the corruption of the Ring, over the military victory that would come from using the Ring.

The Temptation of the Ring: Galadriel and Faramir

The temptations of Faramir and Galadriel are also important. The former stands in stark contrast to the failure of Boromir under similar circumstances, while the latter is one of the more vividly portrayed scenes in *The Fellowship of the Ring*.

Faramir is given his opportunity to possess the Ring when Frodo and Sam stumble into his hands in Ithilien. Though Frodo says nothing about what he carries, Faramir knows enough of the lore, and has enough of the wisdom and power of the true blood of Númenor, that he is able to guess much that Frodo does not reveal. Though he knows not the form of Isildur's Bane—that it is a ring—he knows both that Frodo carries it and that it possesses great power. Unlike Gandalf and Galadriel, Faramir is not offered the Ring, and yet it is certainly in his power to take it. In contrast to his brother, however, he does not attempt to do so. In a statement similar to his earlier comment that he would not snare even an orc with falsehood, he says of the Ring, "I would not take this thing, if it lay by the highway. Not were Minas Tirith falling in ruin and I alone could save her, so, using the weapon of the Dark Lord for her good and my glory. No, I do not wish for such triumphs" (IV/v). Faramir is explicit in stating what was implicit in the refusals of Gandalf and Elrond: he would rather suffer total military defeat than do the evil that would need to be done to win the war by the use of the Ring. In fact, he would sacrifice not only his own life but also his land rather than give in to such moral evil. Given the choice between either doing good and having Minas Tirith fall into ruin or doing evil but winning a triumph on the battlefield, he would choose the ruin. These are not idle words, but ones proven by deeds. Faramir does what his brother could not do: he lets the Ring depart with the Ringbearer. Gentleness may be repaid with death? So be it.

Galadriel's temptation is perhaps the most telling of any of them. For one thing, her temptation is given the most attention and time in the narrative, and the most vivid imagery. Yet there is another factor at work as well. With the others, the moral good of refusing the Ring brings a *risk* of defeat but not a *sure* defeat; though they have no hope of defeating Sauron in military battle, they can hope that Frodo will succeed in his quest and thereby defeat Sauron in another way. Galadriel, however, knows with certainty that if she does not take the One Ring for herself, then whether the Quest of the Ringbearer succeeds or not, whether Sauron is overthrown or comes into complete power, either way she will suffer a defeat. She speaks of this to Frodo: "Do you not see now wherefore your coming is to us as the footstep of Doom? For if you fail, then we are laid bare to the Enemy. Yet if you succeed, then our power is diminished, and Lothlórien will fade, and the tides of Time will sweep it away. We must depart into the West, or dwindle to a rustic folk of dell and cave, slowly to forget and to be forgotten" (II/vii). As Tolkien explains in the book, Galadriel is the bearer of one of the three great elven-rings of power: Nenya, the Ring of Adamant. Like the other elven-rings, it was forged for "understanding, making, and healing, to preserve all things unstained" (II/vii). It is by the power of that ring that Lothlórien itself is preserved unstained.

Unfortunately, though the elven-rings were never corrupted by Sauron, their power is caught up in the power of the One Ring. Sauron forged the One Ring for the very purpose of ruling the others, and Galadriel knows that when the One Ring is destroyed, the Three will fall also, and then all that was made by their power will fade. In fact, Elrond also guesses at this, though he seems less certain than Galadriel: "Some hope that the Three Rings, which Sauron never touched, would then become free, and their rulers might heal the hurts of the world that he has wrought. But maybe when the One has gone, the Three will fail, and many fair things will fade and be forgotten. That is my belief" (II/ii). Saruman also knows this, and when the fall of the Three comes to pass at the end of the book, he gloats over Galadriel: "I did not spend long study on these matters for naught. You have doomed yourselves, and you know it. And it will afford me some comfort as I wander to think that you pulled down your own house when you destroyed mine" (VI/vi). In choosing to help the Fellowship on their quest, Galadriel would be choosing to pull down her own house, and she knows this.

Into this situation steps Frodo. Seeing Galadriel as "wise and fearless and fair" (II/vii), he offers her the Ring. Her response to this temptation is tremendously vulnerable and sincere. In Galadriel's articulation of her thoughts to Frodo, Tolkien gives the reader great insight into just what the temptation is about at many levels.

"I do not deny that my heart has greatly desired to ask what you offer. For many long years I pondered what I might do, should the Great Ring come into my hands, and behold! it was brought within my grasp. . . .

"And now at last it comes. You will give me the Ring freely! In place of the Dark Lord you will set up a Queen. And I shall not be dark, but beautiful and terrible as the Morning and the Night! Fair as the Sea and the Sun and the Snow upon the Mountain! Dreadful as the Storm and the Lightning! Stronger than the foundations of the earth. All shall love me and despair!" (II/vii)

As we consider Galadriel's temptation, we must do so in light of what we have previously seen: that if the Ringbearer even *attempts* the Quest, then whether he succeeds *or* fails, it will mark the end of Lothlórien. Thus his coming to Lothlórien truly is, as she said, the coming of "the footstep of Doom." What the Ring offers to Galadriel is a way out of this doom, a third alternative to having Frodo either fail or succeed. To preserve that land and those works, she would need both to keep the Ring from Sauron and also to keep it from being destroyed. It is an alternative she has long pondered, and even greatly desired, as she admits to Frodo. It is a twofold temptation. Part of her desire for power is, as with Gandalf, the desire to defeat Sauron. It is the desire to do good and to prevent evil. As Sam puts it, she would "make some folk pay for their dirty work" (II/vii). Yet unlike with Gandalf, there is the added dimension of her great desire to take the Ring simply to save her kingdom and all she has worked for from an otherwise sure demise.

Yet with all of this, Galadriel still refuses the temptation. Her refusal is as beautiful and profound as it is simple: "The love of the Elves for their land and their works is deeper than the deeps of the Sea, and their regret is undying and cannot ever wholly be assuaged. Yet they will cast all away rather than submit to Sauron: for they know him now. . . . Yet I could wish, were it of any avail, that the One Ring had never been wrought, or had remained for ever lost" (II/vii). Galadriel might wish the One Ring had never been made or was still lost, but such wishes are of no avail. To preserve Lothlórien, she would need to take the Ring for herself. And yet taking the Ring for herself, she knows, would be a great moral evil. And thus, though using (or at least preserving) the power of the Ring is her one hope to preserve what she has created in Lothlórien, she will accept defeat rather than do what she knows would be evil.

So it is that Galadriel's answer to this temptation is the same as that of the other great Powers: "She let her hand fall, and the light faded, and suddenly she laughed again, and lo! she was shrunken: a slender elf-woman, clad in simple white, whose gentle voice was soft and sad. 'I pass the test. I will diminish, and go into the West, and remain Galadriel'" (II/vii). In these last two passages, Galadriel summarizes the point of this chapter: that moral victory is the more important victory, that it is better to suffer a military defeat and a loss of everything than to suffer a moral defeat, even as it is better to "cast all away rather than submit to Sauron."

5

Human Freedom and Creativity

"But I count you blessed, Gimli son of Glóin: for your loss you suffer of your own free will, and you might have chosen otherwise."

—Legolas

The choice of the wise of Middle-earth to refuse the temptation of the Ring is undeniably important in *The Lord of the Rings*, but it is by no means the only important choice made by the heroes. That Tolkien emphasizes so many choices is significant. Indeed, it is difficult to overlook the extent to which the Middle-earth writings stress the reality of choice. This reality runs through *The Hobbit*, *The Lord of the Rings*, and *The Silmarillion* from bottom to top, beginning to end. It is in their very fabric. As we will explore in this chapter, it is the choices made by the heroes that define their heroism. We might say that the importance of choice in Tolkien's writing is the very thing that defines his writing as heroic literature.

As obvious as this may be, the importance of choice is still worth exploring for two reasons. The first is a reason I explored in another book, *The Mind and the Machine* (which has a chapter on the role of creativity and free will in Tolkien's writings), and also touched on in *Following Gandalf*, the predecessor to this book.[1] There are many famous figures in the world today, as there were during Tolkien's time, who deny that humans have any real freedom to make their own choices. Humans are, they claim, merely programmed machines. As a result, those who deny free choice are suspicious of heroic literature, or of what the twentieth-century psychologist B. F. Skinner (one of Tolkien's famous contemporaries who denied free will) dismissively called "the literature of freedom" (a type of literature that Skinner thought should be rejected).[2] I will not belabor that point here but will note only that while many readers who enjoy Tolkien's works might themselves claim not to believe in free choice, there can be no doubt that Tolkien did believe in it and made it central to his writing. Whatever readers think about the matter, free choice must be understood as central to Tolkien.

The second reason for exploring the importance of choice in Tolkien's work relates to one of my central critiques of Peter Jackson's film adaptations of Tolkien's works. There are fans whose perception of *The Lord of the Rings* comes from Jackson's films rather than from Tolkien's books. Just as fans who have been influenced by the films rather than the books might be more inclined to see the works as glorifying violence, they might also miss the fundamental importance of the free choices of the heroes. This is because with almost every important heroic character in *The Lord of the Rings*, Peter Jackson's film adaptation sadly diminishes the significance of the very choices that (in Tolkien's books) made these characters heroic.

The list of examples is long and, for those who are concerned with the fundamental philosophical ideas behind Tolkien's works, disturbing. At least some are worth mentioning. In Tolkien's works, both Merry and Pippin consciously *choose* to join their friend Frodo in his departure from the Shire, well in advance of when he actually departs, because he needs help. They make this choice even though they also know the journey will be dangerous, and that danger terrifies them. As Merry says to Frodo: "You can trust us to keep any secret of yours—closer than you keep it yourself. But you cannot trust us to let you face trouble alone, and go off without a word. We are your friends. . . . We are horribly afraid—but we are coming with you; or following you like hounds" (I/v). In Jackson's version, by contrast, Merry and Pippin are caught stealing vegetables and get chased by farmer Maggot's dogs, and only accidentally fall in with Frodo and Sam as they head out from the Shire. Though they later do make some heroic choices, this initial choice of heroism and friendship is taken from them.

The devaluing of Gandalf's great heroic choice in the Jackson films is even more egregious. In Tolkien's works, it is Gandalf who wants to lead the Company through the Mines of Moria because he believes it is the best path. Aragorn foresees some disaster awaiting Gandalf there and warns the wizard of it. In the books, therefore, it is Aragorn, not Gandalf, who argues they should instead try crossing the pass of Caradhras to avoid the foreseen harm to Gandalf. Nonetheless, Gandalf is willing to face the danger of Moria for the good of the Company. This free choice of Gandalf's ennobles his later sacrifice at Khazad-dûm in Tolkien's works. By contrast, Peter Jackson portrays Gandalf as so afraid of passing through Khazad-dûm that he pushes the Company to the ill-fated attempt at the pass of Caradhras. And even when this crossing of Caradhras fails, Gandalf forces on Frodo the uncomfortable burden of deciding whether to go through Moria because he is seemingly unwilling to make that choice himself. Gandalf's heroic choices are diminished by Jackson.

And the list could go on. The true Faramir of Tolkien's books would never have attempted to force Frodo to return to Minas Tirith with the Ring. Though he knows the choice to help Frodo on his journey will bring the ire of his father, Faramir makes that difficult choice to let the Ring go because it is the morally *right* choice, as we explored in the previous chapter. Jackson's Faramir instead tries to force Frodo and the Ring back to Gondor, and only later seems to change his mind out of fear rather than out of a heroic choice.

Likewise, Tolkien's Ent Treebeard, once he understands the danger that Sauron poses to the trees of Fangorn Forest as well as to all of Middle-earth, convinces the Ents at the Entmoot to make the great sacrifice of aiding Gondor and Rohan by attacking Saruman at Isengard. He makes this heroic choice even though he fears it might bring about the destruction of the Ents. "Of course, it is likely enough, my friends," he tells Merry and Pippin, "likely enough that we are going to our doom: the last march of the Ents" (III/iv). Indeed, the Ents

97

don't just make this heroic choice; they make it remarkably quickly by Entish standards. Jackson's Treebeard, by contrast, initially refuses to help Merry and Pippin; he must be tricked into attacking Isengard in a fit of rage, more over the loss of his own trees than out of a desire to help others. Likewise with Théoden. Tolkien's Théoden, when he understands the dangers, not only agrees to send Rohan to war at the request of Aragorn and Gandalf, but chooses to lead his army himself, ultimately at the cost of his own life. Peter Jackson's Théoden refuses to aid Aragorn; he chooses instead to go into hiding, and only fights because the war comes to him.

Again and again, where Tolkien's heroes make heroic choices, Jackson's versions of these characters must be tricked or forced or involuntarily stumble into the courses of action that seem to make them heroes. It is important, therefore, to see just how important choice was to Tolkien, and to heroism.

The Reality of Choice

Beyond noting the contrasting portrayals above, we could deepen our exploration of the reality of free will and the importance of choice in Tolkien's writing by taking an obvious route: considering passages that explicitly describe and even emphasize the choices being made. One of my favorite scenes in *The Lord of the Rings* is the first meeting between Gimli and Galadriel, during which the elven queen breaks down the centuries-old enmity between elves and dwarves. Gimli looks into her eyes and sees a friend where once he saw an enemy. So incredible is this reconciliation and healing of wounds that afterward Gimli is ever ready to go to blows against anybody who speaks ill of the Lady of the Wood. If it weren't so noble, it would be almost comic when at their parting the stammering dwarf asks—to the murmuring and astonishment of all present—for a single strand of the Lady's hair rather than for any other gift. Likewise, Gimli's bravado would be ridiculous were it not so moving when Tolkien has him stand up to Éomer and more than one hundred of his mounted Rohirrim over a perceived insult given to Galadriel. Gimli is ready to face certain death to defend the honor of this great elven queen.

In fact, what emerges is a love—though not of a romantic kind—of Gimli for Galadriel, and for the "light and joy" he finds in her kingdom. When he leaves Lothlórien, he is dismayed at the loss. "I have taken my worst wound in this parting, even if I were to go this night straight to the Dark Lord," he bemoans. "Alas for Gimli son of Glóin." The response of Legolas gets at the heart of this chapter: "Alas for us all! And for all that walk in the world in these after-days. For such is the way of it: to find and lose, as it seems to those whose boat is on the running stream. But I count you blessed, Gimli son of Glóin: for your loss you suffer *of your own free will*, and you might have chosen otherwise" (II/viii, emphasis added). Legolas speaks directly of the dwarf's "own free will" and then goes on to further emphasize the reality of that free will by saying that Gimli "might have *chosen otherwise*." Being able to choose between different courses of action is the very essence of what it means to have free will. We also get a taste of what heroism means: the hero is the one who makes the brave choice, even when it brings about his own suffering. For that, Legolas counts Gimli blessed.

Tolkien gives us a similar comment at a very critical moment toward the end of *The Fellowship of the Ring*. In order to escape Boromir, Frodo puts on the Ring and climbs to the top of Amon Hen. There Sauron becomes aware of him, and the Eye begins to seek him out, only narrowly being drawn away at the last moment by some other power—which we later learn is Gandalf. It is as Frodo sits "perfectly balanced" between the "piercing points" of these two powers that "suddenly he was aware of himself again. Frodo, neither the Voice nor the Eye: free to choose, and with one remaining instant in which to do so" (II/x). Here we see again the emphasis that Frodo is "free to choose." But there is even more than that. It is not only that he is free to choose but that the *essence* of his existence as Frodo—what he remembers when he becomes "aware of himself"—is this freedom to choose. He is neither the Voice nor the Eye; he is not *compelled* to do good or to do evil but must choose on his own which he will do. And yet, under the strain of those powers, he almost forgets that. Or, put another way, he almost forgets himself. It is his awareness of himself that makes him aware of his freedom to choose. Why? Because the freedom to choose is fundamental to what it means to be a self.

It is also this "freedom to choose" that makes heroism possible, for it is the choices one makes that determine whether one is a hero. This is what Elrond tells Frodo when Frodo accepts the Quest: "But it is a heavy burden. So heavy that none could lay it on another. I do not lay it on you. But if you take it freely, I will say that your choice is right; and though all the mighty elf-friends of old, Hador, and Húrin, and Túrin, and Beren himself were assembled together, your seat would be among them" (II/ii). As with Legolas's earlier remark to Gimli, we see again in Elrond's words the double emphasis on Frodo's free will: that his action is done "freely" and that it is a "choice." That it is a free choice is exactly what makes Frodo a hero whose seat belongs with the greatest heroes of Middle-earth. Tolkien's Middle-earth is a world where heroism is possible because it is a world where real choices are possible. Tolkien's books are full of the language of heroism, which is to say, the language of choice.

We don't need to travel very long in Middle-earth before we see this. *The Hobbit* is more lighthearted and less deeply heroic than *The Lord of the Rings*. As Gandalf points out at the beginning of that story, "In this neighborhood heroes are scarce, or simply not to be found" (*Hobbit*, 53). Nonetheless, we see the glimmering of heroic traits in Bilbo (and through him, the potential for heroism in all of us simple folk). Interestingly enough, it is not in seeking adventure or danger that Bilbo shows these traits. In fact, he has no desire for adventure or danger. Rather, it is in his willingness to do what he *ought* to do, even when it is uncomfortable, that Bilbo's heroic traits can best be seen. He calls it his "duty," a word used more than once to describe how Bilbo makes his choices. As the story progresses, this sense of heroic duty is developed further. We see it when Bilbo is willing to go back into the goblin caverns after the dwarves, however miserable he feels about it, because he fears they have been left behind and that it is his duty to return for them. In that sense, the dwarves—who are certainly more skilled in battle and more used to danger and adventure than the hobbit—are shown to be much less heroic: they will not choose to do for Bilbo what he is willing to do for them.

Bilbo's greatest act of heroism, according to the narrator, comes when he is in the tunnel preparing to descend into Smaug's lair for the first time: "It was at this point that Bilbo stopped. Going on from there was the bravest thing he ever did. The tremendous things that happened afterwards were nothing compared to it. He fought the real battle in the tunnel alone" (*Hobbit*, 270). What is this brave thing? It is not any of his battles, neither his attempted thievery from the trolls, nor his fight against the spiders in Mirkwood, nor his daring dialogue with Smaug, nor even his small role in the battle against the goblins at the end. It is, simply, the choice to go on, to put one foot in front of the other. This is precisely the sort of "battle" that is important in Tolkien's writing. It is much more important than any military battle. It is a battle that even servants must face—that is to say, a *choice* that even servants are given—as Sam learns when his master falls in Shelob's Lair. In a description closely akin to that of Bilbo in the lair of Smaug, we read that Sam "took a few steps: the heaviest and the most reluctant he had ever taken" (IV/x). Indeed, the observation that this "bravest thing," the "real battle" as it is called, has nothing at all to do with military battle also says much to the subject of whether Tolkien glorifies violence.

The fundamental nature of this relationship between heroism and choice is captured wonderfully in the peculiar wisdom of Sam on the Stairs of Cirith Ungol.

> "But I suppose it's often that way. The brave things in the old tales and songs, Mr. Frodo: adventures, as I used to call them. I used to think that they were things the wonderful folk of the stories went out and looked for, because they wanted them, because they were exciting and life was a bit dull, a kind of a sport, as you might say. But that's not the way of it with the tales that really mattered, or the ones that stay in the mind. Folk seem to have been just landed in them, usually—their paths were laid that way, as you put it. But I expect they had lots of chances, like us, of turning back, only they didn't." (IV/viii)

It is not the big battles and exciting brave adventures that make the hero but the decision to go on and not turn back. It is a decision that is made not just once but continuously, even as the chances of turning back come at the hero continuously. It is also a decision that ordinary "folk" can make, one that turns those ordinary folk into heroes when they do make those choices. Sam and Frodo themselves make this choice, akin in nature to the choice of Bilbo, but more difficult and more significant: the choice to keep going when they were in Mordor and not to give up, to take one step after another across Udûn and up the side of Mount Doom, "every step of fifty miles" (VI/iii). Even when their steps turn to crawling, they go on: "'I'll crawl, Sam,' [Frodo] gasped. So foot by foot, like small grey insects, they crept up the slope" (VI/iii). Why is this heroic? Because they are free. They have the choice to give up or to go on. That they choose the latter is the essence of their heroism.

Aragorn and the Doom of Choice

How important is choice in Tolkien's writing? Choices form the bookends of *The Two Towers*, which ends with a chapter titled "The Choices of Master Samwise" and starts with a chapter that might well have been called "The Choices of Aragorn son of Arathorn." If there is any character in whom, and for whom, the importance and difficulty of choice is especially captured, it is Aragorn. When Éomer first meets Aragorn, he senses something deep and noble about this stranger to Rohan. "What doom do you bring out of the North?" he asks. "The doom of choice," answers Aragorn (III/i). In other words, when Aragorn answers, "The doom of choice," he is really answering, "freedom"; freedom is his fate, his destiny, his punishment. Though only four words long, his answer is truly—like the proverbial picture—worth a thousand words. Many different understandings are layered within it. Even the word *doom* is loaded. In its Anglo-Saxon roots, it refers simply to a law. Yet it can also connote a judgment or sentence passed down, a destiny or fate laid upon one, or some terrible thing that is about to happen. It is also one of the root words of *freedom*, or "free-doom": the state in which one's doom, or destiny, is free for one to choose.

At one level, then, Tolkien is making a statement about the race of men. Choice is our doom. Not only are we free and *able* to choose; it is our destiny as beings of free will that we *must* make choices—and then live with the consequences of those choices! As Aragorn tells Frodo at Parth Galen: "I fear that the burden is laid upon you. . . . Your own way you alone can choose. In this matter I cannot advise you. I am not Gandalf, and though I have tried to bear his part, I do not know what design or hope he had for this hour, if indeed he had

102

any. Most likely it seems that if he were here now the choice would still wait on you. Such is your fate" (II/x). Here Tolkien emphasizes Frodo's choices. Twice Aragorn reminds Frodo of the reality and "burden" of choice: "You alone can choose," he tells him, and "the choice would still wait on you." Choice is Frodo's "fate"—a statement that is itself an ironic twist. Yet Aragorn is also aware of his own choices, and of the "part" he himself has to "bear," especially in Gandalf's absence. Choice is the fate of all in Middle-earth; each "alone" can choose his or her *own way*. Though Frodo is already quite aware of his difficult choices, Tolkien puts this most intense statement of those choices into Aragorn's mouth, probably because Aragorn is so conscious of his own burden of choice. Thus, when Aragorn answers Éomer, he is, as has been pointed out, making a statement about all members of his race, but he is also answering this question in a painful and personal way. He is particularly aware of his own destiny, the many difficult choices he has had to make and those he will soon have to make. Almost from the moment Gandalf falls and Aragorn takes over leadership of the Fellowship, he is plagued by the choice of where and how to lead them. "Would that Gandalf were here!" he says, on the Great River. "How my heart yearns for Minas Anor and the walls of my own city! But whither now shall I go?" (II/ix). Thus, as much as he would like to help Frodo, he seems relieved at Parth Galen that the final choice falls on the Ringbearer, and not himself.

Indeed, Tolkien shows us an Aragorn who is nearly overwhelmed at times by the choices facing him, and who is filled with great human doubt about his ability to make them. On several different occasions, we hear him lament the choices he has made. On the opening page of *The Two Towers*, as the Fellowship is falling apart, he cries: "Alas! An ill fate is on me this day, and all that I do goes amiss" (III/i). A short time later, capturing both his doubt about past decisions and his confusion about current ones, he continues:

Vain was Gandalf's trust in me. What shall I do now? Boromir has laid it on me to go to Minas Tirith, and my heart desires it; but where are the Ring and the Bearer? How shall I find them and save the Quest from disaster? . . .

Are we to abandon him? Must we not seek him first? An evil choice is now before us! (III/i)

The whole war against Sauron is a war to preserve freedom in Middle-earth. Yet we can see why Aragorn might refer to his own free-doom as a doom in the sense of punishment. He has three choices, and all of them come with the possibility of great loss. It is, truly, an "evil choice." Or, as Gimli comments, "maybe there is no right choice" (III/i).

Despite Gimli's words, Aragorn does make a choice, though it comes after much painful deliberation. "I will follow the Orcs," he says, and "my heart speaks clearly at last" (III/i). However hard that choice is, once it is made, Aragorn sticks to it with determination (and several exclamation points): "'Come! We will go now. Leave all that can be spared behind! We will press on by day and dark! . . . With hope or without hope we will follow the trail of our enemies.' . . . On and on he led them, tireless and swift, *now that his mind was at last made up*" (III/i, emphasis added). As with many other choices throughout the books, Tolkien brings emphasis and clarity to the actual moment of decision, showing us just how real the choice itself is and also how important the process of choosing is.

Even after Aragorn makes his choice to pursue Merry and Pippin, and guesses (albeit wrongly) that in making such a choice he may have removed himself from having any significant role in the remainder of the war—commenting that "ours is but a small matter in the great deeds of this time"—he is still very conscious of his choices. "A vain pursuit from its beginning, maybe, which no choice of mine can mar or mend," he says, in deciding whether or not to risk taking a rest. "Well, I have chosen" (III/ii).

There are many heroes in *The Lord of the Rings*, but among the race of men Aragorn represents the greatest. It is thus fitting that the burden of choice is shown to be greatest for him also. But freedom and wisdom do not imply moral infallibility for any created being in Middle-earth—not for the great or the small, neither for Aragorn nor for Sam, not even for wizards.

The Prophecies

Even Gandalf, at times, seems torn by the choices he must make, particularly—as was the case with Aragorn—when he must make those choices without perfect knowledge. He shares this uncertainty at the Council of Elrond: "Whence came the Hobbit's ring? What, if my fear was true, should be done with it? Those things I must decide" (II/ii). As wise as he is, Gandalf does make mistakes in his choices. One such error of judgment is his early inaction with regard to the Ring. "I was at fault," he confesses to the council. "I should have sought for the truth sooner" (II/ii). Another error is his decision, after hearing news from Radagast about the Nine being abroad, to go straight to Saruman rather than returning to the Shire. "Never did I make a greater mistake!" he confesses (II/ii). The choice of which route the Fellowship should use in order to cross the mountains also burdens Gandalf, and it is the subject of debate and disagreement between him and Aragorn. Neither feels certain of the route, and both see evil and great danger in all paths. It is interesting, therefore, to note that Aragorn himself later defends the choices of Gandalf, whom he thinks dead. "The counsel of Gandalf was not founded on foreknowledge of safety, for himself or for others," says Aragorn. "There are some things that it is better to begin than to refuse, even though the end may be dark" (III/ii).

This comment brings us to a deeper subject, on which Tolkien himself was hesitant to tread. Gandalf's plans were not founded on "foreknowledge of safety," and yet they were founded on some sort of knowledge beyond what was plainly visible. There is a strong sense in *The Lord of the Rings*, and even in *The Hobbit*, that the wise of Middle-earth—especially Gandalf and Elrond—have a faith in a power higher than themselves, and that this faith aids them in making the choices they need to make, no matter how difficult. There is both a seen and an unseen reality in Tolkien's Middle-earth. These might be called the *material* plane and the *spiritual* plane. The spiritual plane, though less visible, is no less real to Tolkien. We see this in comments such as those of Gandalf to Frodo: "There was something else at work, beyond any design of the Ring-maker. I can put it no plainer than by saying that Bilbo was *meant* to find the Ring, and *not* by its maker. In which case you also were *meant* to have it. And that may be an encouraging thought" (I/ii). The passive voice used twice for the verb *meant*—made even more important by Tolkien's repeated emphasis of that word—implies an unmentioned and unseen subject of the verb. The subject is not the Ring's maker, Sauron, but rather a greater power that is able to overrule Sauron's will. The words of Elrond, spoken later to those gathered at the council, have similar implications: "That is the purpose for which you are called hither. Called, I say, though I have not called you to me, strangers from distant lands. You have come and are here met, in this very nick of time, by chance as it may seem. Yet it is not so. Believe rather that it is so ordered that we, who sit here, and none others, must now find counsel for the peril of the world" (II/ii). Again, there is a clear indication of some higher power at work—higher than that of Elrond. Indeed, it is a power capable of calling men, dwarves, and elves from all over Middle-earth so that all arrive at Rivendell at just the right time. It is also a power with a purpose beyond chance, which has authority to give moral orders to the inhabitants of Middle-earth.

For Gandalf, the recognition of this higher power at work, above and beyond any design of Sauron, is an "encouraging thought." It strengthens him to his task and to making difficult choices—choices that are not based on foreknowledge of his own safety and that appear to others as a fool's hope. To those who see only in the physical plane, the choices of Gandalf, who also sees in the spiritual plane, may seem foolish. The same could be said about Elrond's vision and his choices.

However, the fact that those present at the Council of Elrond were "called hither" by some higher power, though it should encourage them, does not in any way remove their responsibility and duty to "find counsel for the peril of the world." In other words, the very thought of a power above our own free-doom enables rather than disables that free-doom. One cannot point to that higher power as an excuse to abdicate the responsibility of choosing.

Secondly, while it is clear that this higher power has a hand in shaping events—summoning, by dreams and other means, strangers from distant lands to come to Elrond's council and guiding the footsteps of Sméagol and Bilbo so that the Ring would one day fall into Frodo's hands—the presence, power, and plan of this guiding hand does not in any way remove the reality and significance of the free choices given to individuals in Middle-earth. As Gandalf says to Bilbo at the very end of The Hobbit, "Surely you don't disbelieve the prophecies, because you had a hand in bringing them about yourself?"

(*Hobbit*, 362). Gandalf simultaneously acknowledges the validity of prophecy and the reality of free will. As Tom Shippey points out with regard to prophecy in Middle-earth, Tolkien's characters "have free will but no clear guidance, not from the *palantír*, or from the Mirror of Galadriel. As it happens, all the visions seen in the Mirror by Sam and Frodo seem to be true, though they are a mix of present, past, and future; but . . . they have no effect on anyone's actions."[3] In the age-old theological debate between predestination and free will, Tolkien seems to come down solidly on the side of . . . both.

6

The Gift of Ilúvatar
and the Power of the Ring

> "Did not Gandalf tell you that the rings give power
> according to the measure of each possessor? Before
> you could use that power you would need to become
> far stronger, and to train your will to the domina-
> tion of others."
>
> —Galadriel

In the context of freedom and choice, we now return to the question of the nature of Sauron's One Ring and its particular power.
If Tolkien did not view *all* power as necessarily evil, as I argued
earlier, then what is it about the *particular* power of the Ring that
makes it fundamentally evil and corrupting? And why is it that, in
Tolkien's work, moral victory and personal choices take on greater
significance than do military victories?

Fortunately, the first of these two questions is not difficult to answer and requires little speculation. It is not only hinted at in many
discussions of the Ring but answered rather explicitly by Galadriel:
the power of the One Ring is the power to dominate other wills.

Why that particular power is so evil is a more intriguing question and moves well beyond Lord Acton's claim that power corrupts and absolute power corrupts absolutely. Tolkien's answer can be found, at least in part, in the significance he gives to human free will. Having seen how this reality and importance of choice is expressed throughout *The Lord of the Rings*, and even in *The Hobbit*, and understanding the nature of the One Ring as the power to dominate, we can begin to see why the Ring is so fundamentally evil that no good use of it is possible, regardless of one's underlying motives.

The Domination of Wills

What is the particular power of the Ring that is so fundamentally evil? There are two ways we might go about answering this. The first is by looking at the Ring itself: what is said about it (by the wise) and what effect it has. The second approach is to look at the Ring's creator, Sauron, and to try to understand his power and purpose. We will take both approaches (and find that they lead to the same answer).

Galadriel goes a long way toward describing the nature of the One Ring in her dialogue with Frodo after his encounter with her mirror. She has already explained that Sauron is always searching for her, trying to discover her thoughts. If ever he recovers the One Ring, then her ring, Nenya, and all her works done by the power of Nenya, will be laid bare to him. Frodo then wonders why he himself couldn't see her ring and read her thoughts, since he possesses (and has worn) the One.

> "I would ask one thing before we go," said Frodo, "a thing which I often meant to ask Gandalf in Rivendell. I am permitted to wear the One Ring: why cannot I see the others and know the thoughts of those that wear them?"
>
> "You have not tried," she said. "Only thrice have you set the Ring upon your finger since you knew what you possessed. Do not try! It would destroy you. Did not Gandalf tell you that the rings give power according to the measure of each possessor? Before you could use that power you would need to become far stronger, and to train your will to the domination of others." (II/vii)

Before Frodo could use *that* power—that is, the power of the One Ring—he would need to train his will to domination, specifically to "the domination of others." The essential power of the One Ring, it would seem from Galadriel's words, is thus the power to dominate other wills.

We see this also in a comment Elrond makes about the three elven-rings: "They were not made as weapons of war or conquest: that is not *their* power. Those who made them did not desire strength or *domination* or hoarded wealth, but understanding, making, and healing, to preserve all things unstained" (II/ii, emphasis added). Here, Elrond is contrasting the Three with the One. *Their* purpose, according to Elrond, is *not* conquest or domination. The implication, of course, is that the purpose of the One *is* conquest and domination. This, anyway, is what Saruman sees in the One when he tries to convince Gandalf to help him gain it: "Our time is at hand: the world of Men, which we must rule," he says. "But we must have power, power to order all things as we will, for that good which only the Wise can see" (II/ii). Saruman wants to rule others. This is the central issue in the temptation of the Ring to which he has succumbed. He wants power over other wills. It is not a power whose nature is to do good *for* others, but rather a power to impose (or order) his will *upon* others. Although he uses the word *good*, it is not a good that anybody else can see—that is, it is not a real good that would benefit anyone else—but one that only the wise (by which he means himself) can see. In short, then, the power of the One Ring is the power to rule: the power to conquer, the power to command, the power to order—the power to enslave.

That is the simple answer, and it is consistent with the type of power we saw at work in the temptation of Boromir: "The Ring would give me power of Command," Boromir rightly understands. "All men would flock to my banner!" It is also consistent with what is engraved on the Ring itself: "One Ring to rule them all, One Ring to find them, One Ring to bring them all and in the darkness bind them." The One Ring is about ruling (exercising authority and domination over others) and about binding (forcing, compelling, enslaving). Sauron forged his Ring with the purpose of controlling the other rings and, through them, controlling and enslaving other wills.

110

In a letter written late in 1951 to a potential publisher, Tolkien himself describes the "primary symbolism of the Ring" as "the will to mere power, seeking to make itself objective by physical force and mechanism, and so also inevitably by lies" (*Letters*, 160). One might be tempted to understand the reference to "mere power" as implying that power itself is evil—any power of any type. In this context, however, the phrase "mere power" suggests rather *power for the sake of power*—that is, power for no other reason than to *be* powerful and to *exercise* power. It is the idea of power as an end rather than a means. Contrast this type of mere power with the power of the three elven-ring bearers, Gandalf, Elrond, and Galadriel, whose power always has some other end, such as protecting the lives and freedom of others or preserving beauty and peace. ("The rule of no realm is mine," says Gandalf [V/ii].)

While Tolkien's comment about the symbolism of the One Ring does not explicitly mention domination, it does say that such power is gained through deceit and physical force—through manipulation, we might also say—which strongly suggests such domination. In any case, if we want to look outside *The Lord of the Rings* itself toward Tolkien's letters, earlier in the same letter he gives a clearer picture of the power of the One Ring as well as the other great rings: "The chief power (of all the rings alike) was the prevention or slowing of decay (i.e., 'change' viewed as a regrettable thing), the preservation of what is desired or loved, or its semblance—this is more or less an Elvish motive. But also they enhanced the natural powers of a possessor—thus approaching 'magic,' a motive easily corruptible into evil, a lust for domination" (*Letters*, 152). This last characteristic, a lust for domination, seems especially to be the trait of the One Ring, and of those that it most influenced—namely, the Nine and the Seven, who we learn were *corrupted into evil* by Sauron, while the Three were not. In a personal letter (dated September 1963) Tolkien writes, "It was part of the essential deceit of the Ring to fill minds with imaginations of supreme power" (*Letters*, 332). An exploration of the meaning of magic ("a motive easily corruptible into evil") in Tolkien's writing would itself be worthwhile and might start with the words of Galadriel (this time to Sam): "For this is what your folk would call magic, I believe; though I do not understand clearly what they mean; and they seem also to use the same word of the deceits of the Enemy" (II/vii). However, a full exploration of the meaning of magic and the power of deceit in Tolkien's writing would require at least another entire book![1] For now, the point worth noting is simply the connection, in Tolkien's own words, between the One Ring and domination, will, and power.

The second approach to understanding the nature of the One Ring is to explore Sauron's own power and purpose. Why? Because Sauron and the One Ring are inextricably tied together. It was Sauron's own power that he poured into the Ring when he forged it in secret. "Sauron would not have feared the Ring! It was his own and under his will," Tolkien writes in the 1963 letter. As Elrond says at the council, "It belongs to Sauron and was made by him alone, and is altogether evil" (II/ii). Or as Gandalf tells Frodo, "He made that Ring himself, it is his, and he let a great part of his own former power pass into it, so that he could rule all the others" (I/ii). And as Gandalf later tells the Captains of the West: "If it is destroyed, then he will fall; and his fall will be so low that none can foresee his arising ever again. For he will lose the best part of the strength that was native to him in the beginning" (V/ix). This is why Elrond tells those at the council, "If any of the Wise should with this Ring overthrow the Lord of Mordor, using his own arts, he would then set himself on Sauron's throne and yet another Dark Lord would appear" (II/ii). In other words, if anyone were to take up the Ring, they would not so much *overthrow* Sauron as they would *become* Sauron. Which is also why Galadriel tells Frodo that even the effort to wield the Ring himself would destroy him; it would destroy him by turning him into Sauron—or at least a smaller, weaker Sauron.

What is the power and nature of the Ring, then? It is the power and nature of Sauron himself, for that is what he poured into the Ring. So in order to understand the Ring's nature, we need only to understand Sauron's nature. This is not a difficult task. Tolkien gives illustrations of Sauron's power everywhere. It is the power to force others to his will. We see this in the sharp contrast between the *foes* of Mordor and the *forces* of Mordor. The former fight against Sauron of their own free will. The latter are little more than slaves, driven by fear. Aragorn, Gandalf, Faramir, and even Théoden are always at the forefront of their armies, leading by their own examples of courage. Saruman, Sauron, and, later, Denethor stay in their towers and rule from afar. "He uses others as his weapons," Denethor explains of Sauron. "So do all great lords, if they are wise, Master Halfling. Or why should I sit here in my tower and think, and watch, and wait, spending even my sons?" (V/iv). We see the contrast even in the different types of magic at work in Middle-earth. Tolkien writes in his letters about the differences between elven magic and the magic of Sauron, which are such entirely different things that two different words ought to be used. The elves' magic "is Art, delivered from many of its human limitations: more effortless, more quick, more complete. . . . And its object is Art not Power, sub-creation not domination." While Sauron's magic "is always 'naturally' concerned with sheer Domination" (*Letters*, 146).

In other words, this second path to understanding the Ring—trying to understand Sauron himself—leads us to the same conclusion: the fundamental power of the Ring is the power of domination. It is the power to enslave, the power to rule over other wills. This explains why it is true, as Gandalf says on several occasions, that the Ring can have only one master, not many: many people cannot simultaneously rule over each other.

This raises yet another question about the One Ring. In *Author of the Century*, Tom Shippey raises the point that there are two possible understandings of the evil of the Ring; one he associates with a Boethian view of evil and the other with a Manichaean view.[2] In the Boethian view, evil is internal; the Ring has no innate power of its own to corrupt its bearer, but rather the bearer becomes corrupted by his or her own human sin and weakness, expressed as a greedy desire for the Ring. In a Manichaean understanding, evil is an outside force, and the Ring is actively at work (obeying the will of its master) to corrupt its bearer. Shippey defends the position that Tolkien is ambivalent in his presentation of the Ring's evil, and thus of evil in general, whether it is Boethian or Manichaean. Both aspects of evil seem to be at work at various times: "One can never tell for sure, in *The Lord of the Rings*, whether the danger of the Ring comes from inside, and is sinful, or from outside, and is merely hostile."[3] In this chapter I have claimed that Tolkien associates a particular power and nature with the One Ring: the power to dominate other wills. If this understanding of Tolkien is correct, does that suggest that the debate sways one way or the other, toward the Boethian view or toward the Manichaean? The answer is no. With respect to whether the Ring's evil is internal or external, understanding that the power of the Ring is the power to dominate other wills offers an answer as ambivalent as the one Shippey claims. The corruption associated with the Ring may come entirely from the internal desire of sinful man to dominate other wills, or it may come from some external power at work through the Ring to corrupt the bearer into having a desire to dominate. Or it may be both. As Shippey concludes, "Tolkien's double or ambiguous view of evil is not a flirtation with heresy at all, but expresses a truth about the nature of the universe"— a truth "at the absolute heart of the Christian religion itself." By way of illustration, Shippey suggests that the ambuity can even be found in the Lord's Prayer and the dual request, "Lead us not into temptation / But deliver us from evil," and that there is "no doubt that the Lord's Prayer was in Tolkien's mind" at the very least when he wrote the scene at Sammath Naur—the Chamber of Fire that holds the Crack of Doom—in which Frodo forgives Gollum after the Ring is destroyed.[4]

The Flame Imperishable

Seeing this as the inherent power, or fundamental essence, of the One Ring—the domination of other wills—we still might ask why such a power is fundamentally evil. Why could not Gandalf or Galadriel or Aragorn, or even Boromir or Faramir, put such a power to good use? To answer this question, we must consider again the importance of free will in Tolkien's writing, this time by turning briefly to his other masterpiece, *The Silmarillion*.

The Silmarillion, which recounts the story of the creation of Middle-earth and provides the historical richness that pervades and deepens so much of *The Hobbit* and *The Lord of the Rings*, was not published until 1977, four years after Tolkien's death. It was collected and edited (with considerable care and effort) by J. R. R. Tolkien's son Christopher, from numerous drafts and versions in existence. Because it was published posthumously, and because it was not clear in all instances what were the "final" (or authoritative) versions of various portions of the book, some readers discount the importance and legitimacy of *The Silmarillion* in understanding Tolkien's Middle-earth writing.

There can be no doubt, however, that Tolkien desired *The Silmarillion* to be published (in some form). He sought hard and frequently (though unsuccessfully) to get *The Silmarillion* published during his lifetime. In fact, his original goal was that *The Silmarillion* and *The Lord of the Rings* should be published together! One of the letters from which we quoted earlier in this chapter was actually some ten thousand words long, written to Milton Waldman of Collins publishing company, "with the intention of demonstrating that [the two works] were interdependent and indivisible" (*Letters*, 143). Tolkien had also earlier written a letter to Stanley Unwin (of the publishers Allen & Unwin, who had published *The Hobbit*), in which he had (in his own words) "made a strong point that the *Silmarillion* etc. and *The Lord of the Rings* went together as one long Saga of the Jewels and the Rings" (*Letters*, 139).

Unfortunately, Tolkien's efforts failed, and so we will never know exactly what final form *The Silmarillion* would have taken had the decisions been placed in his hands. (Indications are that even Tolkien himself would have had a difficult time deciding the exact final form, although it is clear from his notes that a certain body of material was part of his canon.) What we do know is that it was his life's work and his life's blood. It was not a piece added on to *The Hobbit* as an afterthought but rather the other way around. The rest of the history of Tolkien's efforts at completing the mythology of Middle-earth (which has been given elsewhere) is not critical to this chapter other than to say that work on *The Silmarillion* began literally decades before *The Hobbit* and *The Lord of the Rings* and continued long after. As his son Christopher wrote in his foreword to the first edition, the "old legends ('old' now not only in their derivation from the remote First Age, but also in terms of my father's life) became the vehicle and depository of his profoundest reflections" (*Silm*, 7). At the very least, Sandra Miesel's remark about Tolkien's old legends should be taken seriously: "Yet, knowing whence his world came and whither it is going greatly enhances the patient reader's pleasure in *The Lord of the Rings*. Indeed, the full scope of Tolkien's achievement cannot be appreciated otherwise."[5]

It is in the *Ainulindalë*—the opening book of *The Silmarillion*, which recounts the Music of the Ainur and the creation of Middle-earth—that we are introduced to both the source and importance of free will in Tolkien's writing. Middle-earth was created by Eru, whose name means "the One" and who is also called Ilúvatar, "Father of All." But before Middle-earth was brought into being, Eru created first the Ainur, or "Holy Ones." These were the first beings, other than Eru Ilúvatar himself, to have wills and selves of their own. We read in the *Ainulindalë*: "Then Ilúvatar said to them: 'Of the theme that I have declared to you, I will now that ye make in harmony together a Great Music. And since I have kindled you with the Flame Imperishable, ye shall show forth your powers in adorning this theme, each with his own thoughts and devices, if he will'" (*Silm*, 15).

For those who have not (yet) read *The Silmarillion*, a little background may be helpful. The Ainur are spiritual beings, most closely akin to angels in the biblical concept of Tolkien's Christian faith. When Eru creates Eä, the physical or material universe, and Arda, the earth itself, he gives the Ainur the opportunity to enter into this created order in order to assist Ilúvatar in creation. Many choose to do so, and those who make that choice have the ability to take incarnate forms like the stuff of Arda, and make them into the image of the coming Children of Ilúvatar (that of elves in particular). Greatest among those who go to Arda are the Valar, or the Powers of Arda. Manwë is their King, and Varda, also called Elbereth, is their queen. These Valar, and lesser spirits known as the Maiar, take up their residence in Valinor in the far West of Arda. Gandalf, in fact, is one of the Maiar, known originally as Olórin.

Of critical importance here is the idea of the Flame Imperishable, with which Eru "kindled" the Ainur. What is this Flame Imperishable? It is closely associated with the gift of existence itself—that is, the gift of a *separate* existence, with a separate will, an awareness of self, and the freedom to act.[6] Thus, each of the Ainur has "his own thoughts." Even more, Ilúvatar gives each the choice of whether or not even to participate in this Music of the Ainur. Each may do so, not under compulsion, but "*if* he will" (emphasis added). That one of the Ainur, namely, Melkor, soon rebels against Eru, seeking to "increase the power and glory of the part assigned to himself," shows us quickly just how real this freedom is (*Silm*, 15–16). Creation now has beings who, though dependent on Eru for their existence, have wills of their own to choose and to act and even to rebel. (One cannot miss the echoes, in Tolkien's creation account, of Genesis 1–3 as well as of Milton's *Paradise Lost*.)

It is also important to realize that this Flame Imperishable is a gift—indeed, it is the great gift—given by Eru Ilúvatar to his created beings. It is this freedom that enables them to participate in Ilúvatar's Music and to assist in sub-creating new beauty. In fact, so great a gift is it that none other than Eru Ilúvatar himself can give it. Not even Manwë can create beings having their own free will. Both Melkor and Aulë try, and both fail. As we read in the *Ainulindalë*, Melkor "had gone often alone into the void places seeking the Imperishable Flame; for desire grew hot within him to bring into Being things of his own. . . . Yet he found not the Fire, for it is with Ilúvatar" (*Silm*, 16). We later learn that this Flame Imperishable is also the gift given to elves and men (the Children of Ilúvatar): "For the Children of Ilúvatar were conceived by him alone. . . . Therefore when [the Ainur] beheld them, the more did they love them, being things other than themselves, strange and *free*" (*Silm*, 18, emphasis added). In other words, elves and men are also beings of free will. This, then, is the source of their nature, which we discussed in the context of *The Lord of the Rings* in chapter 5. This is the significance of the "doom of choice" that Aragorn has.

We see more of the significance and meaning of this great gift of freedom when it is bestowed on the dwarves also. It is the Vala Aulë who first creates the dwarves (in form, at least). But Aulë, though he has as a gift his own free will—which is exhibited in his choice to attempt such a thing on his own without the command of Ilúvatar—has neither the authority nor the power to complete his task and give these creatures their own independent being. That is, though Aulë creates the *form* and *features* of the dwarves, he cannot give them free will. They are simply his puppets, moving when he thinks to move them and sitting idle when his thought is elsewhere. In repentance, therefore, he prepares to destroy his own creation. But Ilúvatar, in his mercy, bestows on the dwarves the same gift of free will that he has designed for his other Children: elves and men.

Then Aulë took up a great hammer to smite the Dwarves; and he wept. But Ilúvatar had compassion upon Aulë and his desire, because of his humility; and the Dwarves shrank from the hammer and were afraid, and they bowed down their heads and begged for mercy. And the voice of Ilúvatar said to Aulë: "Thy offer I accepted even as it was made. Dost thou not see that these things have now a life of their own, and speak with their own voices? Else they would not have flinched from thy blow, nor from any command of thy will." (*Silm*, 43–44)

What it means for beings to have this gift of freedom—their own free will—is that they can shrink even from the hand of their Creator. Ilúvatar's created beings can choose to participate in the Music in keeping with their part in the Theme of Ilúvatar, or they can choose to rebel and bring about discord. As we saw in chapter 5 in our discussion of Aragorn, it is the *destiny* of beings with free will that they *must* make choices. But we also see that this freedom, in Tolkien's writing, is a gift as well as a doom: a gift that even Melkor and Sauron envy.

The importance of the gift of freedom can be seen even in the relationship between the Children of Ilúvatar (especially the elves) and the Valar. "For Elves and Men are the Children of Ilúvatar. . . . For which reason the Valar are to these kindreds rather their elders and their chieftains than their masters; and if ever in their dealings with Elves and Men the Ainur have endeavored to force them when they would not be guided, seldom has this turned to good, howsoever good the intent" (*Silm*, 41). The Valar, though older and more powerful than elves, men, or dwarves, are not given the right to take away this gift of freedom given to the Children. They are allowed to advise the Children, and to teach them, and to share wisdom with them, but any attempt made at *compelling* the Children to some course of action, no matter what the intention, leads to an evil result.

The clearest example of this in *The Silmarillion* is the summons the Valar issue to the elves (who call themselves the *Quendi*, in their own tongue), that they should come to Valinor.

Then again the Valar were gathered in council, and they were divided in debate. For some, and of those Ulmo was the chief, held that the Quendi should be left free to walk as they would in Middle-earth, and with their gifts of skill to order all the lands and heal their hurts. But the most part feared for the Quendi in the dangerous world amid the deceits of the starlit dusk; and they were filled moreover with the love of the beauty of the Elves and desired their fellowship. At the last, therefore, the Valar summoned the Quendi to Valinor, there to be gathered at the knees of the Powers in the light of the Trees for ever; and Mandos broke his silence, saying: "So it is doomed." From this summons came many woes that afterwards befell. (*Silm*, 52)

The choice here is between being "left free," though in a "dangerous world," and being safe, but with a loss of freedom. Freedom is held the higher gift than safety! And the desire of the Valar, even if phrased in terms of "love" and "fellowship," still involves the elves at their knees, which is a place of subservience. For this very reason, Ulmo, ever one of the wisest of the Valar, argues against such a summons, and Mandos foretells what doom will come of the Valar exercising authority over the Children. We see this same principle behind the refusal of the wise of Middle-earth to wield the Ring. The power of the Ring is the power to compel other wills to one's own will. There is never a good use for such a power.

Now, much more could be said about this freedom and about what it really means under the authority of Eru Ilúvatar, who promises that "no theme may be played that hath not its uttermost source" in him, nor can any "alter the music in [his] despite" (*Silm*, 17). Again, there are strong biblical echoes, this time of passages such as Romans 8:28: "And we know that to them that love God, all things work together unto good, to such as, according to his purpose, are called to be saints." The depth of this theology could be (and has been) pondered for centuries, and we will return to it in the last chapters of this book. In regard to the specific topic of freedom as a gift of Ilúvatar to his Children, men and elves, there are two concerns worth exploring before concluding this chapter.

The Firstborn and the Followers

The first issue pertains to the differences between the two Children of Ilúvatar: elves, who are called the Firstborn, and men, who are called the Followers.[7] Or, as elves and men are known in the elven tongue: the Quendi, meaning "those who speak with voices," and the Atani, meaning "the second people." The following passage is one of the longest cited in this book, but it is included because it lays much of the foundation for understanding the races:

> For it is said that after the departure of the Valar there was silence, and for an age Ilúvatar sat alone in thought. Then he spoke and said: "Behold I love the Earth, which shall be a mansion for the Quendi and the Atani! But the Quendi shall be the fairest of all earthly creatures, and they shall have and shall conceive and bring forth more beauty than all my Children; and they shall have the greater bliss in this world. But to the Atani I will give a new gift." Therefore he willed that the hearts of Men should seek beyond the world and should find no rest therein; but they should have a virtue to shape their life, amid the powers and chances of the world, beyond the Music of the Ainur, which is as fate to all things else. . . .
>
> But Ilúvatar knew that Men, being set amid the turmoils of the powers of the world, would stray often, and would not use their gifts in harmony; and he said: "These too in their time shall find that all that they do redounds at the end only to the glory of my work." . . .
>
> It is one with this gift of freedom that the children of Men dwell only a short space in the world alive, and are not bound to it, and depart soon whither the Elves know not. Whereas the Elves remain until the end of days, and their love of the Earth and all the world is more single and more poignant therefore, and as the years lengthen ever more sorrowful. For the Elves die not till the world dies, unless they are slain or waste in grief. . . . But the sons of Men die indeed, and leave the world; wherefore they are called the Guests, or the Strangers. Death is their fate, the gift of Ilúvatar, which as Time wears even the Powers shall envy. But Melkor has cast his shadow upon it, and confounded it with darkness, and brought forth evil out of good, and fear out of hope. Yet of old the Valar declared to the Elves in Valinor that Men shall join in the Second Music of the Ainur; whereas Ilúvatar has not revealed what he purposes for the Elves after the World's end, and Melkor has not discovered it. (*Silm*, 41–42)

Some things are clear in this passage, but many others are less so. What is clear is that elves and men are different. The obvious difference—one that could be understood even from a quick reading of *The Lord of the Rings* without the additional understanding to be gained from *The Silmarillion*—is that elves are given immortality, whereas men die of old age. Interestingly enough, it is also stated that mortality and immortality, as well as freedom, are all gifts. That is, they are all *meant* as good things; the ability of men to "shape their life" is a "virtue," not a vice. As stated, however, Melkor seeks to turn men (and elves) away from Ilúvatar by making the gifts look bad or by making each envious of the gifts of the others. Yet the very fact that he must use deceit to make the gifts appear evil is a demonstration that they are indeed good. In any case, this reinforces the earlier observation that freedom is a good gift from Ilúvatar to his Children.

What is less clear, but is nonetheless hinted at, is that men somehow have a greater or more meaningful freedom than do elves. It is what Ilúvatar calls "a new gift." To the elves, the Music of the Ainur is fate; no choices of elves have the power to change what has already been foreseen (and foresung) in this Music. Men, by contrast, have the power to "shape their life" beyond the Music. In fact, free will goes hand in hand with mortality: "It is one with the gift of freedom that the children of Men dwell only a short space in the world alive."

Does this mean the elves do not have free will? How are men more free? What does this "new gift" really mean? Tolkien does not spell out the answers to these questions. He was, after all, writing story and history, not theology or philosophy. So we can only guess or infer the answers from other passages. What I think becomes clear from the rest of *The Silmarillion* is that the elves do indeed have free will, even though all their choices will ultimately lead to the fulfillment of what has already been seen. If this were not the case, then the debate of the Ainur about whether to summon the elves to Valinor or to leave them free to wander Middle-earth would be meaningless. In particular, the elves are responsible for their choices. We see this especially in the case of Fëanor, "mightiest in all parts of body and mind, in valour, in endurance, in beauty, in understanding, in skill, in strength and in subtlety alike, of all the Children of Ilúvatar," who finally rebels against the Valar and against Ilúvatar himself. When his rebellion and haughty words are made known to the Valar, Manwë weeps in sadness but then proclaims that some good will still be brought into the world through Fëanor's evil. To this statement Mandos, the judge of spirits, replies, "And yet [that evil of Fëanor will] remain evil" (*Silm*, 98). That Fëanor rebels at all shows that he, like men, has freedom. That he and his evil will be judged shows not only that he is free but also that he is responsible for his freedom.

Free Will and Creativity

A second issue that relates to the Flame Imperishable and the gift of free will is the possibility of real creativity. Although puppet masters and computer programmers may be creative, neither the puppets controlled by the masters nor computer programs written by the programmers are themselves creative. When Eru Ilúvatar gives the gift of freedom to the Ainur, the Quendi, and the Atani (as well as to the dwarves), enabling them to have thoughts of their own and to act of their own initiative, he gives them the gift of creativity. The Ainur were to "adorn" the Theme of Ilúvatar. *Adorn* is a word that is full of artistic and creative connotations. Moreover, each is to do so with "his own thoughts and devices." And the elves are to "conceive and bring forth more beauty than all [Ilúvatar's] Children."

There can be no doubt that creativity, and more specifically creative art, plays a very important role in Tolkien's writing. Throughout *The Silmarillion* we are moved by story after story of one of the great of Middle-earth pouring thought and effort into some creative work of beauty. The whole history of the First Age of Middle-earth, told in *The Silmarillion*, revolves around two great creative acts. The first is that of Yavanna, the Vala who creates Telperion and Laurelin, the Two Trees of Valinor. The second is that of Fëanor, the elf who creates the Silmarils, the living jewels in which dwells the mingled light of Telperion and Laurelin. So important are these two creative acts that it is written of the Two Trees, "Of all things which Yavanna made they have most renown, and about their fate all the tales of the Elder Days are woven" (*Silm*, 38). The importance of Fëanor's jewels can likewise be understood from what is said about them, that they were "most renowned of all the works of the Elves." We learn that "Varda hallowed the Silmarils, so that thereafter no mortal flesh, nor hands unclean, nor anything of evil will might touch them" (*Silm*, 67). Indeed the book itself gets its title from these jewels. And these, though the most important in the history of the elves, are merely two of many creative labors we read about in *The Silmarillion*. We could also speak of the white ships of the Teleri elves; of the Nauglamír, the great necklace of the dwarves; of Iluin and Ormal, the mighty lamps of the Valar; of the fountains of Gondolin; and so on. The great among men, dwarves, elves, and Valar are often known by what they create. In other words, what we begin to see here and elsewhere is that creativity is a great and highly prized gift.

One of the most moving acts of creation is the making of dwarves by Aulë, alluded to earlier. When Tolkien writes of Aulë picking up his great hammer to smite the dwarves, one should picture Tolkien sitting beside the huge pile of papers comprising the manuscripts of his unfinished work and holding a lit match to it. Both Aulë and Tolkien deeply loved their work, and both sought to give their work a life of its own. (By the grace of Ilúvatar, Aulë succeeded beyond what he could have imagined. Those reading this book might agree that Tolkien succeeded, perhaps by the same grace.) And Tolkien, like Aulë, often doubted whether he had the power and authority to do what it was he was trying to do in his creative work. You can see this expressed both in his tale of Aulë and Yavanna and in his very personal and deeply moving short fairy tale "Leaf by Niggle." In the same letter to Milton Waldman quoted earlier, Tolkien writes:

> Do not laugh! But once upon a time (my crest has long since fallen) I had a mind to make a body of more or less connected legend, ranging from the large and cosmogonic, to the level of romantic fairy-story—the larger founded on the lesser in contact with the earth, the lesser drawing splendour from the vast backcloths—which I could dedicate simply: to England; to my country. . . . I would draw some of the great tales in fullness, and leave many only placed in the scheme, and sketched. The cycles should be linked to a majestic whole, and yet leave scope for other minds and hands, wielding paint and music and drama. Absurd. (*Letters*, 144–45)

So we picture Tolkien, crestfallen, looking at his unpublished work, thinking it absurd, and lighting a match. "And he wept."

But we must also picture Tolkien defending what he had done, as Aulë does before Ilúvatar.

> Then Aulë answered: "I did not desire such lordship. I desired things other than I am, to love and to teach them, so that they too might

perceive the beauty of Eä, which thou has caused to be. . . . And in my impatience I have fallen into folly. Yet the making of things is in my heart from my own making by thee; and the child of little understanding that makes a play of the deeds of his father may do so without thought of mockery, but because he is the son of his father." (*Silm*, 43)

In this one little speech by Aulë, Tolkien answers (with considerable profundity) one of the most important philosophical questions of history: why are we creative? Or, put another way, where does our creativity come from? This is, of course, part and parcel of the question, from whence comes our free will? Tolkien not only affirms both free will and creativity but tells us from whence they came. Unlike a rock or mountain, men (and also elves and dwarves and the Ainur) have from Ilúvatar the gift of the Flame Imperishable. Indeed, the first task of the Ainur after hearing the Theme of Ilúvatar's Music is to *create* music of their own. To broaden the answer from Ainur to man, the making of things is in our hearts because of the way in which the Maker made us as making-creatures. We are children of a Father—Ilúvatar, the "Father of All"—who is a Creator. As his children, it is only natural that we also create. A message similar to that found in the story of Aulë and Yavanna can also be found in Tolkien's essay "On Fairy-Stories": "We make in our measure and in our derivative mode, because we are made: and not only made, but made in the image and likeness of a Maker" ("Fairy," 145). Tolkien's powerful short story "Leaf by Niggle" has some equally wonderful meditations on the value of human art and creativity.

And this relates to our earlier discussion of why the Ring is so fundamentally evil. Its power, like the power of Sauron himself, is the power to dominate other wills. It is the power to take away freedom. Sauron is no different from his master, Melkor, in whose image both Sauron and the Ring take their shape. Of Melkor we read, "But he desired rather to subdue to his will both Elves and Men, envying the gifts with which Ilúvatar promised to endow them; and he wished himself to have subjects and servants, and to be called Lord, and to be a master over other wills" (*Silm*, 18). The essence of the desire and power of the Ring is to master other wills: to have subjects and servants, to subdue others and ultimately remove their freedom. This is a fundamentally evil desire. Why? Because the gift of Ilúvatar—this gift of freedom, and the creativity that goes with it—is such a great gift.

And this, finally, is our answer to the second question posed at the start of the chapter. If the greatest gift to the race of men is that of freedom, and with it the gift of creativity, then the greatest evil—the evil of Melkor, his servant Sauron, and Sauron's One Ring—is the taking away of that gift of freedom.

7

Moral Responsibility and Stewardship

"Good and ill have not changed since yesteryear; nor are they one thing among Elves and Dwarves and another among Men. It is a man's part to discern them, as much in the Golden Wood as in his own house."

—Aragorn

In J. R. R. Tolkien's world of Middle-earth, free will is real. It is not only a gift, but a great gift, highly valued. It is a gift that can be given only by Eru Ilúvatar himself, and therefore it is a gift that should never be taken away from someone else. This, in part, is an answer to the question posed in the previous chapter. It is why choice is so important in Tolkien's works. Or, put another way, free will is what makes heroism possible in Middle-earth, and the choices made by heroes are what define them as heroes. It is also an answer to the question of why the One Ring is so inherently evil: its power is to dominate other wills and to steal the gift of freedom.

It is worth noting that Tolkien's emphasis on the choices of his characters is also the reason many critics—in particular, those who believe that humans are merely complex biochemical computers or machines, products of blind, purposeless chance who have no free will—are often so adamantly opposed to his stories, and more broadly to any heroic literature, or "literature of freedom." While Tolkien's vision of reality may be appealing to many readers because his underlying philosophy rings true (whether or not we are consciously aware of it), to modern materialists his vision of humans as beings of free will, created with a purpose, is deceptive and dangerous. And that, rather than any stylistic issue, is at the core of most criticisms of the Middle-earth *legendarium*.

There may be only one aspect of Tolkien's underlying philosophy that draws even more ire from critics, and that aspect is yet another reason why free will is so important in Middle-earth. We inched close to it in the first chapter of this book in our discussion of the treatment of prisoners and ethics in war. It is the notion of objective morality and moral responsibility. Objective morality—or what some people call "moral absolutes"—is a definition of good and evil that is real and true for every person (and every culture), regardless of whether that person (or culture) happens to *believe* it to be true. In the first chapter I wrote of torture as an ethical issue. But it would be more accurate, and more to the point of this chapter, to speak of it as a moral issue. Torturing prisoners may simply be morally wrong, for all people at all times. Whether it is Sauron or Gandalf doing the torturing makes no difference, Tolkien's stories tell us. Nor does it matter if the tortured prisoner has important information that could be used for a good purpose. Torture is wrong. Evil means are still evil; they are not justified by a good end. That, at least, seems to be Tolkien's view.

Objective morality stands in sharp contrast to subjective morality, or moral relativism. Objective morality is independent of the individual subject or subjects (whether it is a person, nation, culture, or era). Fëanor's evil deeds, for example, especially the tragic Kinslaying at Alqualondë, are going to be judged. But on what basis are they to be judged? Looking at the question another way, the discourse between Manwë and Mandos about Fëanor speaks of both good and evil: Manwë claims that Ilúvatar will bring some good out of the evil of Fëanor, and Mandos replies that the deeds themselves will yet remain evil. But the "good" and "evil" of which Manwë speaks are moral categories independent of any particular character, and this implies some standard for judgment that is likewise independent. What is the standard? Whatever it is, it is something outside of Fëanor. And, in fact, it is above even Manwë himself.

Before exploring the reality and importance of objective moral categories in Tolkien's works, first identifying the relationship between free will and morality, and then outlining the prevailing worldviews regarding morality will help us to see just how sharply the writings of Tolkien contrast with today's dominant cultural views. We begin with the way that many popular strands of contemporary thought deny the very existence of free will, and the relationship between free will and moral responsibility.

Consider a computer virus. No matter how inconvenient or destructive it is, a computer virus is just an impersonal collection of computer code composed of bits (zeros and ones) on a computer. A virus has no will of its own and cannot be considered evil or immoral. The *person* who creates a virus, by contrast, might well be considered evil, especially if the virus is designed with malicious intent. Put another way, if we have suffered the results of a malicious computer virus, we may seek to have the programmer of the virus punished (perhaps by a fine or by jail time), but we probably don't seek to punish the bits (zeros and ones of computer code) that compose the virus.

Now suppose that a person who commits a heinous crime is only acting as he or she is *programmed* to do, as a materialist worldview states is the case. (For the sake of this discussion, it is irrelevant whether that programming comes by nature or nurture.) Then by no means can that *person* be evil; only the *programmer* of that person can be evil. In this case, however, the programmer is believed to be a blind, impersonal force. In short, where there is no choice at all, there can be no moral (or immoral) choice. In a merely material world, we may at worst consider another person's actions as inconvenient to us; we cannot call them "evil" or "immoral." Or, if we do, then we are really only calling "immoral" the universe itself: the impersonal universe that programmed the person. In any case the word *immoral* has no meaning in this context. We are stuck saying, as the famous twentieth-century materialist philosopher Bertrand Russell writes, "When a man acts in ways that annoy us we wish to think him wicked, and we refuse to face the fact that his annoying behavior is a result of antecedent causes."[1] The language of "good" and "evil" (or "wickedness") has been replaced by that of "convenience" and "annoyance." If we start with the presupposition of materialism that denies free will, then we can immediately conclude that there is no such thing as objective morality, and we are left with the popular position of moral relativism (or with no morality at all).

It must be pointed out that one need not believe in materialism in order to hold a view of moral relativism. One may be a theist, a deist, a polytheist, and so on, and still hold to relativism. Also, there are many forms of moral relativism, including cultural forms, that claim that good and evil are defined by society and not the individual and thus may be defined differently by different societies. The point is only that the prevailing credo of our time is this: right and wrong are personal choices, like the type of ice cream we prefer. This view was already widely popular when Tolkien was thinking about a sequel to *The Hobbit*. Anthropologist Ruth Benedict, author of *Patterns of Culture* (1934), aptly expresses this relativistic worldview.

> It is a point that has been made more often in relation to ethics than in relation to psychiatry. We do not any longer make the mistake of deriving the morality of our locality and decade directly from the inevitable constitution of human nature. We do not elevate it to the dignity of a first principle. We recognize that morality differs in every society, and is a convenient term for socially approved habits. Mankind has always preferred to say "it is morally good," rather than "it is habitual," and the fact of this preference is matter enough for a critical science of ethics. But historically the two phrases are synonymous.[2]

Benedict dismisses any notion that morality may be a first principle—that is, an objective reality from which other principles may be derived—and instead reduces moral virtue, or goodness, to mere habit. This view permeates modern thinking. The only remaining virtue still accepted as objective is tolerance; intolerance is the only thing we are free not to tolerate. Whether or not one comes to the question of morality from a materialist worldview, in the modern world objective morality is out and subjective morality is in: good and evil, if they exist as categories at all, are only personal or at best societal.

Tolkien, of course, does use the language of objective good and evil. This language is woven into the very fabric of his works, from start to finish. He rejects altogether the thinking behind Benedict's quote. Indeed, I think he must have had some notion of that form of relativism in mind when he wrote the dialogue between Gandalf and Saruman when Saruman's treachery is first made known. Gandalf recounts this dialogue to the council.

> "'I looked then and saw that his robes, which had seemed white, were not so, but were woven of all colours, and if he moved they shimmered and changed hue so that the eye was bewildered.'
> 'I liked white better,' I said.
> 'White!' he sneered. 'It serves as a beginning. White cloth may be dyed. The white page can be overwritten; and the white light can be broken.'
> 'In which case it is no longer white,' said I. 'And he that breaks a thing to find out what it is has left the path of wisdom.'" (II/ii)

Black and white have long been images of evil and good. Saruman rejects the very notion of white, saying that it is something that may be dyed, overwritten, broken. By doing so, he is denying—perhaps in an attempt to justify his own actions, which otherwise must be seen as treacherous and evil—the existence of any higher moral law, or at least any higher law that applies to *him*. Saruman's sneering disdain for white in each of the three metaphors (cloth, paper, and light) and his preference instead for that which is multicolored is, then, a preference for relativism. Gandalf's rebuttal gives us a good idea of what Tolkien probably thinks of this: such moral relativism is a departure from the path of wisdom. With the dialogue seen in this light, Saruman's fall may be seen as a fall away from objective morality into subjectivity and may well represent Tolkien's view of the downfall of our whole society.

Now for those who question the particular interpretation of the symbolism of black and white given in the previous paragraph, the case for the reality and importance of objective morality in Tolkien's writing does not rest just in this one passage. The existence of objective morals—definitions of good and evil that are true for everybody regardless of whether any person or culture believes them true—is central to *The Lord of the Rings* and *The Silmarillion*. Objective moral principles are referred to time and again. Speaking of his encounter with Saruman and his subsequent captivity, Gandalf later comments, "There are many powers in the world, for *good* or for *evil*" (II/i, emphasis added). Fëanor will be judged, and not by his own personal standards, or even by the standards of the Noldor; he will be judged by a transcendent law. "Ye have spilled the blood of your kindred unrighteously and have stained the land of Aman," Mandos the Judge tells Fëanor. "For blood ye shall render blood" (*Silm*, 88).

Objective Morality and Judgment

We get glimpses of this objective morality even in *The Hobbit*. Consider the array of morality words used throughout the book: *evil*, *good*, *wicked*, *fair*, *unfair*, and so forth. "Evil things did not come into that valley" (*Hobbit*, 94), the narrator tells us of Elrond's domain of Rivendell, while of wood-elves we are told, "Still Elves they were and remain, and that is Good People" (*Hobbit*, 219). By contrast, the narrator also tells us that goblins "are cruel, wicked, and bad-hearted" (*Hobbit*, 108). The casting of these moral judgments *by the narrator*, without any diminishing of their strength by qualification in some particular subjective or cultural or even situational context, suggests a moral authority that is above the characters within the story.

Tolkien also makes an important comment about Bilbo's understanding of morality at the end of his riddle game with Gollum: "He knew, of course, that the riddle-game was sacred and of immense antiquity, and even wicked creatures were afraid to cheat when they played at it" (*Hobbit*, 126–27). What Bilbo's thoughts convey is that the definitions of good and evil are known not only by those who are good but even by those who are evil, or "wicked." "Wicked creatures" may choose to disobey the "sacred" moral laws, but even in their disobedience the law itself is not invalidated. Indeed, such is Gollum's knowledge of this moral law that when he breaks it— murdering his brother, thieving from his neighbors, not keeping his

131

bargain with Bilbo—he makes excuses for why it is justifiable for him in his particular circumstance to do what he does, rather than just pretending that no such law exists (the Ring was a gift, Bilbo's question wasn't fair, etc.). Tolkien believed the influence of moral law to be so powerful as to be understood even in an imaginary universe, and even by the wicked creatures there.

In *The Lord of the Rings*, we see moral language and the contrast between good and evil in many places. Tom Shippey makes a point about the orcs that is similar to the one just made about Gollum. Drawing on the dialogue between Gorbag and Shagrat after they take Frodo prisoner, he writes that Gorbag "is convinced that it is wrong, and contemptible, to abandon your companions."³ Shippey goes on to conclude, "Orcs here, and on other occasions, have a clear idea of what is admirable and what is contemptible behaviour, which is exactly the same as ours. They cannot revoke what [C. S.] Lewis calls 'the Moral Law' and create a counter-morality based on evil, any more than they can revoke biology and live on poison. They are moral beings, who talk freely and repeatedly of what is 'good,' meaning by that more or less what we do."⁴ Of course, the orcs rarely come close to living up to that moral law—there is no indication that they even make any effort—but this failure to put the law into *practice* by living good lives denies neither the existence of that objective law nor their knowledge of it. Tolkien also shows us glimpses of this objective moral law in the internal debate between Sméagol's two sides (which is given such prominence in *The Two Towers*). The foundation for this debate is laid by Gandalf early in *The Fellowship of the Ring*: "There was a little corner of his mind that was still his own, and light came through it, as through a chink in the dark. . . . But that, of course, would only make the evil part of him angrier in the end—unless it could be conquered" (I/ii). That the two sides or "parts" of him are not merely different but *morally distinguishable*, with only one part being seen as "evil," gives insight into the moral nature of Middle-earth.

The objective distinction between good and evil in Middle-earth is so clear and powerful that those among Tolkien's characters who are morally attuned may even sense it externally at times. "You have frightened me several times tonight," Frodo says to Aragorn shortly after they meet, "but never in the way that servants of the Enemy would, or so I imagine. I think one of his spies would—well, seem fairer and feel fouler, if you understand" (I/x). Aragorn later has the same experience when he meets Gandalf after the wizard's return from death: "Aragorn felt a shudder run through him at the sound, a strange cold thrill; and yet it was not fear or terror that he felt: rather it was like the sudden bite of a keen air, or the slap of a cold rain that wakes an uneasy sleeper" (III/v). Evil has a feel to it, and it is different from the feel of good.

Tolkien's morality is also a morality that is not situational. Consider the words of Faramir when he discovers what it is that Frodo is carrying: "We are truth-speakers, we men of Gondor. We boast seldom, and then perform, or die in the attempt. *Not if I found it on the highway would I take it*, I said. Even if I were such a man as to desire this thing, and even though I knew not clearly what this thing was when I spoke, still I should take those words as a vow, and be held by them" (IV/v). We see that Faramir recognizes that it is wrong to break one's vow. Not even a situation in which breaking his vow were the only way for Faramir to save his country would turn the evil of breaking it into a good. Breaking a vow is an objective moral ill, independent of the situation. There are also echoes here of earlier words spoken by Faramir, that he would not speak a falsehood even to snare an orc. Men of Gondor speak the truth, whatever the situation. Thus, the main conclusion of chapter 4, that moral victory is more important than military victory, is just one application of this broader principle: morality is objective and does not change with the shifting winds or with different situations; even the situation of military battle does not justify breaking moral law.

Tolkien gets even more specific in his articulation of objective morality. One of the most important passages among those that deal with the nature of morality is the dialogue between Éomer and Aragorn when the two first meet on the Plains of Rohan. We have already considered this passage in our discussion of free will and the "doom of choice" in chapter 5, and we now resume our explorations from that starting point. Remember Éomer's question to Aragorn: "What doom do you bring out of the North?" After replying, "The doom of choice," Aragorn goes on to add, "You may say this to Théoden son of Thengel: open war lies before him, *with Sauron or against him*" (III/ii, emphasis added). I grant that there is not yet any explicit

133

mention of good, evil, or morality in this passage. Yet Aragorn, in the context of a statement about "choice"—and in particular about the "doom" of those who must make choices—states that ultimately there are only two choices to be made in Middle-earth at this time: to fight "with Sauron or against him." As Aragorn tells us, there is no neutral ground: for Théoden, the dividing barrier between black and white is a sharp line, with no gray territory. There are, of course, many different strategies and tactics the king might choose to use in the war, for one side or the other, but the distinction between the sides cannot be any clearer than Tolkien has painted it. This is an objective standard for making a choice. And Aragorn lays upon Éomer another equally clear choice: help the three hunters on their quest to find and free the captured hobbits, or hinder them.

We don't, however, have to risk stretching Aragorn's words beyond what they were intended to mean in order to reveal the existence of an objective moral basis for judgment. Because of the paralysis of his king and uncle, Éomer has not yet been faced with the many difficult decisions Aragorn has had to make, and has not yet acquired the wisdom that comes with making those decisions. At a loss for whether or not to help Aragorn, he asks, "How shall a man judge what to do in such times?" Aragorn's answer is the key passage in this chapter: "As he has ever judged. Good and ill have not changed since yesteryear; nor are they one thing among Elves and Dwarves and another among Men. It is a man's part to discern them, as much in the Golden Wood as in his own house" (III/ii). Here is our straightforward proclamation of moral absolutes: "good and ill" are the same, not only across cultures (of dwarf, man, elf), but across times and eras as well, from yesteryear to today. Morality is neither spatially relative, temporally relative, nor culturally relative. The meaning of right and wrong does not, and has not, changed. "And this deed was unlawful," Mandos tells Fëanor, before pronouncing his judgment, "whether in Aman or not in Aman" (*Silm*, 71).

Now a moral law such as what I have described in Middle-earth is sometimes referred to as part of "natural law"; the hobbits of the Shire sometimes call this "The Rules." If by "natural law" one means no more and no less than what I have said above—namely, moral laws that are not only universally in effect for all eras and all peoples but also seem to be commonly known or felt even among those who

134

disobey them—then "natural law" is a correct term. However, if by "natural law" we mean a law whose source is nature itself, where nature is an impersonal object, then it is the wrong term. In Tolkien's Middle-earth, the law has come down from Ilúvatar through Manwë, and thus it bears the authority not just of nature, but of the *Creator* of nature. We see this in the words of the Vala Mandos when he reminds Fëanor both that Manwë is king over all Arda and that Mandos himself is the judge. Even the simple hobbits, who never dwelt in Valinor with the Valar and have little contact with the elves who did, have a vague understanding of this: "For they attributed to the king of old all their essential laws; and usually they kept the laws of free will, because they were The Rules (as they said), both ancient and just" (Prologue). So it is that Gandalf can reply to Pippin, after Pippin tries to defend his looking into the *palantír* with the plea that he had no idea what he was doing: "Oh yes, you did [. . .]. You knew you were behaving *wrongly* and foolishly; and you told yourself so, though you did not listen" (III/xi, emphasis added).

We should also note that even though Tolkien makes it clear that the distinction between good and evil is real and objective, when it comes to individuals—whether elf, dwarf, man, or hobbit—there are none who are either completely good or completely evil. Sauron alone might be considered completely evil, but even he was not so in the beginning, we are told. The ambiguity of good and evil doesn't lie in the law itself but in the moral state of those who follow (or disobey) the law. Indeed, the criticism that objective moral law in Tolkien's universe leads to simplistic black-and-white characters so greatly misses the mark that one wonders if those who make this criticism even see the target. Boromir may fail morally at a critical point, but he is by no means completely evil, as is evident when he gives his life to save Merry and Pippin. Gandalf may have great moral character, yet he is not above pride, and in desperation possibly even gives in to the temptation of resorting to the evil of torture. Or consider the opposite and complex trajectories of Denethor and Théoden, *both* of whom display good motives as well as evil ones. Or consider Pippin's falling to temptation with the *palantír*, or the behavior of some of the Shirrifs (in "The Scouring of the Shire") who may not be wholly corrupt and yet who collaborate in some way with Sharkey. The reality of a moral standard enlivens and richens rather than simplifies and diminishes Tolkien's characters. It makes their choices that much more important. Which brings us back to the discussion of this chapter.

Moral Responsibility

Now we can begin to see even more deeply the significance of the gift of free will. One's choices mean more than which of two (or ten, or twenty) flavors of ice cream he or she will consume. There is good, and there is ill, and as Aragorn says, "It is a man's part to discern them, as much in the Golden Wood as in his own house." That there are objective moral standards by which our choices may be *judged* is also to say that there are real—that is, moral—consequences to our actions, and where we have free will and moral consequences, we have *moral responsibility*. Aragorn and Éomer are free, and they must make choices; and because there is an objective definition of good and ill, Aragorn says, they have a moral responsibility—a "man's part"—to discover what that "good" is and to act accordingly.

Once again, though Tolkien gives these ideas a fuller expression in *The Lord of the Rings*, and a mythological (or theological) basis in *The Silmarillion*, we can see the notion of moral responsibility even in *The Hobbit*. For example, *The Hobbit* is full of references to *duty*, a word that refers to an obligation or responsibility of a moral or legal type. Time and again, we see Bilbo making moral choices about what he ought to do, usually in contrast to what he wants to do: "He had a horrible thought that the cakes might run short, and then he—as the host: he knew his duty and stuck to it however painful—he might have to go without" (*Hobbit*, 38). Like many instances early in *The Hobbit*, the consequences of Bilbo's choice are not presented as especially significant at the moment; the issue at stake is only whether or not Bilbo or the dwarves will get the last of the hobbit's supply of cakes. Yet in basing even such small decisions on moral responsibility, Bilbo is training himself, so that when the more significant decisions are placed before him—whether or not he ought to risk going back into the goblins' caves to rescue the dwarves, for example—he is ready to perform his duty. This is exactly what we see: "He had just made up his mind that it was his duty, that he must turn back—and very miserable he felt about it—when he heard voices" (*Hobbit*, 137). Though these two choices involve consequences of entirely different magnitudes, Tolkien uses a similar voice in presenting them to the reader. In both cases, the contrast is between doing what is comfortable and doing what is right, and Tolkien interrupts the sentence to let the reader know that the right thing is a "painful" or "miserable" choice. We also must note that in both cases there is no legal obligation on Bilbo to act in some particular way; in other words, the obligation implied by duty is a moral one.

Because of this connection between duty and moral obligation, the notion of duty and Tolkien's use of the concept is interesting. When teaching courses on Tolkien's works, I have occasionally had students criticize Bilbo for acting *only* according to the dictates of duty, without having any warm feelings or heartfelt desire corresponding to his actions. According to this popular view, acting only in duty is somewhat less morally admirable: Bilbo should have *felt* like doing good rather than ill; he should have been happy to watch the dwarves eat the rest of his cakes even if he went without. Some go so far as to say that acting only in duty is hypocritical, in that our actions are not in unity with our real feelings and emotions. But it is clear that Tolkien portrays dutiful actions as virtuous and makes this a mark of those characters in Middle-earth who are most heroic. In another sense, however, a case could be made that Bilbo really does want to do his duty; he may want to be comfortable as well as do his duty, but his actions show us that his desire to do his duty is greater than his desire to be comfortable. Whether one agrees with this understanding or not, the significant issue is that in this notion of duty Tolkien is emphasizing Bilbo's moral responsibility.

In *The Lord of the Rings*, Tolkien gives a more profound and explicit elucidation of this responsibility. In the important dialogue between Gandalf and Frodo in "The Shadow of the Past," near the start of *The Fellowship of the Ring*, Frodo laments that the burden of the Ring has fallen onto him.

> "I wish it need not have happened in my time," said Frodo.
> "So do I," said Gandalf. "And so do all who live to see such times. But that is not for them to decide. All we have to decide is what to do with the time that is given us." (I/ii)

This, in a nutshell, is the summary of what moral responsibility means to every individual in Middle-earth. None can choose the time into which they are born, nor can they choose what great events or great crises will come to pass in the time that is theirs. The times and their corresponding choices are beyond their control; they are given to them. They may be pleasant choices, such as those Bilbo faced throughout the majority of his long life, or they may be painful choices, such as those faced by Frodo. In short, the characters in Tolkien's stories are not responsible for the actions and decisions of others. What they are responsible for—what they have to discern, as Aragorn says—is what to do with the choices given to them.

This is such an important concept that Tolkien repeats it often throughout his work. Gandalf lays out this moral responsibility to the Captains of the West in "The Last Debate," using the imagery of gardening: "Other evils there are that may come; for Sauron is himself but a servant or emissary. Yet it is not our part to master all the tides of the world, but to do what is in us for the succour of those years wherein we are set, uprooting the evil in the fields that we know, so that those who live after may have clean earth to till. What weather they shall have is not ours to rule" (V/ix). Again, the captains are not responsible for the decisions of others; they needn't "master all the tides of the world." Their responsibility— their "part"—is for how they act in "those years wherein [they] are set." Each age (and even each person) will face a different set of evils, a different set of weeds in the gardens that they till. They needn't worry about the evils that others face in their own earth, and they needn't worry about the choices that others must make in the face of those evils; they are responsible only for the "evils in the fields that [they] know."

Gandalf gives even more insight in this speech when he speaks of doing "what is in us." The suggestion is that each person has been given certain strengths and abilities—a set of gifts, if you will—and each is responsible for how those strengths and gifts are used. The implication is that more will be expected of those to whom more has been given: more of Denethor than of Pippin, more of Faramir than of one of his soldiers.

Another Word on (or against) Judgment

Before turning to the issue of stewardship, one important point needs to be made about objective morality and judgment. While Tolkien makes it clear that there is a real difference between good and evil and that it is a person's part to learn to discern, or judge, what that difference is and to act accordingly, the characters of his story are also strongly warned not to judge one another. That is, they can (and indeed must) judge between good and evil *actions*—and they themselves will be subject to the judgment of Ilúvatar for how well they choose—but they are not given authority to judge other *persons*. Frodo is given this lesson in stern fashion by Gandalf when Frodo suggests that Gollum ought to have been put to death for his crimes.

> "Do you mean to say that you, and the Elves, have let him live after all those horrible deeds? Now at any rate he is as bad as an Orc, and just an enemy. He deserves death."
>
> "Deserves it! I daresay he does. Many that live deserve death. And some that die deserve life. Can you give it to them? Then do not be too eager to deal out death in judgement." (I/ii)

Gandalf presents to Frodo a rather stern admonition against judging others. Though Gollum is the narrow topic of conversation, Gandalf's phrasing suggests a much broader and more general application. For example, he speaks not just of Gollum's evil but of the "many" others who have committed evil deeds as well. Certainly his final sentence is phrased in a general way. Given the wisdom with which Gandalf is portrayed, readers might well imagine such a stern admonition coming from Tolkien himself, to all his readers. Don't be eager to judge others.

Now an admonition such as the one Tolkien puts in Gandalf's mouth may be motivated by at least three different beliefs, and an understanding of which of these three beliefs motivated (or did not motivate) Gandalf will help us understand the philosophies beyond Tolkien's vision. One possible underlying philosophy that would make judging others ludicrous is the philosophy of materialism, or materialistic determinism—namely, that none of us are actually free to make choices. No matter how much the actions of others bother us, if we know they are not actually free to choose otherwise—their genetic and social programming leaves them no choice but to act in annoying ways, as Bertrand Russell has suggested is the case—then it makes no sense to judge them for their choice. So we must admonish against judging. Which, as we noted above, is just what Russell does.

Another possible reason not to judge others is simply that there is no objective moral basis on which any actions may be judged. If all of our decisions are ultimately personal preferences, such as what flavor of ice cream we are going to eat, then there are no grounds for judging others for any particular decision they might make. We can express a personal preference against actions we find annoying, but we cannot judge those actions as right or wrong, and thus certainly cannot judge a person as deserving of death. This understanding makes Gandalf's admonition against judging others a very popular one in a society that has rejected objective morality and recognizes tolerance as the only virtue. It is therefore not surprising that, out of the entire long dialogue between Gandalf and Frodo in chapter 2 of *The Fellowship of the Ring*, in which the wizard tells the young hobbit much of the history of the Ring, this one line of Gandalf's was chosen to *remain* (word for word) in the script of Peter Jackson's film while many other important portions were cut. If morality is purely subjective, then holding tolerance as the highest (and perhaps only) virtue makes sense: *of course* we must "tolerate" someone choosing chocolate over vanilla, we argue, as we must do of all *seemingly* moral choices if indeed there is no basis for morality. Of course if this is true, then we must also realize that there is no *moral* basis for claiming that tolerance itself is good, and we must be careful not to judge people for intolerance.

In any case, it is clear that Gandalf's (and Tolkien's) reason for abstaining from "dealing out death in judgment" is different from either of the two above. His reason is certainly *not* that there is no objective moral basis for judgment, nor that there is no such thing as free will; the passages explored earlier in this chapter should make this very clear. In Tolkien's Middle-earth, free will is real and there is an objective basis for moral judgment. Indeed, even in this very passage in which we hear Gandalf's admonition against judging others, the wizard's own words acknowledge that there is an objective moral basis for judging actions: there are some who "deserve death," the wizard bluntly states, and others who deserve life. Thus

Tolkien's reason for sparing judgment on others is *not* that there is no objective basis for such a judgment, or that people don't *deserve* to be judged.

As an infantryman in World War I, and later as a citizen of England in a war against Hitler's Nazi Germany, Tolkien confronted what he understood to be real evil in his world, and he understood that evil as something to be opposed. If nothing else, *The Lord of the Rings* forces the reader to confront real evil in Middle-earth. We see it not only in Mordor but also in Isengard, in Bree, and later in the Shire itself. Tolerance of a certain type in many situations may be virtuous, and a sign of humility, but tolerance *of evil* is not a virtue. A decision by one of the enemies of Sauron, such as Boromir, to possess and use the Ring is no more to be tolerated than Sauron's enslavement of all Middle-earth.

In fact, Gandalf's admonition isn't even a blanket statement covering all instances of judgment. He does not say never to judge—though certainly a blanket admonition against being judgmental might well have come from Gandalf's lips. Rather, the wizard in this instance warns only against dealing out death in judgment. And even then, he doesn't say it could never be done but only that Frodo must not be quick to do it.

What, then, is the motivation for this admonition? Gandalf's primary reason for not dealing out death in judgment seems to be that nobody in Middle-earth has the wisdom or authority to enact such justice. For one thing, no finite being in Middle-earth—not even the wise wizard Gandalf—has the wisdom to know fully who deserves life and who deserves death. Even acts of judgment involving punishments less severe than death may often be beyond the wisdom of one person. In a comment Faramir makes to Gollum after the incident at the Forbidden Pool, we see something like this at work: "Nothing?" Faramir asks, when Gollum claims to have done nothing wrong. "Have you never done anything worthy of binding or of worse punishment? However, that is not for me to judge, happily" (IV/vi). First, Faramir is saying (as did Gandalf) that there *are* moral crimes worthy of punishment; second, he is guessing that Gollum has indeed committed some of these. Yet Faramir is also confessing a lack of the knowledge and wisdom necessary to judge Gollum for anything beyond a very limited area in which he has been invested with authority to judge.

A second reason that nobody within Middle-earth can claim the ultimate authority of judgment—the sentencing to life or death—is that life, like free will, is so valuable a gift, given by Ilúvatar himself. It is too valuable for one person to take from another. Judgment must be served at times, as Mandos does with Fëanor. For a society to function, it must have laws and a means of enforcing those laws. But dealing out *death* in judgment is beyond mortal authority. Even the Valar, when faced with the outright rebellion of the men of Númenor at the end of the *Akallabêth*, choose to abdicate their authority in Middle-earth and turn to Ilúvatar to judge rather than themselves dealing out death in judgment. Neither do they deal out death in judgment on Fëanor and the rebelling Noldor, even after the Kinslaying at Alqualondë.

Third, and finally, no one in Middle-earth has fully lived up to the moral law. In other words, everyone is deserving of some judgment, and so who can act as the judge? Tolkien spells out this last point in one of his letters, even as he affirms that there is an objective moral basis for judgment.

> Gollum was pitiable, but he ended in persistent wickedness, and the fact that this worked good was no credit to him. His marvellous courage and endurance, as great as Frodo and Sam's or greater, being devoted to evil was portentous, but not honourable. I am afraid, whatever our beliefs, we have to face the fact that there are persons who yield to temptation, reject their chances of nobility or salvation, and appear to be "damnable." . . . But we who are all "in the same boat" must not usurp the Judge. (*Letters*, 234)

Tolkien explicitly states that Gollum, though he deserved pity, is nonetheless wicked and also deserving of death. As with Fëanor, good is brought out of his wickedness, but also as with Fëanor, that is "no credit to him"; it does not change the fact that he chose evil. And here Tolkien is very explicit in holding views that are immensely unpopular today: "Whatever our beliefs, we have to face the fact that there are persons who yield to temptation . . . and appear to be 'damnable.'" This thread of thought, spelled out explicitly in this letter, runs implicitly through *The Lord of the Rings*. But Tolkien also then points out something all his readers should likewise realize, that "we who are all 'in the same boat' must not usurp the Judge."

The Steward of Middle-earth

And now we turn to the issue of stewardship, which is an important concept in *The Lord of the Rings*. It is important, in part, because the stakes are high. The greater the evil that must be confronted, the more wisdom necessary to make good choices. The greater the gifts that one is given—with freedom being the greatest of them all—the more wisdom is needed to use those gifts well. Stewardship refers to the responsibility one has for those things that have been placed under one's care. The word *steward* comes from the Old English *stigweard*, which itself is derived from two words: *stig* and *weard*. Though it later comes to mean an "inn," a *stig* in its earlier meaning is a "hall," as in a mead hall where an English or Saxon chieftain or king would rule. Beorn's home in *The Hobbit*, as well as Meduseld in Rohan where king Théoden ruled, are both modeled after Anglo-Saxon mead halls. *Weard* means "lord" or "keeper," and has a modern derivative in *warden*. Thus, a steward, or *stigweard*, is the keeper or warden of the mead hall. The word implies a certain set of responsibilities. The Anglo-Saxon *stigweard* was a host in charge of taking care of the guests of the hall. In *The Fellowship of the Ring*, Barliman Butterbur is something of a steward in this sense. He is the host of an inn, or mead hall of sorts (the Prancing Pony of Bree), and is responsible to his guests. This can be seen especially in his response after the attack of the Black Riders. "I'll do what I can," he tells the hobbits, and he does. He buys a new pony for them (though he must pay three times its value for it), and he gives Merry another eighteen pence as compensation for his lost animals (I/xi). In short, though he was not to blame for the losses, as the innkeeper (steward), he takes personal responsibility to make reparations to Frodo and company.

In contemporary usage, *steward* means one who manages the possessions or affairs of another, oftentimes in the absence of that other. To be a steward of something implies both that you have a responsibility over that thing and that it belongs to another. A steward has authority, but it is an authority granted by and subject to some other, higher authority. As Gandalf says to Denethor:

> "Well, my lord Steward, it is your task to keep some kingdom still against that event, which few now look to see. In that task you shall have all the aid that you are pleased to ask for. But I will say this: the rule of no realm is mine, neither of Gondor nor any other, great or small. But all worthy things that are in peril as the world now stands, those are my care. And for my part, I shall not wholly fail of my task, though Gondor should perish, if anything passes through this night that can still grow fair or bear fruit and flower again in days to come. For I also am a steward. Did you not know?" (V/i)

This is as close as Gandalf comes to explicitly identifying his own role and purpose in Middle-earth: he is a steward. Of what? Of "all worthy things." Of anything "that can still grow fair or bear fruit or flower." In short, he is the steward of Middle-earth itself, or of all that is good in Middle-earth. His responsibility—his "task," as he himself names it—is to care for those things and to make good and wise choices concerning them. As the imagery suggests, he is like a gardener caring for a garden, helping it grow to maturity and produce fruit. Thus, the essence of stewardship is really the essence of moral responsibility. But Gandalf's task is also to train others to be good stewards: first, to help the people of Middle-earth to realize that they *are* stewards, each one of them, and then to help them grow in the wisdom to be *good* stewards. This is at the heart of many of his speeches. As he tells the Captains of the West gathered as representatives of the peoples of Middle-earth, they are all responsible for what they do with the freedom, the time, and the power given them. They are stewards of these things—time, skills, freedom, abilities—just as Gandalf himself is a steward. To be a steward, however, is to acknowledge the higher authority of another, just as Denethor, as Steward of Gondor, is (or ought to be) responsible to the king of Gondor if he should ever return: "to keep some kingdom still against that event."

Here is where there is a sharp contrast between Gandalf and Denethor, who holds the official role as Steward of Gondor and yet does not hold to the meaning of the word *steward*. For Denethor has begun to see himself more as lord (*weard*) than as steward (*stigweard*): "Yet the *Lord* of Gondor is not to be made the tool of other men's purposes," he says of himself to Gandalf. "And the *rule* of Gondor, my lord, is mine and no other man's, unless the king should come again" (V/i, emphasis added). Although he gives lip service to the possibility that "the king should come again," he does not act as if that is even desirable. He is more concerned with his own rule and power. Indeed, when the king does return, Denethor will not even consider his claim to the throne. "With the left hand thou wouldst use me for a little while as a shield against Mordor," he says to Gandalf, "and with the right bring up this Ranger of the North to supplant me." He sees the return of the king not as the hoped-for event for which he is to prepare, but as a threat to "supplant" his power. Ironically, it is in clinging to the title of Steward that Denethor refuses to do the very thing a steward is called to do: to uphold the king's authority. "I will not step down to be the dotard chamberlain of an upstart. . . . I will not bow to such a one, last of a ragged house long bereft of lordship and dignity" (V/vii).

Ultimately, under the pretense of stewardship, Denethor claims an authority that not even the wise kings of old had: to take his own life and the life of his son. Gandalf chastises him for this, but to no avail. "'Authority is not given to you, Steward of Gondor, to order the hour of your death,' answered Gandalf. 'And only the heathen kings, under the domination of the Dark Power, did thus, slaying themselves in pride and despair, murdering their kin to ease their own death'" (V/vii). It is interesting that Tolkien uses the word *heathen* to describe Denethor's behavior; a heathen is an "unbeliever," one who does not acknowledge God. If Tolkien really meant this word, then it implies that Denethor's real fault is deeper than his refusal to acknowledge the authority of a king; it is a refusal to acknowledge the divine authority that is over even a king's, the authority of Ilúvatar. Amandil, the grandfather of Isildur and the sire of the race of kings of Gondor, speaks of Ilúvatar's ultimate authority even over earthly kings: "For there is but one loyalty from which no man can be absolved in heart for any cause" (*Silm*, 275). This is the loyalty that Denethor does not seem to acknowledge, though his son Faramir does. In any case, a central point Gandalf is making is that there is authority given to all stewards no matter what they are stewards of, and that authority is bestowed with the title, but there is also authority that a steward does not have. The moral responsibility of those in Middle-earth is to be good stewards of their gifts—that is, of those things under the authority that has been given them—and not to usurp authority that is not theirs. Denethor eventually fails in both of these.

Gandalf, unlike Denethor, is the ideal steward. He does not claim any lordship or authority over others. "The rule of no realm is mine," he says, and his actions validate that claim. Earlier, in examining Gandalf's wisdom, I quoted a personal letter in which Tolkien himself describes who Gandalf is: "There are naturally no precise modern terms to say what he was. I wd. venture to say that he was an *incarnate* 'angel.'" This same letter also gives insight into Gandalf's role and nature as a steward, a role that is closely tied to his wisdom. In the letter, Tolkien leads into this description of Gandalf by explaining something about Gandalf's sacrifice at Khazad-dûm.

> Gandalf really "died," and was changed: for that seems to me the only real cheating, to represent anything that can be called "death" as making no difference. "I am G. the *White*, who has returned from death." Probably he should rather have said to Wormtongue: "I have not passed through death (*not* 'fire and flood') to bandy crooked words with a serving-man." And so on. I might say much more, but it would only be in (perhaps tedious) elucidation of the "mythological" ideas in my mind. . . . G. is not, of course, a human being (Man or Hobbit). There are naturally no precise modern terms to say what he was. I wd. venture to say that he was an *incarnate* "angel." . . .
> . . . At this point in the fabulous history the purpose was precisely to limit and hinder their exhibition of "power" on the physical plane, and so that they should do what they were primarily sent for: train, advise, instruct, arouse the hearts and minds of those threatened by Sauron to a resistance with their own strengths; and not just to do the job for them. . . .
> [But] the crisis had become too grave and needed an enhancement of power. So Gandalf sacrificed himself, was accepted, and enhanced, and returned. (*Letters*, 201–3)

This comment speaks to two different aspects of Gandalf's stewardship. We see that his own power is enhanced after his death and return. Some of the limitations on his exhibition of "angelic" power

146

have been removed, which is to say he is now more powerful on the physical plane. As a result, he is now responsible for the stewardship of an even greater gift—namely, his *enhanced* power. We might say that Gandalf had proven to be a faithful steward with the smaller gifts he originally had been given, and so he was given even more over which to be a steward.

And he remains a good steward! He does not use his enhanced power to claim more rule or authority over others. Indeed, his relationship to those around him remains fundamentally the same as before his power was enhanced. He does not command, but he trains, advises, instructs. And, most especially, he arouses "the hearts and minds of those threatened by Sauron to a resistance with their own strengths." This is what he does with Théoden, first in Meduseld and later on the way to Isengard. As we mentioned earlier, it is also what he does on the walls of Minas Tirith. It is what he does with the hobbits throughout the Quest, especially Frodo and Pippin. In other words, inasmuch as it is Gandalf's role to be a steward, it is also his role to train those around him to be stewards themselves. His goal is to see each person use his or her own time and abilities to fight against Mordor. He wants each person to understand the moral responsibility that comes with free will, and to choose well. This is why he does not do people's jobs for them. If he did others' jobs for them, so that they needn't use their own strength, then he would be removing their moral responsibility. It might make Gandalf's life simpler and accomplish his "military" goals more quickly if he were to exercise more power and do more, but his goal is not to make his own life simple. His ultimate aim is for the moral good of those around him, which is to say for their training in moral responsibility.

This returns us to the earlier conclusion that moral victory is more important than military victory, and to the importance of free will and choice. If there is no objective right and wrong, then one is free to win the military victory by whatever means is possible; power is what matters, not right and wrong. This is the path Saruman takes. Likewise, if there is no right or wrong—if all choices are equally good—then choice itself and our free will to make choices become less important; it is not the choosing that matters but only the outcome. But in Tolkien's Middle-earth, there is objective morality. There is a standard for judgment. As a result, moral decisions are important.

147

8

The Seen and the Unseen

Salvation and Social Justice

"But that, of course, would only make the evil part
of him [Gollum] angrier in the end—unless it could
be conquered. Unless it could be cured."

—Gandalf

At this point, we are ready to touch on a dangerous subject. At
least it is dangerous for a writer discussing J. R. R. Tolkien's work
because it approaches ground that might be called *religious*. Tolkien
largely avoided anything explicitly religious in his own fiction. And
he did so consciously and by intention. We can gain some insight
into his reason for avoiding or removing explicitly religious elements
from his writing by looking at three shortcomings Tolkien sees in
the Arthurian legends, the third of which in particular makes these
legends inadequate (in his opinion) as a mythology for England
(*Letters*, 144).

Tolkien's first criticism of Arthurian legend is that it is not English
enough. Though it is vaguely associated with the soil of Britain,
it is not associated with the English people, culture, or language.

Mallory's fifteenth-century *Le Morte d'Arthur*, probably the most influential, best-known medieval version of the Arthurian legends, though written in Middle English, draws most heavily on earlier French sources. Other influential early Arthurian grail legends, such as Wolfram's thirteenth-century tale, *Parzival*, and Chrétien de Troyes's unfinished late twelfth-century romance, *Perceval, le Conte du Graal*, were not even composed in English.

Second, the fairy elements of the Arthurian legends are (in Tolkien's opinion) too lavish, incoherent, and repetitive.

Tolkien's third criticism, and the most important both to him and to this chapter, is that Arthurian legend contains too much *explicit* religion: religion in the same form as in the primary world. This is what he termed the legend's "fatal error" (*Letters*, 144). In the final chapter we will deal more with *why* explicit religion is a problem in myth and fantasy. For now we need only note that Tolkien was critical of the presence of too much explicit religion in Arthurian legend. (Thus, a critic must follow a careful path in observing meanings within Tolkien's own work that bear what one might call a religious significance.) In a similar vein, as I noted in the introduction to this book, Tolkien had a well-known dislike for allegory, and probably especially for religious allegory. "But I cordially dislike allegory in all its manifestations," he writes in his foreword to the second edition of *The Lord of the Rings*, "and always have done so since I grew old and wary enough to detect its presence" (Foreword).

And yet, as I also noted in the introduction, though he disliked allegory, Tolkien felt—as he goes on to say in the foreword—that his works should have "applicability to the thought and experience of readers." His stories are full of meaning, and, furthermore, much of that meaning relates directly to themes that are theological, philosophical, and even religious in nature. In the same letter in which he criticizes Arthurian legend for its explicit religion, Tolkien affirms that myth and fairy stories "must contain elements of moral and religious truth (or error)." Here Tolkien is suggesting that there is an objective truth in the universe, even with respect to religion. Religious claims may be true or false. Not only that, but myth *must* contain elements of that truth (or attempts at it). Yet the religious elements should not be "in the known form of the primarily 'real' world" (*Letters*, 144). In other words, Tolkien's works may be replete with

important philosophical and religious themes and reflections, but
we should not expect to find them (usually) expressed in the same
language and terminology, or with the same external practices, as
in our primary world. In short, then, what Tolkien thought was
inappropriate in fantasy literature—or the literature of Faery as
he called it—was the portrayal of explicit religious practices and
sacraments in the form they are known in our world. *The Lord of
the Rings* does not show us churches in Middle-earth, or priests
or rabbis carrying on clerical duties; Tolkien does not present immediately recognizable Christian customs or practices; we get only
rare and indirect glimpses of various practices of religious worship.
(The *Akallabêth* is a notable exception to this.) What Tolkien did
believe was acceptable, and even necessary, by contrast, was an element of religious truth that would be applicable to our world as
moral truth—just not presented using the religious terminology and
practices and ceremonies of our modern world.

As Tolkien himself suggests toward the end of his essay "On
Fairy-Stories," part of the danger of the subject we explore in this
chapter does not stem from its lack of importance but rather from
its being too important.[1] It was vitally important to Tolkien, anyway,
and that alone makes it worth exploring in his writing. Furthermore,
the subject of this chapter flows naturally from the central ideas
discussed earlier in this book, which themselves—if I have reasoned
correctly so far—are fundamental to the understanding of the story
and are fully woven into its fabric. For Tolkien's writing, as we have
now seen, clearly rejects the materialist presuppositions that lead
to a denial of human free will or moral responsibility. In the worldview reflected in the mythology of Middle-earth, people are more
than physical beings. And if more than physical, then what do we
call that "more"? The usual word to use is *spiritual*: men and elves
both are creatures of spirit as well as of body. Tolkien writes in his
commentary on "Athrabeth Finrod Ah Andreth" in *Morgoth's Ring*,
"There are on Earth 'incarnate' creatures, Elves and Men: these are
made of a union of *hröa* and *fëa* (roughly but not exactly equivalent
to 'body' and 'soul')" (*Morgoth*, 330).

While the natures of the bodies and spirits of elves and men dif-
fer slightly, as we saw from *The Silmarillion*, it is clear that both
races have a spiritual nature in addition to the physical. Men have

mortal bodies that die, but their spirits live on and "leave the world," eventually to take part in the Second Music of the Ainur. Elves do not die a natural death (of illness or old age), but their bodies may be slain, and if this happens their spirits are gathered to the halls of Mandos. The point is that in both cases, with elves and men, their nature is more than physical, and individuals continue on as self-aware individuals even after bodily death. What we really begin to see, in fact, is that there are two aspects of the created world: a spiritual plane and a physical plane. Both the spiritual and the physical are real, and they are interrelated; what happens on the spiritual plane affects what happens on the physical, and vice versa. One of the greatest marks of wisdom in Middle-earth can be understood as an eternal perspective: a realization that reality includes both of these planes, and that while it is not quite right to say that the spiritual plane is more important than the physical (an important concern we will return to in the final chapter), it is certainly true that one's spiritual life, being eternal, carries more weight than one's present and temporal bodily life. This relates very closely to the earlier conclusion that moral victory is more important than military victory.

This spiritual reality also relates to objective morality and the fact that the choices of men, dwarves, and elves (and also hobbits) are subject to judgment. What does it mean to be judged? With respect to our moral battles, does judgment have to do with the definition of victory? Many of the answers become clearer in an exploration of the notion of salvation in *The Lord of the Rings*. Indeed, the very concept of spiritual (moral) victory that is at the heart of Tolkien's writing may be defined by this word: *salvation*.

The Salvation of Boromir

As I said, writing about salvation in *The Lord of the Rings* is a dangerous task—dangerous in part because it has clear religious connotations. In particular, the notion of salvation is fundamentally important to the Christian faith, including both to Catholic forms, such as that practiced by Tolkien, and to Protestant forms, such as that practiced by his friend C. S. Lewis. A discussion of salvation cannot avoid religious ground. It is also dangerous in the specific examples that follow because the words *salvation* (or *saved*) and, its opposite, *damnation* are not the words Tolkien uses in his fiction to describe this spiritual victory. Indeed, these are the sorts of words he would avoid because of their explicit modern religious usage. Nonetheless, he uses many words and concepts—for example, *cured* and *escaped* and their opposite, *fallen*—to imply spiritual salvation. These words, in context, carry the meaning of salvation but without the explicit form of religion in our own world (although at times, as we shall see, Tolkien comes very close to that form).

To start with, salvation implies being saved *from* something, presumably from something bad. If we are speaking of bodily salvation, then the ultimate salvation is from physical death. If we are speaking of spiritual salvation, then the objective reality of good suggests a salvation from its opposite: evil. That is certainly what is at stake for Boromir, as Frodo realizes after Boromir's attempt to take the Ring by force: "Boromir has fallen into evil," Frodo contemplates, as he tries to decide his course (II/x). This is, of course, a statement coming from a framework of objective morality. It also must be a statement about spiritual (and not physical) reality because at the time Frodo is saying this nothing physically bad has yet happened to Boromir. So for Boromir to be saved, he must be saved spiritually from this evil.

This is precisely what happens, although Boromir himself might not realize it. We see this in Aragorn's reply to Boromir's dying words. "Farewell, Aragorn! Go to Minas Tirith and save my people! I have failed," Boromir says, with his dying breath. Aragorn's reply is telling. "'No!' said Aragorn, taking his hand and kissing his brow. 'You have conquered. Few have gained such a victory. Be at peace!'" (III/i). This is a short passage, and yet it speaks more to the central ideas of this book than almost any other. Boromir sees himself as having failed. And in every physical and military way, he has failed. He fails in his task to bring Aragorn and "the sword that was broken" back to Minas Tirith. He fails to bring Isildur's Bane back to his father. Indeed, he fails to return to Minas Tirith at all. In short, he fails to do *anything* to save Gondor from military defeat. Or at least at the time of his death, this would seem to be the case. He even fails in the last thing he attempts: to save Merry and Pippin from capture by the orcs. From a physical or bodily viewpoint, he suffers the greatest possible failure: he dies. So in the material plane, Boromir's final words are true. He fails. He has lost the physical battle. He has lost the military battle.

Yet Aragorn contradicts him emphatically: "No!" Aragorn argues instead that Boromir has "conquered," that he has won a "victory." Of what victory does Aragorn speak? Not a military victory, but a moral one; not a bodily victory, but a spiritual one. Whereas Boromir is speaking about the material plane, Aragorn is speaking of the spiritual plane.

Now one might suggest that Aragorn's words are little more than comforting sounds for a dying man, devoid of any more significant meaning. Suppose for a moment we were to ignore how important words are to Aragorn and to suggest that he is a flatterer, one who speaks falsely in order to make someone feel better. Although Aragorn's character suggests otherwise, this suggestion is at least worth considering. It is, after all, the only time in all the books that we hear Aragorn's words to a dying man, and if there were ever an instant to provide comfort with flattery, this would be it. The problem with this interpretation of the events is that at a later point Gandalf says the same thing about Boromir, that in his death he has won an important victory: "It was a sore trial for such a man: a warrior, and a lord of men. Galadriel told me that he was in peril. But he escaped in the end. I am glad. It was not in vain that the young hobbits came with us, if only for Boromir's sake" (III/v). Whatever motive we may attribute to Aragorn's earlier words, we cannot reasonably say that Gandalf is merely comforting a dying man with these words. For Gandalf's words are spoken several days after Boromir's death; Boromir is not even present. Yet Gandalf says Boromir has "escaped." And the wizard's words suggest strongly that what Boromir escaped from was a moral or spiritual rather than a physical danger. Indeed, readers know that the "sore trial" was the temptation of the Ring, since Boromir knew how desperately such power would be needed. Gandalf even goes on to point out that it was good for Boromir's sake that Merry and Pippin came on the journey. Why? If Gandalf were speaking of Boromir in physical or military terms, it would make no sense. The failed attempt to protect the two young hobbits cost Boromir his life. And yet the opportunity to give his life to save them may have been a large part of his spiritual victory.

153

And Gandalf is not the only other person to comment, after the fact, on some moral or spiritual victory that Boromir had won in his final moments even as he lost his life. Faramir also, in discussing his brother with Frodo and Sam, notes, "Now I loved [Boromir] dearly and would gladly avenge his death, yet I knew him well." He goes on with wisdom and insight to acknowledge his brother's faults and that Boromir might well have attempted to take Isildur's Bane by force. Then Faramir proceeds to comment on what he observed in his vision when the dead Boromir floated by on a boat: "Whether he erred or no, of this I am sure: he died well, achieving some good thing. His face was more beautiful even than in life" (IV/v). Faramir is painfully honest about his brother's faults and yet sees from his brother's face that in his death he has moved from the "evil" that Frodo has seen in him to "some good thing." The good thing Faramir sees in Boromir's death is something moral, not something physical. Faramir sees his spiritual condition.

So we must agree that Boromir, in some important spiritual sense, has "conquered," "won a victory," and "escaped," having achieved "some good thing." We will use the term *salvation* to refer to this spiritual victory. What is the essence of this salvation? What does Boromir do to achieve it? The answer is fairly simple. First and foremost, Boromir acknowledges his evil and apologizes for it. "I tried to take the Ring from Frodo," he confesses. "I am sorry" (III/i). This path to what Aragorn describes as a "victory" strongly corresponds to the Christian notion of salvation, which comes through repentance of sin. "Repent and believe" is the essential response called for in the proclamation of the gospel (see, for example, Mark 1:15). In that sense, Aragorn's words can be used as a central piece of evidence supporting the thesis that in Tolkien's work moral victory is more important than military victory. Boromir's moral victory is repentance.

There is one other thing we might associate with Boromir's victory, though it represents perhaps more of a stretch and is not immediately clear from this passage alone. From the start, Boromir has a strong dependence on his own strength and importance and on military might (his own, that of Gondor, etc.). In giving his life to save the two hobbits, he is giving up his own quest to save Gondor, much as Aragorn will do a short time after Boromir's death when he chooses to pursue Merry and Pippin rather than aid Frodo and Sam or take his sword to Minas Tirith. Gandalf also makes a similar choice when he sacrifices himself on the Bridge of Khazad-dûm, allowing the responsibility to pass from him. Boromir is acknowledging that the fate of Gondor is no longer in his hands. This too might be associated with the gospel: that people can be saved by faith in God's work and not by their own strength or actions (see, for example, Eph. 2:8–9). In any case, Boromir is seen as having been saved from a great evil, and salvation as something that happens on the spiritual and moral plane. And since such salvation is an important thing to Aragorn, Gandalf, Faramir, and—through them—to Tolkien, it may also be important to Tolkien's readers.

The Salvation of Sméagol

Gollum-Sméagol also makes for an interesting study, in part because so many passages in *The Lord of the Rings* deal with what might be called his salvation (including much of book 4, beginning with "The Taming of Sméagol"), in part because—unlike with Boromir—Gollum's salvation is never achieved, and also in part because Tolkien has shared some of his own thoughts about Gollum's salvation in his personal letters.

As mentioned, there are numerous references throughout *The Fellowship of the Ring* and *The Two Towers* to Gollum's "cure." Gandalf in particular speaks of it on several occasions. Even before Frodo leaves the Shire, he says: "'But that, of course, would only make the evil part of him [Gollum] angrier in the end—unless it could be conquered. Unless it could be cured.' Gandalf sighed. 'Alas! there is little hope of that for him. Yet not no hope. No, not though he possessed the Ring so long, almost as far back as he can remember'" (I/ii). And a short time later, for extra emphasis, Gandalf adds: "I have not much hope that Gollum can be cured before he dies, but there is a chance of it. . . . In any case we did not kill him: he is very old and very wretched. The Wood-elves have him in prison, but they treat him with such kindness as they can find in their wise hearts" (I/ii).

Cured is a different word than *saved*, of course, and usually refers to a physical illness rather than a spiritual condition. Likewise, the word *conquered* more often refers to an enemy, though it is also used of physical diseases such as cancer. In this case, however, there is no particular medical problem that Gollum suffers. Rather, we see that it is a moral condition of evil—or "the evil part of him"—that needs a cure. That the "treatment" is "kindness" also suggests that the illness is not physical at all, but spiritual. This treatment of kindness suggested by Gandalf is also later administered by Frodo and is at the center of the taming of Sméagol. One part of Frodo's kindness is treating Gollum with dignity and trust, which includes the simple act of calling him by his given name: Sméagol.

We also must note that as little *hope* as Gandalf sees for Gollum's cure, there can be no question that he *desires* that cure and still works toward it with some shred of hope. He shows noticeable sympathy for the creature, lamenting that his tale is "a sad story" (I/ii) and sighing about how deeply he has fallen into evil. As Legolas shares at the Council of Elrond, "Gandalf bade us hope still for his cure, and we had not the heart to keep him ever in dungeons under the earth, where he would fall back into his old black thoughts" (II/ii). Admittedly, there are not many others who share Gandalf's vision for Gollum's salvation. At the start, not even Frodo does. To the contrary, he wishes Gollum dead. By the end of the book, however, Frodo shows mercy to Gollum and works toward his cure. It is Frodo's kindness to him—"good Master," "nice Master," "kind Master"— that leads to the whole inner debate between his Sméagol-side and his Gollum-side, and to the change that takes place in him. It is a change that Tolkien illustrates in several ways, and of which Frodo is aware. After the famous debate between his two voices in "The Passage of the Marshes," "Gollum welcomed [Frodo] with dog-like delight. He chuckled and chattered, cracking his long fingers, and pawing at Frodo's knees. Frodo smiled at him" (IV/ii). Initially, Frodo may only be using Gollum as a guide, out of necessity. By the time they reach Faramir, however, it is clear both that Frodo has grown considerably in his understanding of and pity for the poor creature and that he truly desires his salvation. This is especially evident in Frodo's anguish at the Forbidden Pool, when in order to save Gollum's life he has to lure him away from the water to be captured: "His heart sank. . . . What Frodo did would seem a treachery to the poor treacherous creature. It would probably be impossible ever to make him understand or believe that Frodo had saved his life." He knows from the start that Gollum will feel betrayed and guesses (correctly) the damage that sense of betrayal will do to Gollum's repentance process. Thus, when it is over, Frodo is "feeling very wretched" and tells Sam, "I hate the whole business" (IV/vi).

In the end, despite the incident at the Forbidden Pool, Gollum comes very close to the salvation that Gandalf and Frodo seek and hope for in him. In one of the most poignant passages of *The Lord of the Rings*, Tolkien shares this moment with the readers.

> Gollum looked at them. A strange expression passed over his lean hungry face. The gleam faded from his eyes, and they went dim and grey, old and tired. A spasm of pain seemed to twist him, and he turned away, peering back up towards the pass, shaking his head, as if engaged in some interior debate. Then he came back, and slowly putting out a trembling hand, very cautiously he touched Frodo's knee—but almost the touch was a caress. For a fleeting moment, could one of the sleepers have seen him, they would have thought that they beheld an old weary hobbit, shrunken by the years that had carried him far beyond his time, beyond friends and kin, and the fields and streams of youth, an old starved pitiable thing. (IV/viii)

The interior debate, we may guess in hindsight, is whether or not to go through with his plan of leading Frodo to Shelob. We may also guess that Sméagol (that is, the Sméagol side of Gollum) is on the verge of winning this debate. The "gleam," a sign of his sneaking slyness, fades from his eyes. The pawing becomes "almost . . . a caress"—a sign of love and affection—and for "a fleeting moment" he is no longer the slinking, stinking Gollum of secret caves but the hobbit-like creature he once was, associated with "friends and kin, and the fields and streams of youth."

Unfortunately, the fleeting moment of near-salvation slips away. For Sam, who does not take part in administering the treatment of kindness, also does not see the promising results of that treatment. Mistaking this moment of sorrow, compassion, and near-repentance on the part of Gollum for mere "pawing at his master," Sam continues with his unkind and untrusting treatment. As a result, "Gollum withdrew himself, and a green flint flickered under his heavy lids. Almost spider-like he looked now, crouched back on his bent limbs, with his protruding eyes. The fleeting moment had passed, beyond recall" (IV/viii). Gollum has come so near to salvation but has turned away in the end. Suddenly, the imagery associates him more with Shelob-kind than with hobbit-kind.

Just how important salvation is to Tolkien is illustrated in a letter he wrote in 1963 describing this scene, in particular Sam's lack of understanding and his possible lack of mercy.

> Sam was cocksure, and deep down a little conceited. . . . He plainly did not fully understand Frodo's motives or his distress in the incident of the Forbidden Pool. If he had understood better what was going on between Frodo and Gollum, things might have turned out differently in the end. For me perhaps the most tragic moment in the Tale comes . . . when Sam fails to note the complete change in Gollum's tone and aspect. "Nothing, nothing," said Gollum softly. "Nice master!" His repentance is blighted and all Frodo's pity is (in a sense) wasted. (*Letters*, 329–30)

It is quite telling that among all the episodes in the three volumes, including the deaths of Boromir, Théoden, and Denethor, Tolkien would refer to Gollum's failure to come into his cure as "the most tragic moment in the Tale." It speaks volumes about what is really important to the author. He says almost the same thing—though more briefly—in another, earlier letter to his son Christopher, written in 1945 while *The Lord of the Rings* was still in progress: that he was "most moved" by "the tragedy of Gollum who at that moment came within a hair of repentance—but for one rough word from Sam" (*Letters*, 110). In short, it is not only Gandalf who seeks and hopes for Gollum's salvation but Tolkien himself.

This also contributes to our understanding of why Gandalf restricts his own use of power in the war against Sauron, seeking instead to encourage each person in Middle-earth to use his or her own strength. If the path toward (or away) from salvation relates to moral choices (and not to physical or material victory), and if salvation truly is the highest and most important end, then it will avail nothing for Gandalf to do the work of others for them; with regard to salvation, the laboring itself—that is, the *choice* to do good—is as important as the result of that labor. So Gandalf seeks for each person to make good choices, even when he could accomplish the outcome of those choices more quickly himself. Or, looking at this from the point of view of those whom Gandalf is helping, the way to escape judgment is not to abdicate choices and responsibility to the wizard, but rather to make good choices.

Saruman, Denethor, and Damnation as Un-Salvation

Indeed, Tolkien shows Gandalf as having a desire for the salvation of all in Middle-earth, no matter how far they may have fallen. As we saw, Gandalf rejoices at Boromir's "escape" even though it comes about only at Boromir's death, for what was accomplished on the spiritual plane is more important than what was lost on the physical plane. Likewise, he seeks and hopes for Gollum's cure. He is also chiefly responsible for bringing about Théoden's awakening, which we saw in the first chapter with respect to the vivid portrayal of Théoden's death and the battle between Éowyn and the Nazgûl.

Gandalf hopes even for the cures of Saruman and Wormtongue. "Dangerous, and probably useless; but it must be done," he says, as he readies for his conversation with Saruman after the fall of Isengard to the Ents (III/x). Why does it *have* to be done? Gandalf's words to Saruman give us some hints: "I do not wish to kill you, or hurt you, as you would know, if you really understood me. And I have the power to protect you. I am giving you a last chance" (III/x). Despite the evil that Saruman has done to Gandalf, and indeed to all of Middle-earth, Gandalf does not intend any retribution. Following his own admonition to Frodo, Gandalf does not seek to deal out death in judgment, no matter how thoroughly it may be deserved by Saruman. Instead, he offers kindness: an opportunity for freedom and a chance to turn (as Boromir does) away from the evil he has chosen. It seems even that Gandalf feels a moral *duty* to offer Saruman "a last chance," even though the attempt is "dangerous." A last chance at what? At salvation: "You have become a fool, Saruman, and yet pitiable. *You might still have turned away from folly and evil*, and have been of service. But you choose to stay and gnaw the ends of your old plots" (III/x, emphasis added). Gandalf's language here has strong Christian connotations. The word *repent*, which is at the core of the message preached by Jesus and is also the word used by Tolkien to describe what nearly happened with Gollum, simply means to "turn away from evil." Thus Gandalf could equally have said to Saruman, "You might still have repented."

This is particularly significant in light of two other aspects of Gandalf's words here. In his reference to "folly and evil," we see yet again the objective nature of morality; Saruman is not free to define his own good and evil, but rather there is an objective good and evil above and beyond both Gandalf and Saruman, to which Gandalf may refer. We also see again an emphasis on the freedom to "choose" and the importance of the moral choice to turn away from evil or, in Saruman's case, to "choose to stay and gnaw the ends of [his] old plots."

As for his desire to see Saruman's repentance and salvation, Gandalf's words to Pippin as he departs from this encounter reinforce what we have already seen: "But I had reasons for trying; some merciful and some less so. . . . What will become of him? I cannot say. I grieve that so much good now festers in the tower" (III/x). Yes, Gandalf has personal motives for seeking Saruman's repentance: Saruman is still powerful and knowledgeable and could be of great help in the war against Sauron. But Gandalf also has compassionate motives. He grieves that Saruman turns away from salvation. Indeed, we might well conclude that to Gandalf, this salvation from evil—a spiritual salvation that comes not from physical might or military victory but from repenting of the evil and choosing the good—is the highest and greatest end for all in Middle-earth. As he says to Denethor, he pities even Sauron's slaves.

That Frodo really learns the virtue of mercy is shown as much (or more) in Saruman's case as it is in Gollum's. With Gollum, it may be easier for Frodo to feel pity because Gollum is so weak and miserable and also so similar to the hobbits in his origins. Also, as a Ringbearer, Frodo knows the torment that Gollum has experienced, and in clinging to a hope for Gollum he is thereby also clinging to some hope for himself. But Saruman has no such excuse. He is of a wise and powerful order, and he is never burdened with the One Ring (much though he desires it). Furthermore, the evil that Saruman does to Frodo strikes much closer to home. Indeed, it literally does strike home. When they finally meet near the end of the trilogy, Saruman is coming out of the home that once belonged to Bilbo and

Frodo. Nor does Saruman ever take even the smallest steps toward repentance—not even repentance that is later blighted, like that of Gollum. Nonetheless, Frodo follows Gandalf's path and offers Saruman yet another chance at being "cured": "He is fallen, and his cure is beyond us; but I would still spare him, in the hope that he may find it" (VI/viii). Frodo's words not only shed added light on the desire of the more noble characters to help others find their cure—this spiritual salvation of which I wrote—but also suggests that one of the reasons mercy is so important, and shown to be so virtuous, is that mercy leaves open the door to salvation. Once a sentence of death has been carried out, there is no longer the possibility of repentance.

At this point, one must wrestle with the reality that salvation has an opposite, or alternative, which is damnation. This, at least, is what Tolkien believed to be the truth about the primary reality of this world, as is illustrated in the letter quoted earlier: "There are persons who yield to temptation, reject their chances of nobility or salvation, and appear to be 'damnable.'" And as unpopular a notion as this is in modern times, it is the reality in Middle-earth. Indeed, our earlier observations on moral responsibility and judgment at least suggest the possibility of damnation in Tolkien's writing, for judgment means nothing if there are not consequences to our choices: good consequences for good choices and evil consequences for evil. Even our affirmation of free will suggests the possibility of damnation, for if created beings are to be truly free, then they cannot be *forced* to follow their Creator, and damnation is nothing but the natural eternal consequence of rejecting that Creator. Of course, that salvation is a possibility but not a necessity, as has been shown in this chapter, affirms something like damnation as the alternative: the "un-salvation."

We see several hints of this final judgment in *The Lord of the Rings*. We see it in the imagery surrounding the deaths of Denethor and Gollum, two characters who fail to come to salvation and who both perish in their evil. Both of them end in flames, a *consummation* of their wickedness in both the literal and figurative meaning of that word. In the case of Denethor, he "leaped upon the table, and standing there wreathed in fire and smoke he took up the staff of his stewardship that lay at his feet and broke it on his knee. Casting the pieces into the blaze he bowed and laid himself on the table" (V/vii). Gollum ends in the greatest flames in Middle-earth: the fires of

Mount Doom. Both of these scenes bring up unmistakable images of the flames of hell, which is the image of eternal damnation.

Equally interesting are the words of Gandalf when he faces the Lord of the Nazgûl at the gates of Minas Tirith: "Go back to the abyss prepared for you! Go back! Fall into the nothingness that awaits you and your Master. Go!" (V/iv). The imagery of these words also calls up the notion of damnation, not only for the Nazgûl but also for his master, Sauron. Though once a man, the Lord of the Nazgûl has long ago ceased to be of human kind, but is of the spirit realm. In the Bible, the "abyss" is another name for hell, the place where evil spirits in rebellion against God will be sent. It is a place of damnation. In Luke 8:31, the legion of demons possessing the man of the Gerasens pleads with Jesus "that he would not command them to go into the abyss." It is not only evil spirits who are sent to the abyss, however. Later, in the parable of the sheep and the goats, Jesus speaks of the final judgment of the goats (those who did not serve God) in words that should strike a familiar chord with anyone who has just read the words of Gandalf: "Then he shall say to them also that shall be on his left hand: Depart from me, you cursed, into everlasting fire which was prepared for the devil and his angels" (Matt. 25:41).

The point here is not to dwell on damnation. Tolkien's writing certainly does not. The focus is rather on salvation. Nevertheless, we must acknowledge that just as salvation is a real possibility in Tolkien's world, so is the alternative. For free beings in a moral universe, having a choice between salvation and damnation seems inevitable. However, when a being follows a path toward damnation and seems to receive it as a punishment, there is no gloating, only sorrow. Gandalf grieves at the demise of Denethor, his face "grave and sad" (V/vii). Frodo shows similar sadness at the death of Gollum—"Let us forgive him," he says (VI/iii)—and even later at the failure of Saruman to turn from his evil. Salvation is not only a possibility; it is the hope for everyone in Middle-earth.

Bilbo and Frodo: Mercy for the Merciful

The possibility of one's own damnation is yet another reason that mercy is so important in Middle-earth. Not only might the showing of mercy lead to the salvation of others—the recipients of that mercy—but it may be the most important instrument in the salvation of the one who is showing mercy. This seems to be the case with both Bilbo and Frodo. Before Gandalf comments about the effect on Gollum of Bilbo's mercy, and the possibility of Gollum's cure, he discusses the effect of that mercy on Bilbo himself: "Pity? It was Pity that stayed his hand. Pity, and Mercy: not to strike without need. And *he has been well rewarded*, Frodo. Be sure that *he took so little hurt* from the evil, and *escaped in the end*, because he began his ownership of the Ring so. With Pity" (I/ii, emphasis added). Again, Tolkien does not use the religiously laden term *salvation*, but Gandalf is certainly speaking of something on the moral (rather than physical) plane, and he uses three different phrases that all suggest something similar to salvation. Bilbo is "well rewarded." What reward can be greater than salvation and the gift of heaven? This is an illustration of one of the principles of Jesus's teaching: "Blessed are the merciful: for they shall obtain mercy" (Matt. 5:7). Or, looking at the passage in terms of the opposite possibility, Gandalf sees that Bilbo "took so little hurt" from evil and that he "escaped." In fact, Bilbo is one of only two bearers of the One Ring who ever freely relinquish it (the other being Sam, who possesses the Ring for only a fraction of the time that Bilbo does). We can only guess what might have happened had Bilbo not begun his ownership of the Ring with an act of mercy, but we can "be sure" that things would have gone worse for him. Indeed, we need look only as far as Gollum, who begins his ownership of the Ring with murder. We can also be sure that Gandalf cares at least as much for Bilbo's salvation as he does for Gollum's.

Frodo's case is not very different. Here, I will rely on Tolkien's own explanation of the situation. In a letter describing what happens at the Crack of Doom, he writes: "But at this point the 'salvation' of the world and Frodo's own 'salvation' is achieved by his previous *pity* and forgiveness of injury. . . . By a situation created by his 'forgiveness,' he was saved himself, and relieved of his burden" (*Letters*, 234). Up to this point, I have claimed that Tolkien, without explicitly using the word *salvation*, nevertheless uses the language and imagery associated with the Christian concept of salvation. In this letter, however, Tolkien himself explicitly uses the word twice, with each use conveying a different meaning. With respect to "the world," Tolkien is probably using the word to mean something more akin to military victory—namely, salvation from the dominion of the Dark Lord Sauron. The peoples of Middle-earth have been saved from slavery. But with respect to Frodo, the word has a double meaning. Frodo is physically saved; what he could not do himself, Gollum does for him, and had he not shown mercy, then Gollum would not have been alive to do what he does. But Frodo is also spiritually saved from enslavement to the evil of the Ring, and here it is not the outcome of the act of mercy (the fact that Gollum is still alive) but rather the *showing* of mercy itself that keeps Frodo from sinking even further under the dominion of the Ring.

Thus in this subject of salvation are tied up the notions of moral victory, free will, objective morality, and judgment. Frodo follows a path toward salvation in his moral choices to do right, even when it is inconvenient or dangerous. Yet ultimately his salvation comes by mercy, when he is unable to complete his task and Gollum does it for him. Indeed, it comes through mercy in two ways: the mercy Frodo has consistently shown to Gollum and the mercy shown to Frodo by Ilúvatar, who intercedes and brings about the destruction of the Ring when he fails. "Blessed are the merciful," Jesus taught, "for they shall obtain mercy."

Social Justice and a Rejection of Gnosticism

The practice of mercy brings us to a final topic I now believe is necessary to avoid a misunderstanding of Tolkien, or of the central points of this book *about* Tolkien and his *legendarium*.[2]

For some readers, the concept of salvation in a religious (and especially Christian) context conjures visions of a future ethereal heaven: a world of disembodied spirits hovering on clouds and playing harps, as heaven is often depicted in television commercials, comics, and even films. To express this in more philosophical terms, a discourse on the importance of a spiritual reality—especially when the eternal nature of that spiritual reality is contrasted with the temporal nature of our present bodies—leads to a legitimate concern about gnosticism or certain forms of Platonism.

Gnosticism is a millennia-old philosophical belief system that had (and has) adherents in many religions. At its core is a type of dualism, a belief that there is some nonphysical reality (a spiritual reality, or just a world of pure ideas and forms) that is superior to the physical world, and that salvation is achieved by escaping the physical world. Indeed, according to gnosticism, the very thing we are saved from *is* the physical world, and the thing that may be saved is our nonmaterial soul. Gnosticism, as with certain forms of Platonism, maintains that the physical world, along with our physical bodies that inhabit the physical world, is evil or impure. The goal is to save the soul by freeing it from the body.

Looking only at a small handful of passages of Tolkien's writing removed from their context, it might be possible to read a type of gnosticism into his works—or to mistakenly think that I am attributing a gnostic view to Tolkien. After all, I earlier argued that some sort of moral victory is more important to Tolkien's heroes and wise characters than military victory. *The Lord of the Rings*, then, seems to place a certain emphasis on the spiritual (battle) rather than the physical (battle). And earlier in this chapter I argued for the importance in Tolkien's writings of a spiritual salvation. Does that make Tolkien a gnostic? Far from it!

First and foremost, gnostics denied the goodness of the physical world and sought the escape of the soul from the body. Tolkien, by contrast, affirms time and again the goodness and beauty of the physical world of Middle-earth.[3] In Tolkien's Middle-earth cosmogony, *Eä* (his term for the entire material universe) is the good creation of a good Creator, Eru Ilúvatar. Eä is full of beauty, including the beauty of *Arda*, the term for the earth containing the inhabited world of men and elves: Middle-earth. Though Arda was created as a habitation for elves and men, collectively called the Children of Ilúvatar, Tolkien's cosmogony and mythology as expressed in the *Ainulindalë*, the *Valaquenta*, and the early portions of *The Silmarillion* suggest that the Children of Ilúvatar exist as much to care for and enrich the beauty of Arda ("with their gifts of skill to order all the lands and heal their hurts" [*Silm*, 52]) as Arda exists to provide habitation for them ("And amid all the splendours of the World . . . Ilúvatar chose a place for their habitation in the Deeps of Time and in the midst of the innumerable stars" [*Silm*, 18]). It is a mutual belonging: Arda belongs to the Children of Ilúvatar, and even in some way to the Valar, but the Children belong also to Arda. Sandra Miesel, in addressing Tolkien's creation myth and the spiritual reality in his writing, also points out that he "avoids Gnosticism" in several ways. Regarding Tolkien's Arda, Miesel writes, "Despite its contamination by Melkor, matter as such is still good, so good that some of the blessed spirits wish to enter into Arda and bind themselves to it until its ending."[4] Tolkien's portrayal of the world itself is anything but gnostic.

What evil there is in Eä and Arda is not attributed to its materiality but rather to the fact that the fallen spiritual being Melkor, later known as Morgoth, waged war on Ilúvatar's creation. Ilúvatar's servants—both the spiritual beings known as the Ainur and also the elves and men who are material beings, or rather beings of both spirit and flesh—were called to care for Arda and heal the hurts caused by Melkor. A spiritual being is the cause of evil. The physical world is good and should be cared for.

As a side note, physical (or bodily) pleasure is also not portrayed by Tolkien as evil. The goodness of the physical world is meant to be enjoyed (though not exploited) by bodily beings who can experience (as hobbits of the Shire do) the taste of strawberries and cream, and the scent of flowers, as well as the taste and scent of fresh-baked mushrooms and freshly brewed beer and seed-cakes. The physical place is good and beautiful and is worth enjoying and saving.

Which, indeed, is the purpose of the existence of Ents as well; because the trees and flowers and plants of Middle-earth are also good and valuable and worth saving, and can be victims of moral wrongdoing, Ents were sent by Ilúvatar to protect the plants of Middle-earth (especially the trees) and to punish those who wrongfully destroy the earth. Some scholars have suggested that Middle-earth itself is as much a hero of the tales as any of the elves, hobbits, dwarves, or men. There is certainly some truth in that.

Perhaps my favorite expression of the worth of the physical world comes from Frodo. When he accepts from Gandalf the burden of leaving his home and bringing the Ring to Rivendell, he speaks of his desire to save the Shire: "I should like to save the Shire, if I could—though there have been times when I thought the inhabitants too stupid and dull for words" (I/ii). As the second part of this sentence makes clear, when Frodo speaks of the Shire he wishes to save, he does not mean merely its sentient hobbit inhabitants (though they are certainly included); he means the Shire itself in its fullness, with its woods and fields and rivers, as well as its farmlands and mushroom fields and inns that brew beer—and, of course, its hobbit inhabitants too, though his phrasing makes it clear that the Shire itself means much more than that. Saving the Shire is worth the cost of his life.

In short, the importance of the spiritual reality does not deny the goodness or importance of the physical reality. And this points to another way in which the philosophy underlying Tolkien's writing is decidedly not gnostic. Salvation, according to Tolkien—though it may be thought of in some way as a spiritual state—does not mean separation from the body. Tolkien expresses this belief clearly in his important and authoritative commentary on "Athrabeth Finrod Ah Andreth," a dialogue published in *Morgoth's Ring: The Later Silmarillion* (which I will introduce and explore in more detail in the final chapter of this book). In this essay, commenting on the nature of bodily beings in Middle-earth, Tolkien writes, "There are on Earth 'incarnate' creatures, Elves and Men: these are made of a union of *hröa* and *fëa* (roughly but not exactly equivalent to 'body' and 'soul')" (*Morgoth*, 330). In denying an *exact* equivalence of *fëa* with soul, I suspect that Tolkien was trying to avoid a Platonic understanding, since for many philosophically astute readers the body-soul dichotomy would suggest Plato's discourse in the *Phaedrus* and elsewhere, and thus a Platonic and possibly even gnostic view.

In fact, the elvish word *fëa* corresponds more closely with a Judeo-Christian concept of *spirit* than with a Greek or Platonic notion of *soul*—hence the translation of the name Fëanor as "spirit of fire." In any case, Tolkien's essay goes on to explain that *hröa* and *fëa* ("body" and "spirit") "were designed each for the other, to abide in perpetual harmony" and that "the separation of *hröa* and *fëa* is 'unnatural,' and proceeds not from the original design, but from the 'Marring of Arda,' which is due to the operations of Melkor" (*Morgoth*, 330–31). Thus it is not at all the case, in Tolkien's philosophical framework, that spirit is good and body evil, or that the spirit is meant to be separated from the body. Quite the contrary.[5]

Another way in which the physical and bodily reality is closely related to the spiritual—and another way in which Tolkien's work is firmly anti-gnostic—emerges from clarifying the observation that moral victory, in Tolkien's world, is more important than military victory. This is not at all the same as saying that his heroes win spiritual battles by ignoring or denying the physical reality. Neither Aragorn, nor Gandalf, nor Faramir, nor Frodo, nor any of the other hobbit heroes try to live as entirely spiritual beings, isolating themselves from the troubles of the physical world in which they live. In fact, it is quite the opposite. The physical world is the very place in which all moral and spiritual victories are won! Physical bodies are the very vehicles through which goodness (including both spiritual and moral goodness) is lived out. Or, put another way, the very means by which Tolkien's heroes pursue peace, and uphold virtues of gentleness, and show love to other beings, and exercise stewardship is by taking care of the physical bodies of others—and the physical world as well.

Why is it morally wrong to torture a prisoner in Tolkien's Middle-earth, as we argued in the first chapter? Suppose that only *ideas* were good and pure and important (as forms of Platonism suggest) and that our bodies were impure and unimportant. Then it might be easy to justify torturing the worthless and impure body of a prisoner for the sake of a valuable idea. But, in fact, our bodies and the bodies of others do matter. Why is Frodo willing to give so much to save the Shire? He does not make his sacrifice for an abstract idea, like freedom, but for a physical place and bodily beings.

Indeed, just as there is (as I argued in *Ents, Elves, and Eriador*) a strong environmental thread in Tolkien's writings, a close look at his books also shows a strong undercurrent of what might today be called "social justice": a concern for the oppressed and poor, a valuing of justice and fairness, pity for slaves and an effort to free them, redress of social wrongs. Consider the ways that Tolkien portrays Sauron and Saruman as evil, or even how he portrays the lesser evil of Lotho Sackville-Baggins (a "wicked fool" [VI/viii]) and the corruption of the Shire. Sauron not only rules by fear, but he also feeds his army with slave-based agriculture; he has "great slave-worked fields away south" and "tributary lands, from which the soldiers . . . brought long wagon-trains of goods and booty and fresh slaves" (VI/ii). On a smaller scale, Lotho gets rich through oppression of his fellow hobbits who grow the food but don't get to eat much of it, and live instead under a set of oppressive rules, suffering unjust treatment and often imprisonment in the Lockholes (VI/viii). One of the primary purposes of a king is to ensure justice. A good king, such as Aragorn becomes, understands this.

On the other side, moral and spiritual victories are won in Middle-earth not by disengaging from the physical world but by engaging it deeply: feeding the poor (providing physical food to physical bodies), nurturing the sick (spiritually as well as physically), building houses for the dispossessed or offering shelter to those whose bodies are cold, offering release to prisoners, abstaining from torture (no matter how desperate the need for knowledge), planting trees, cleaning rivers, and performing all sorts of daily tasks using hands and feet and bodies. This, at least, is the sort of activity we see in the peace and love and justice practiced by the four hero hobbits at the end of *The Lord of the Rings*. It is also what we see from heroes like Aragorn and Faramir and Gandalf, and even Treebeard and the Ents in their management of Isengard.

It is the moral victory of being gentle and pursuing peace in the midst of war, activities that are every bit as much physical and bodily as they are spiritual.

9

A Shift in Tone

Free Will and the Hand of Ilúvatar

> "Surely you don't disbelieve the prophecies, because
> you had a hand in bringing them about yourself?
> You don't really suppose, do you, that all your ad-
> ventures and escapes were managed by mere luck,
> just for your sole benefit? You are a very fine person,
> Mr. Baggins, and I am very fond of you; but you are
> only quite a little fellow in a wide world after all!"
>
> —Gandalf

Even the casual reader of J. R. R. Tolkien is likely to observe a significant difference between the narrative tone of *The Hobbit* and
that of *The Lord of the Rings*. While the former is a lighthearted
fairy tale that could well be labeled as children's literature, the latter
is a heroic romance more akin to an epic. The difference between
The Lord of the Rings and *The Silmarillion* is even more striking,
although those who knew Tolkien and his goals would not be surprised by this difference. In Tolkien's 1951 letter to Milton Waldman of Collins—a letter of some ten thousand words, mentioned in
chapter 6—he recounts his desire to "make a body of more or less
connected legend, ranging from the large and cosmogonic, to the
level of romantic fairy-story" (*Letters*, 144). These three works—*The*

Hobbit, *The Lord of the Rings*, and *The Silmarillion*—represent three distinct parts of that range: the lighthearted fairy tale, the epic romance, and the large and cosmogonic myth.

This book has focused on the middle, in part because it *is* the middle (and thus provides the common ground that allows us to see something of the whole range), and in part because it is the longest. It is also a deeper and more profound work than *The Hobbit*, but unlike *The Silmarillion* it is told from the perspective of hobbits who provide modern eyes to look into Tolkien's ancient world and heroes that are more accessible to modern readers. Nonetheless, we have seen something of both ends of Tolkien's *legendarium*. We have explored *The Silmarillion* and found in the roots of this work some deeper and clearer answers to various questions raised in *The Lord of the Rings*. And we have turned to *The Hobbit* to see that some of the profound ideas explored in more depth in the other books are so important to Tolkien that they can be found even within the more lighthearted of his works.

As we approach the end of this book and get closer to the roots of some of the themes we have explored, we begin to draw more heavily from *The Silmarillion* and the roots of Middle-earth. Yet we see that hints of these deeper ideas—whether by the design of the author or not—can be found even in *The Hobbit*. And our starting point is to notice that even within *The Hobbit* there is a marked change in narrative tone between the start of the book and the end. Indeed, the change within *The Hobbit* is almost as significant as the change from *The Hobbit* to *The Lord of the Rings*, except that the change within *The Hobbit* happens gradually. If I were to pick a specific place where this change begins to be noticeable, it would be the moment the reader first meets Elrond in Rivendell. A full articulation of all aspects of this shift in tone is beyond the scope of this book, but the shift can be illustrated in a few ways.

A Deepening of Voice

One way we see the change in tone is in the songs and poetry. The first song we read in *The Hobbit* is that of the dwarves at the "unexpected party." This song begins:

Chip the glasses and crack the plates!
Blunt the knives and bend the forks!
That's what Bilbo Baggins hates—
Smash the bottles and burn the corks!
Hobbit, 42

It is a lighthearted piece—almost a child's rhyme—with a singsong rhythm and no particularly profound meaning. It might be argued that it has, in fact, no meaning at all, which is to say that the dwarves do not *mean* the words they are singing, since they actually do "none of those dreadful things" (*Hobbit*, 43). They sing the song only to mock and tease their anxious host.

Now contrast this with the last poem of the book, found in the final chapter:

Roads go ever ever on,
Over rock and under tree,
By caves where never sun has shone,
By streams that never find the sea;
Over snow by winter sown,
And through the merry flowers of June,
Over grass and over stone,
And under mountains in the moon.

Roads go ever ever on,
Under cloud and under star,
Yet feet that wandering have gone
Turn at last to home afar.
Eyes that fire and sword have seen
And horror in the halls of stone
Look at last on meadows green
And trees and hills they long have known.
Hobbit, 359–60

The difference between the somber, contemplative tone of this poem and the mocking, humorous tone of the earlier one is striking. Indeed, not only *might* this later poem fit comfortably in the context of *The Lord of the Rings*, but a version of it *is* sung in the trilogy—twice, in fact! And far from being without significance, its final lines touch on those things that are most important in life, in a way reminiscent of the dying words of Thorin: "If more of us valued food and cheer and song above hoarded gold, it would be a merrier world" (*Hobbit*, 348). When Bilbo finishes this poem, the wizard says, "My dear Bilbo! Something is the matter with you! You are not the hobbit that you were." We can almost hear Tolkien's own voice saying, "My dear me, this is not the story it once was."

But does this contrast between songs really illustrate a change in narrative tone? One might suggest that the latter poem is intentionally given a more somber tone only to illustrate the change that comes over Bilbo from the start of the quest to the end and that it is not reflective of any overall change in narrative voice. Certainly we must acknowledge, as Gandalf does, that Bilbo has changed over the course of the book from the innocent hobbit who tries to "good morning" a wizard to the one who has lived through the deaths of Thorin, Fili, Kili, and many worthy elves. We could also point out that it is the dwarves who sing the former song, while the latter is sung by a hobbit, and thus the difference between the songs might only serve to illustrate the differences in character between two of the races of Middle-earth, not a difference between the start of the book and the end. Both of these observations would be well taken, except that the same point could also be illustrated with contrasts between several other pairs of songs and poems. Furthermore, these contrasts in poems are only a few among many examples of the dramatic change in voice, and when all of the different aspects are taken as a whole, they are hard to ignore.

Consider, for example, the song sung early on when Thorin's company first approaches Rivendell. The song begins:

> O! What are you doing,
> And where are you going?
> Your ponies need shoeing!
> The river is flowing!
> O! tra-la-la-lally
>   here down in the valley!
>   *Hobbit*, 91

This is the third song or poem appearing in the story, and the last before we meet Elrond. Of particular importance is the fact that it is not a song sung by dwarves but by elves! To put it very plainly, this is not a song we could really imagine being sung by the elves of Rivendell in *The Lord of the Rings*. It is another song of teasing, with a refrain of nonsense syllables, much more akin to the early song of the dwarves than to anything we would later come to associate with the nobility, splendor, wisdom, or grace of the elven race. I don't think I put it too strongly if I say that it is entirely out of character for those of the high House of Elrond. Of course at the time this song appears, we haven't met Elrond yet!

By contrast, consider the first song sung after the appearance of Elrond (not counting the rhymes of goblins). This song comes after the departure of the company from Rivendell, when they are resting in the house of Beorn, and it is the dwarves who sing it. The first stanza suggests both the mood and the theme of the song.

> The wind was on the withered heath,
> but in the forest stirred no leaf:
> there shadows lay by night and day,
> and dark things silent crept beneath.
> *Hobbit*, 177

This song has a much more serious and somber tone than the "tra-la-la-lally" rhyme, as it goes on to speak in mythic imagery of the journey of the wind. The words speak not only of shadows and dark things that creep silently beneath the forest, but also of wind that roars and rolls like a tide, of the tearing and rending of clouds, and of cool heavens and wide seas. It also has nature imagery of living and growing things: leaved forests and the branches of trees, hissing grasses, rattling reeds. These are imaginings one might associate with elves. It even ends with a reference to the stars, which are also an elven love. The point simply is this: in this contrast the more serious song is sung by the dwarves and comes after the departure from Rivendell, while the more lighthearted song is sung by the elves and occurs before the meeting with Elrond. Not surprisingly, then, the elven songs also take a more serious tone after the meeting with Elrond. Consider the striking *similarity* between the first line of that last dwarvish song, with its wind/heath[er] imagery, and the second line from the last elven poem to appear in the book: "The

wind's in the tree-top, the wind's in the heather" (*Hobbit*, 357).
The common theme in the contrasts between the poems has naught
to do with races but with where the poem falls with respect to the
meeting with Elrond.

Admittedly, not every poem in the book adheres strictly to this general pattern. Another "tra-la-la-lally" song, for example, is repeated
at the end of the story when Bilbo returns to Rivendell. One might
think that Tolkien has returned to the pre-Elrond lightheartedness.
Yet even the post-Elrond "tra-la-la-lally" song is much more serious
than the earlier one, and deals with ultimate values.

> Though sword shall be rusted,
> And throne and crown perish
> With strength that men trusted
> And wealth that they cherish,
> Here grass is still growing,
> And leaves are yet swinging,
> The white water flowing,
> And elves are yet singing
>   Come! Tra-la-la-lally!
>   Come back to the valley!
>   *Hobbit*, 355

This is a song that reflects on the vanity of the mortal pursuits of
power and treasure, and on the timelessness of nature. Other than
the shared refrain, it is a different song entirely than the earlier one
that continues on to make fun of the wagging beards of the dwarves.

Another significant difference between the tone of the book before
and after Elrond's entrance can be seen in the monsters faced by
Bilbo.[1] In *The Hobbit* there are five significant enemies or groups of
enemies that might be deemed "monsters":[2] the trolls who appear
near the start of the tale, the goblins who appear several times, Gollum, the spiders of Mirkwood, and, of course, the dragon Smaug.[3]

Of these five, only the trolls appear in the tale before Elrond, and
these three trolls are as out of place in Middle-earth as the "tra-la-la-
lally" song is out of place in Rivendell. They have common English
names: Tom, Bert, and William. They speak with cockney voices. And
they border on being silly. They come from the world of children's
nursery stories and not from the heroic landscape of Middle-earth.

We see nothing of their kind in *The Lord of the Rings*. (The cave-trolls encountered in Moria are of another kind altogether.) Even if we did later encounter trolls like these, we could not imagine Elrohir or Elladan, the sons of Elrond, or the great warrior Glorfindel of Rivendell (who stood up to face several Ringwraiths), or for that matter any of Elrond's folk as we know them from *The Lord of the Rings*, "hurrying along for fear of the trolls," as Gandalf claims Elrond's folk were doing (*Hobbit*, 83)—not if the trolls were Tom, Bert, and Bill! Tolkien, when he later realized where *The Hobbit* had taken him, even regretted the choice of their names.

Here it must also be pointed out that the hobbits themselves, along with their beloved Shire, are also anachronistic; they don't fit into the heroic world created in *The Silmarillion* any more than Tom, Bert, and Bill do. Indeed, their presence in Middle-earth is quite by accident. But it is a wonderful accident that may be the most important ingredient in making *The Lord of the Rings* the successful work that it is. For part of the wonder of the hobbits' existence in Middle-earth is precisely their anachronistic nature. Despite their diminutive size, they really do function as regular and recognizable people (like common English men and women of the late nineteenth through middle twentieth century) who are placed in heroic situations requiring heroic actions, such as the facing of monsters who are fierce enough to demand real heroism of any who would face them.[4]

Returning to the monsters, those we meet *after* Elrond are much more worthy enemies than the three trolls, with natures more fitting to the heroic world of Middle-earth. The goblins come first. When we first meet them, shortly after the company departs from Rivendell and gets ambushed in a cave, the goblins have not yet become the orcs described in *The Lord of the Rings*. They are more like the diminutive and comic goblin creatures of George MacDonald's delightful children's fairy tale, *The Princess and the Goblin*—which is to say, they have not fully become monsters worthy of a heroic age. (In a personal letter, Tolkien even acknowledges this similarity[5]—though there is indication that he later regretted this portrayal much as he regretted the portrayal of the three trolls.) But they are a step in that direction. They are more serious, less modern, and more dangerous than the three trolls. And, indeed, my argument is not that the narrative tone changes *instantly* when we meet Elrond but only that from the meeting in Rivendell on, when Tolkien discovers that he is actually in Middle-earth, the tale *begins* to change from the low and comic to the high and heroic.

Gollum is next. Though in stature and origin he is akin to hobbits, in some regards Gollum is actually a considerably more frightening "monster" than the trolls, and he appears in a more frightening situation. Like the trolls, his goal is to eat the hobbit. He is certainly more crafty and intelligent than the trolls, as he proves in the riddle game. Most importantly, perhaps, he also speaks riddles taken from a heroic age: riddles that Tolkien borrowed and adapted from Old English and Old Norse and other medieval poetry. In other words, while the three trolls belong in the nursery, Gollum belongs in a medieval heroic poem. Even his underground lake abode links him to Grendel, though he is certainly less strong and fierce than the monster from *Beowulf*.

And the narrative tone continues to change. After Gollum, we meet the goblins again when they trap Gandalf, Bilbo, and the company of dwarves up in the trees. This time they are darker and more sinister and come riding on wolves, more like the warg-riding orcs of *The Lord of the Rings*. They are not going to be fooled by a simple trick, and the company must be rescued by the great eagles.

Likewise, the spiders of Mirkwood that come next in the tale, though lesser in size and power than the great spider Shelob who appears at the end of *The Two Towers*, are akin to her and to Ungoliant, the horrific spider-beast that destroys the two trees of Yavanna and nearly devours the Silmarils. We could also add that the were-bear character, Beorn, though by no means a monster, also was born in medieval heroic times and belongs much more fully to the heroic world of Middle-earth than do the three trolls, or even the MacDonald-inspired goblins as they first appear in the tale. We will return to Beorn later in this chapter.

As for dragons, they are the archetypal monsters of the heroic world. Smaug is of the same type as Glaurung, the bane of Túrin. By the time Smaug appears, the shift in tone is complete, and we find that we are reading a rather different tale from the one we started (even if we didn't notice any exact instant of change). And then the goblins appear a third time. As we discover at the end of the book, the goblins are vicious enemies, nothing less than the orcs of

The Silmarillion and *The Lord of the Rings*. They are motivated by vengeance and hatred, not by the desire for a good leg of mutton. It is as if, once we meet Elrond, we have suddenly stepped into an older, larger, more heroic world including the appropriate villains. In fact, that is exactly what has happened—accidentally, as it turns out, for Tolkien did not initially set the story in Middle-earth—and the narrative tone changes to reflect that.

Even the quest itself takes on a much greater significance after the meeting with Elrond. Initially, the quest is a private affair of Thorin, centered on personal revenge on the dragon Smaug and on recapturing the treasure of Thorin's ancestors. Gandalf's comment at the unexpected party, regarding the possibility of a direct approach to Smaug's front gate, gives insight into how insignificant Thorin and company are, despite the dwarf-king's sense of self-importance: "That would be no good, not without a mighty Warrior, even a Hero. I tried to find one; but warriors are busy fighting one another in distant lands, and in this neighbourhood heroes are scarce, or simply not to be found" (*Hobbit*, 53). To the reader it is a humorous comment, giving a glimpse of Gandalf's lighter side. To the characters themselves, however—Thorin especially—it is a condescending and even insulting statement. Gandalf is stating outright that none of them are great warriors or heroes in a classical or medieval tradition. Furthermore, in telling the dwarves that the real heroes and warriors are all off doing more important things, Gandalf is also letting them know that their quest is not so important: certainly not important enough to warrant the time of a hero.[6] Gandalf makes a similar comment later in the conversation with respect to the Necromancer: "Here is an enemy quite beyond the powers of all the dwarves put together, if they could all be collected again from the four corners of the world. . . . The dragon and the Mountain are more than big enough tasks for you!" (*Hobbit*, 58).

It is after the meeting with Elrond that this quest for dragon's gold takes on greater significance than Gandalf hints at with the dwarves—and likely more than the author himself initially supposed. Elrond, for example, has motives much different from those of the dwarves when he gives them his help as they pass through Rivendell: "For if he did not altogether approve of dwarves and their love of gold, he hated dragons and their cruel wickedness, and he grieved to remember the ruin of the town of Dale and its merry bells, and the burned banks of the bright River Running" (*Hobbit*, 95).

In any case, at least the unintended consequences of the quest become more important than earlier imagined. The discovery of the One Ring, the death of Smaug, and the Battle of Five Armies all turn out to be important events in the history of Middle-earth. As the narrator tells us when Bilbo departs with the elf-host, "The northern world would be merrier for many a long day. The dragon was dead, and the goblins overthrown, and [the Elves'] hearts looked forward after winter to a spring of joy" (*Hobbit*, 352). None of this was in the mind of Thorin—nor was it, we might guess, in the mind of Tolkien—when Thorin set out from Hobbiton with his company of fourteen.

The common theme in all of the changes we have just discussed is Elrond. Before we meet Elrond, the story seems to be one thing. After we meet Elrond, it changes to something else. Again, it is not that the change is immediate. As Tom Shippey explains, Tolkien could be quite stubborn even with his bad ideas.[7] Nor is it a complete change in direction. It is more a deepening, a sending down of roots—a movement from children's story to something bordering on the heroic romance genre of *The Lord of the Rings*. The shift starts in chapter 3, "A Short Rest," when we meet Elrond, but it takes time to really set in. It seems to be complete about two chapters later, when Bilbo acquires the Ring and meets Gollum. Thus, as noted, the goblins of chapter 4 have not yet become the goblins of the Battle of Five Armies in chapter 17. This explains why many readers associate the shift more with the appearance of Gollum or the discovery of the Ring than with the appearance of Elrond. Also, Tolkien's revisions before the first edition and the substantial revisions between the first edition and the second edition—especially with respect to the Ring and the outcome of the game of riddles—obscure the exact moment in which the shift occurs. Nonetheless, the shift in narrative voice cannot be doubted, and the beginning of that shift can be traced to Elrond.

Attaching a Leaf

Why, then, is this meeting with Elrond so important? And why does it spawn such a significant shift in the tone and voice of the narrative?

Much of the answer to this lies in the genesis and roots of *The Hobbit*. For many years before Tolkien began writing this story, he had been working on a deep and profound mythology for his created world of Middle-earth. Some of his surviving stories date back at least to 1916–17. Though at the time he was very private about his writing, there is evidence that he had been working on what was later to become *The Silmarillion* from as early as 1914. Certainly by the 1920s he had done a significant amount of work on the languages and early histories of Middle-earth. Surprisingly, however, when he began *The Hobbit* he didn't realize that this story would eventually fit into the larger (and much more serious) framework to which he had already devoted so much time! *The Hobbit* begins with a voice much more akin to that of Tolkien's fairy tale *Farmer Giles of Ham* than to that of *The Silmarillion*.

The situation can be explained using imagery from Tolkien's short masterpiece "Leaf by Niggle" (see "Niggle," 75–78). Imagine a painter who has a broad canvas on which he is painting a tree. Imagine further that he has been working on this tree for many years; it is his passion and life's interest. Imagine also that this painter has several smaller canvases on which he paints leaves. He has quite a collection of them. Some of these leaves remain works of art in their own right. Other leaves, however, turn out to belong to the great tree. When the painter realizes this, he attaches them to that other, broader canvas. This is precisely what happened with *The Hobbit*. Some readers are under the impression that Tolkien began with *The Hobbit* and then later went back and added the histories that were to become *The Silmarillion*. It was the other way around: the myths and histories of Middle-earth had been around for about two decades already when Tolkien began *The Hobbit*, and *The Hobbit* merely got added on to them like a small leaf glued to the giant mural of the tree. At what exact point Tolkien "realized" that this new story involving Bilbo Baggins was part of his other canvas, I don't know for sure, but the arguments I've given in this chapter suggest that it happens when the company meets Elrond at Rivendell. In any case, Elrond is the obvious connection to the preexisting myth. He is "one of those people whose fathers came into the strange stories before the beginning of History, the wars of the evil goblins and the elves and the first men in the North. In those days of our tale there were still some people who had both elves and heroes of the North for ancestors, and Elrond the master of the house was their chief" (*Hobbit*, 93–94). Readers of *The Silmarillion* will realize at once that those "people who had both elves and heroes of the North for ancestors" refers to the offspring of Beren and Lúthien, and of Tuor and Idril, from which spring not only Elrond's line but also the line of the kings of Númenor and thus Aragorn himself. The great hidden kingdom of Gondolin—the tale of which is told in *The Silmarillion*—is also mentioned by name; it is from there, we learn, that Gandalf's and Thorin's swords come. In short, it is right here, when Bilbo meets Elrond, that we are suddenly plunged more fully into the thematic depth and importance of Middle-earth.

It is even interesting to note that the narrator's comment "in those days of our tale" follows immediately after a reference to "the strange stories before the beginning of History." It would seem, therefore, that the phrase "those days" refers to this earlier history, when Elrond's forefathers were alive. If this is the case, then the phrase "our tale" encompasses both the strange stories of Elrond's past and the current story of Bilbo's adventure, implying that it is all one tale. And it is one, though Tolkien himself didn't realize this when he began writing *The Hobbit*. We are told, for example, that Gandalf's sword, Glamdring, belonged to the king of Gondolin, who was Turgon, the father of Idril Celebrindal, the mother of Eärendil the Mariner, the father of none other than Elrond himself. Thus the story comes full circle, and Elrond identifies the sword of his great-grandfather and begins the living connection tying us to the past.

Aragorn's tale also comes full circle. When he sits by the fire on the edge of Weathertop near the beginning of *The Lord of the Rings* and sings to the four hobbits the tale of Beren and Lúthien Tinúviel, he is singing his own song about a mortal man who falls in love with an elf maiden and goes through many perils and hardships to earn the right to wed her. "Why to think of it," Sam says to Frodo on the Stairs of Cirith Ungol, "we're in the same tale still! It's going on." This is a fundamental aspect of Tolkien's work. It is one great story. We simply keep stepping into it at different spots. Time and again Tolkien connects us with the deep past of Middle-earth's history, and yet does so in a way that relates that history to the present situation.

"Don't the great tales never end?" Sam goes on to ask. "No," Frodo replies, "they never end as tales" (IV/viii).

And it is as Tolkien brings Thorin and company into contact with this deeper and richer preexisting history, embodied in Elrond, that their quest—which in and of itself is not of great significance to any but themselves—suddenly takes on more importance. In fact, it is much more important than Tolkien himself realized when he began writing *The Hobbit*. But once this story begins to be intertwined with the existing landscape and history that was so dear to Tolkien's heart, it naturally takes on much greater importance to the author. This later realization accounts for numerous changes Tolkien made to the book after its first edition. One can only wonder why he didn't make more changes.

The Presence of Ilúvatar

Now if the story and characters of *The Hobbit* suddenly find themselves entering a world and history both deeper and more important than the one Tolkien thought they were in when he began writing the book, it should not be surprising to find that the narrative also begins to take up themes that are more important. At the start of *The Hobbit*, for example, the author is concerned with such things as the invention of golf. In a line that is more cute than profound, we learn that Bullroarer Took, in the Battle of the Green Fields, knocked the head of the goblin-king clean off, whereupon "it sailed a hundred yards through the air and went down a rabbit-hole, and in this way the battle was won and the game of Golf invented at the same moment" (*Hobbit*, 48). By the end of the story, however, we have begun at least to encounter issues of much greater import: themes such as the objectivity of moral law, the importance of free will, the role of fate, the value of life and friendship, and even salvation. That is, we begin to see the moral, philosophical, and theological themes that become much more prevalent in *The Lord of the Rings* (and that are the focus of this book).

One thing we begin to get hints of in *The Hobbit* is something mentioned in the introduction to this book: that reality consists not only of a physical plane (a *seen* world) but also of a spiritual plane (an *unseen* world). And this unseen world is vitally important. Indeed, the spiritual and physical planes are intimately related: what happens on the spiritual plane affects what happens on the physical, and the decisions made on the physical plane have spiritual import. In a few critical places in *The Hobbit*, Tolkien shows the contrast between temporal (physical) values and eternal (spiritual) values and challenges his readers to begin to understand the world through the eternal values. This is seen especially in Thorin's sad downturn, where we witness in him the destructive nature of greed. In his parting speech to Bilbo, he glimpses in the face of death the realization of what is really important: "'Farewell, good thief,' he said. 'I go now to the halls of waiting to sit beside my fathers, until the world is renewed. Since I leave now all gold and silver, and go where it is of little worth, I wish to part in friendship from you, and I would take back my words and deeds at the Gate'" (*Hobbit*, 348). First, Thorin is professing a belief that the end of his bodily life does not mean the end of his spiritual existence. His present bodily life is temporal, but his spiritual life is eternal. Of course Tolkien is not gnostic; the value of this spiritual reality does not diminish the value of the physical reality. Dwarves, like elves and men, are meant to be embodied creatures; embodiment, not an existence as disembodied souls or spirits, is the good and proper state. Thus Thorin looks forward to a renewed world. His spirit will have a time of waiting, and then (so he believes) he will be reembodied in this renewed world.

Still, the eternal nature of the spiritual reality gives weight to moral decisions and provides a different value system. Gold and silver, though they have worth in the physical plane, have no value in the spiritual plane. Friendship, by contrast, does have spiritual worth and significance. It is sad that Thorin must face death—that is, he must come face-to-face with the reality of his finite existence in the present material plane and his eternal existence in the spiritual plane—before he contrasts temporal values with eternal values and realizes the greater importance of the latter.

Another place we get hints in *The Hobbit* of something going on in the spiritual plane is in the long-standing battle against the evil embodied in the Necromancer. We see this at the edge of Mirkwood when Gandalf leaves Thorin's company in order to play some role in this battle. We learn in the final chapter of the book not only that

Smaug is defeated but also that the Necromancer is "at last driven . . . from his dark hold in the south of Mirkwood" and that as a result the land would "be freed from that horror for many long years." We also learn that this is not merely a physical war against a bodily enemy but rather a battle against a spiritual evil that has gone on for many lives of men and whose end, Elrond guesses, "will not come about in this age of the world, or for many after" (*Hobbit*, 357).

Perhaps the most important spiritual idea that Tolkien gives a glimpse of in Bilbo's story is the presence of some sovereign or divine hand at work in the events of the world. The hint of this is expressed by Gandalf in the penultimate paragraph of the book, a paragraph that may be the most important of *The Hobbit* when it comes to understanding Tolkien's Middle-earth.

> "Then the prophecies of the old songs have turned out to be true, after a fashion!" said Bilbo.
>
> "Of course!" said Gandalf. "And why should not they prove true? Surely you don't disbelieve the prophecies, because you had a hand in bringing them about yourself? You don't really suppose, do you, that all your adventures and escapes were managed by mere luck, just for your sole benefit? You are a very fine person, Mr. Baggins, and I am very fond of you; but you are only quite a little fellow in a wide world after all!" (*Hobbit*, 362–63)

At one level, this passage could be compared with the realization that comes to Théoden when he first sees Ents: the world is much bigger than he imagined, and his own little problems are somehow less significant. Or, rather, the significance of his problems must be understood in the context of the bigger problems of the world around him. Bilbo, like Théoden, is "only quite a little fellow in a wide world."

There is much more at work in this passage, however. We first note that Gandalf is not at all surprised that the prophecies should be fulfilled. The very fact that Tolkien includes prophecies, and that they come true, suggests that in Middle-earth some reliable foreknowledge of future events is assumed. Gandalf himself trusts the source of this foreknowledge, and he is not alone. When Boromir arrives at the Council of Elrond and shares the prophecy that came to him in a dream—"There shall be shown a token / That Doom is near at hand"—no one at the council doubts the significance of those words; the importance of prophecy is taken for granted (II/ii). Now, prophecy may spring from impersonal fate, but at least it raises the possibility that there is some sort of plan with a purpose. In the Christian worldview of Tolkien's Catholicism, for example, prophecy does not come from an impersonal source but from the Creator of the world whose plans are communicated through the prophecy. It is out of trust in the Creator that one would also trust the prophecy. And so the presence of trustworthy prophecy may be a first piece of evidence, even within *The Hobbit*, that there is a divine hand at work in Middle-earth.

Admittedly, the reference to "prophecy" might be interpreted in many ways, some of which could spring from a nonmonotheistic notion of fate, such as that held in Greek mythology or in *Beowulf*, Tolkien's own beloved Germanic legend. But there is more than just this one hint of the divine. For Gandalf goes on to challenge Bilbo's belief that all his adventures and escapes were "managed by mere luck." Throughout the story there have been many references to luck and to its importance in bringing Bilbo and the dwarves to the successful completion of his quest. Gandalf himself has spoken of luck on numerous occasions, as has the narrator. Apart from the deeper consequences of the quest—consequences the author wouldn't know about until the quest stumbled its way into Middle-earth—*luck* (meaning an impersonal chance) is the appropriate word. However, here at the end of *The Hobbit*, after it has completed its transition from being a children's story to being a more mature tale contributing to the broad heroic landscape of Middle-earth, Gandalf says something much more important. In one blow, with the mere use of the word *mere*, he lays to rest all notions that the course of events is determined by "luck"—if by the word *luck* we mean blind, purposeless chance. For in his appeal to prophecy, Gandalf is referring to a power behind the luck, so that however lucky (or unlucky) certain events appear, it is not "mere luck."

More importantly, Gandalf's reference to the events being "managed" implies the presence of a *manager*! In other words, there is some hand at work in all of the events of the story, leading the events (and the characters) to their prophesied (and planned or managed) conclusion. This manager, then, has both the *desire* to act—a care

185

and concern for Middle-earth and its people—and the *power* to bring about his purposes. Although to characters within the story, who are merely experiencing something beyond their control and their ability to understand, this manager's actions may appear as luck.

Given how powerful and wise Tolkien portrays Gandalf to be, some readers might infer that Gandalf himself is the manager hinted at by the author. (This interpretation would make this aspect of the story more palatable to Tolkien's nontheistic readers.) After all, Gandalf certainly seems to know more than any of the others, as is evident in the final moments leading up to the Battle of Five Armies. However, it cannot be the case that Gandalf is the manager responsible for all of the supposedly "lucky" events, for not only is he absent from many of them, but he is also as surprised as any of the dwarves by Bilbo's reappearance after his finding of the Ring, and again by Bilbo's survival of the Battle of Five Armies. Furthermore, Gandalf is as helpless as Bilbo and the dwarves when the company is caught by the goblins in the burning trees in the chapter "Out of the Frying-Pan into the Fire." He is truly frightened and expects to die.

At this point we must note that while Gandalf affirms the presence of a managing hand at work in the events of the world, and simultaneously affirms the validity of prophecy and of certain predestined events, he also affirms the reality of free will. He admits that even little Bilbo, by his choices and actions, had a hand in bringing about the prophesied events: events that within the manager's purposes are much more significant than any of Thorin's company expected. In other words, Bilbo's free will—emphasized several times and most especially in his choice to continue down the tunnel to Smaug's lair—is not an illusion but is somehow used by the manager to bring about the very events that were fated and foretold by prophecy. If we return to *The Silmarillion*, we must understand this in the context of Ilúvatar's gift of freedom. Ilúvatar can use for his own ends the good choice of Bilbo to show mercy to Gollum as well as the evil choices of Fëanor bound up in his oath, and yet in both cases the individuals are still free to act.

Of course, even at the end, *The Hobbit* remains a more light-hearted work than its sequel, and many of these deeper matters are only suggested in a way peripheral to the story. Gandalf's concluding words to Bilbo, though they carry the added weight of being concluding words, are really the only significant reference we see in *The Hobbit* to any sort of God or Creator or divine hand. Had Bilbo's story never found its way into Middle-earth, we might not have seen even that glimpse of greater theological concerns in *The Hobbit*.

When we move to the deeper heroic work that is *The Lord of the Rings*, however, we begin to see many more examples of this managing hand at work in the history of Middle-earth: evidence of Providence, or of a Creator's care for his creation. We see examples in how the wise of Middle-earth speak of Frodo's role: Gandalf refers to him as having been "chosen" (I/ii); Elrond speaks of him as having been "appointed" (II/ii); and even Frodo sees himself as having been chosen, though he wonders why. But just as events being *managed* implies the existence of a manager, Frodo having been *chosen* and *appointed* implies that there is a chooser and appointer. And both Gandalf and Elrond make it clear that this chooser is neither of them but is instead a much higher and more powerful being. Aragorn uses a word even more laden with spiritual connotation when he says to Frodo, "It has been *ordained* that you should hold it for a while" (II/ii, emphasis added). The term *ordination* usually implies a spiritual calling from a supreme being.

Elrond also hints at this higher power when he welcomes the visitors to the council: "That is the purpose for which you are called hither. Called, I say, though I have not called you to me, strangers from distant lands. You have come and are here met, in this very nick of time, by chance as it may seem. Yet it is not so. Believe rather that it is so ordered that we, who sit here, and none others, must now find counsel for the peril of the world" (II/ii). Though Elrond does not explicitly name a divine being in this passage, he suggests one in several ways. Using the passive voice, he speaks of each person present as having been "called," but denies being the one who called them. *Calling*, like *ordination*, connotes a spiritual purpose and vocation. The phrase "by chance as it may *seem*" (emphasis added) is a clear implication that it is not by chance at all but by some greater intentional purpose that only seemed like chance. Then we get another reference to the strangers being "ordered" to have been there. In fact, we see a pattern here that no explicit subject is given for any of these verbs: *chose, called, managed, ordained,* and *ordered*. Yet for all of them, a higher power is suggested and implied. It is also clear that this power is actively involved in the affairs of Middle-earth.

Those who have read *The Silmarillion* know the name of this power: Eru Ilúvatar, the Creator of Middle-earth in Tolkien's mythology. Or at the very least it is lesser authorities (the Valar) working on behalf of Ilúvatar. Why Tolkien did not give more explicit details in *The Lord of the Rings* as to the identity and nature of this manager-ordainer-chooser-caller-prophesier, but left all references to Ilúvatar vague and indirect, is an interesting and important question to which we shall return in the final chapter. But first we must explore the importance of this presence in Middle-earth and in *The Lord of the Rings*.

The Purpose of Ilúvatar

Though Ilúvatar is not mentioned by name in *The Lord of the Rings*, the evidence of his presence and of his concern for the peoples of Middle-earth is significant to the tale and to the characters within it. Among other things, awareness of the great purpose of the Creator, and of the scope of his concerns, becomes at times a source of hope in that it gives a very different perspective to some of the troubles encountered by the characters. This hope is vitally important; it is what keeps the characters from giving up and ceasing to do what they are called to do, what is necessary for the defeat of Sauron.

Not surprisingly, it is in Gandalf that we see this understanding most clearly manifested. He is able to see beyond one day and one battle, one victory or one defeat, as we saw in the passage cited earlier: "And for my part, I shall not wholly fail of my task, though Gondor should perish, if anything passes through this night that can still grow fair or bear fruit and flower again in days to come" (V/i). Thus he is able to expand the vision of many of those with whom he comes into contact, such as Théoden, whose healing was discussed earlier: "For not only the little life of Men is now endangered, but the life also of those things which you deemed the matter of legend. You are not without allies, even if you know them not" (III/viii).

It is a scene in Minas Tirith, as we approach the siege, where Gandalf's awareness of the spiritual plane is most clearly and beautifully captured: "Pippin glanced in some wonder at the face now close beside his own, for the sound of that laugh had been gay and merry. Yet in the wizard's face he saw at first only lines of care and sorrow; though as he looked more intently he perceived that under all there was a great joy: a fountain of mirth enough to set a kingdom laughing, were it to gush forth" (V/i). This scene takes place at one of the most despairing moments in the story. Sauron's darkness is coming upon the land. Frodo has been captured. The terrible siege of Minas Tirith is about to start, and there is no sign of Aragorn or the Rohirrim or Faramir. Denethor is showing signs of the evil coming upon him. And on the outside, Gandalf himself is showing the great burden on him. Yet beneath that terrible weight, there is a spiritual side to the wizard. That spiritual side shows in the incredible joy—a joy that is inexplicable from the point of view of the current *physical* reality of his situation. This joy can be explained in no other way than that Gandalf has a deeper understanding, one of the *unseen* reality beyond what is seen. Indeed, the imagery here of Gandalf's fountain of mirth is explicitly biblical. As Jesus told the woman at the well, "But the water that I will give him shall become in him a fountain of water, springing up into life everlasting" (John 4:14).

In a personal letter quoted in chapter 3, Tolkien explains a bit more of Gandalf's spiritual understanding and that the wizard dwells in part in the spiritual plane. Writing of Gandalf's sacrifice at Khazad-dûm, Tolkien explains how the wizard's understanding of Ilúvatar's purposes enables him, or frees him, to do what he does.

> For in his condition it was for him a sacrifice to perish on the Bridge in defense of his companions, less perhaps than for a mortal Man or Hobbit, since he had a far greater inner power than they; but also more, since it was a humbling and abnegation of himself in conformity to "the Rules": for all he could know at that moment he was the only person who could direct the resistance to Sauron successfully, and all his mission was vain. He was handing over to the Authority that ordained the Rules, and giving up personal hope of success. . . .
> . . . In the end before he departs for ever he sums himself up: "I was the enemy of Sauron." He might have added: "for that purpose I was sent to Middle-earth." But by that he would at the end have meant more than at the beginning. He was sent by a mere prudent plan of the angelic Valar or governors; but Authority had taken up

this plan and enlarged it, at the moment of its failure. "Naked I was
sent back—for a brief time, until my task is done." Sent back by
whom, and whence? Not by the "gods" whose business is only with
this embodied world and its time; for he passed "out of thought and
time." (*Letters*, 202–3)

Here, Tolkien refers to the Authority—that is, the divine Creator,
Ilúvatar—and to his purpose, and how it exceeds even the understanding of the Valar, the angelic beings who govern Middle-earth
from Valinor. Gandalf's return is akin to a resurrection, though it
is not quite the same thing, since the wizard is not of mortal kind
but is one of the Maiar, the lesser angelic beings who serve the
Valar. Tolkien makes his intention clear in this letter: it is Ilúvatar
and not the Valar who send Gandalf back. For it is the Authority's
purpose to rescue Middle-earth from Sauron. As mentioned earlier,
Ilúvatar has both the desire and the divine power to do this. So he
completes his plan by sending Gandalf back, at the very moment
of Gandalf's failure.

Yet even as we get a glimpse of Ilúvatar's plan, we also see Gandalf's faith in that Authority, and his understanding of the Authority's plan—that its scope far exceeds his own personal definition of
"success." In Gandalf's limited knowledge (limited compared to that
of Ilúvatar, not to that of mortal beings of Middle-earth), there is
no one else capable of doing what he, as a wise, knowledgeable, and
powerful wizard, can do. It would be easy for him to believe that
the entire resistance to Sauron depends on his own strength. But
he knows the Authority and has faith in him, and this knowledge
broadens his vision so that he can see that even he, Gandalf, is not
responsible for the fate of Middle-earth. Thus, he subordinates his
own mission and purposes.

In many ways, this discussion of Gandalf's faith and knowledge
relates to the reality behind the prophecies that we looked at earlier
in this chapter. In knowing something of Ilúvatar's purposes, Gandalf is able to have faith that the plan will be accomplished and the
prophecies fulfilled. Interestingly enough, far from making Gandalf
care less about the little individuals of Middle-earth (hobbits, for
example!), his understanding of Ilúvatar's bigger purposes gives him
a greater care for each individual—and, we might add, for the flowers

and plants and trees of Middle-earth. Or, to phrase this another way, his love for the Creator (Ilúvatar) gives him a deep love and concern for the creation (Arda and Middle-earth).

Even Sam, in his simple understanding, takes courage from the little glimpse he gets of the larger reality of Ilúvatar's plans. In another of the most beautiful passages of the trilogy, we are shown Sam's thoughts.

> Far above the Ephel Dúath in the West the night-sky was still dim and pale. There, peeping among the cloud-wrack above a dark tower high up in the mountains, Sam saw a white star twinkle for a while. The beauty of it smote his heart, as he looked up out of the forsaken land, and hope returned to him. For like a shaft, clear and cold, the thought pierced him that in the end the Shadow was only a small and passing thing: there was light and high beauty for ever beyond its reach. His song in the Tower had been defiance rather than hope; for then he was thinking of himself. Now, for a moment, his own fate, and even his master's, ceased to trouble him. (VI/ii)

What exactly does Sam see? Just a single star. No more. Nor is there any deep philosophical dialogue about the meaning of that star. Rather, it is one simple thought, reaching him at a level much more intuitive and visceral than intellectual: the evil of Sauron was only a small and passing thing; light and high beauty really existed, and Sauron could never destroy it. Like Sam himself, the realization is simple, but also profound. For it tells him that even if he fails in his quest, it will not mean that evil will triumph forever. The scope of Ilúvatar's plan is much broader than that. And in light of the greater scope, his own troubles are put in a new perspective. Like Théoden, he moves from thinking of himself to thinking of others. In other words, he moves from selfishness to unselfishness. And the less he focuses on himself, Tolkien is saying, the less his own fate troubles him. And hope returns to him.

The Power of Ilúvatar

Now it is not only the abstract notion of some broader *plan* of the Creator that gives hope (both to the characters within the story and

191

to its readers); the evidence of Ilúvatar's *power* at work in practical and visible ways provides an even greater hope. Again, although the power is not explicitly identified as Ilúvatar's, evidence of the workings of the Creator's power in *The Lord of the Rings* is significant even if not abundant.

Consider the finding of the One Ring. As Gandalf tells Frodo, "It was the strangest event in the whole history of the Ring so far: Bilbo's arrival just in time, and putting his hand on it, blindly, in the dark" (II/ii). This comment alone does not necessarily point to Ilúvatar's power at work. In the context of *The Hobbit*, it might be seen merely as one additional lucky event in a long chain of lucky events. In this case, however, the event—the finding of that "tiny ring of cold metal" in the midst of all the vast underground chambers and tunnels—seems rather far-fetched even for Bilbo's luck. Suppose a whole army of hobbits was sent underground beneath the mountains and told to look for the Ring. We would still have to say their chances of finding it were rather slim. How many readers have ever dropped a ring or similar object in the safe confines of their living room and been unable to find it? Now add the fact that Bilbo isn't even looking for the Ring at the time he discovers it. He just places his hand down in exactly the right place where it has been dropped on the hard floor of the tunnel, and not six inches to one side or another. This is so astronomically unlikely that the word *luck* cannot even describe it. Indeed, though the reader is told, for example, that the riddle game is won by "pure luck" (*Hobbit*, 125), the finding of the Ring is one place in *The Hobbit* where Tolkien specifically does not use the word *luck* (*Hobbit*, 115).

If not luck, then what is behind this event? It is hinted in the hindsight offered by *The Lord of the Rings* that this event was the result of a higher power. Gandalf explains this to Frodo.

> There was more than one power at work, Frodo. The Ring was trying to get back to its master. . . .
>
> Behind that there was something else at work, beyond any design of the Ring-maker. I can put it no plainer than by saying that Bilbo was *meant* to find the Ring, and *not* by its maker. In which case you also were *meant* to have it. And that may be an encouraging thought. (I/ii)

This is as close as Gandalf comes to explaining to Frodo the theology of Middle-earth. Those who have read *The Silmarillion* can more fully grasp what Gandalf is speaking of. Up to this point, he has been telling Frodo about the power of Sauron. Now suddenly he speaks of *another* power at work: one, we are led to understand, that is greater and higher than the Dark Lord. It is this *other* power that overrules the will of the Ring to return to its master and the will of the master to recover the Ring and instead leads the Ring to Bilbo, and thence to Frodo. For that other power has its own purpose, in which the Ring is meant to go to Frodo (and not to Sauron, its maker) and *acts in power* to bring this purpose to fulfillment. In fact, in part 3 of appendix A to *The Lord of the Rings*, it is hinted by Gandalf that the entire quest of *The Hobbit* was brought about by similar involvement of this Authority, at work in a seeming "chance-meeting" between Gandalf and an important dwarf named Thorin at an inn in Bree. The meeting, however, was no more "chance" than was the Council of Elrond. In any case, when the characters of Middle-earth believe that there is a caring and powerful Creator at work in the events of Middle-earth, it is indeed an encouraging thought, one that creates a sense of hope.

At times this Creator grants an apparently supernatural power to those serving him. Gandalf, as an angelic being—one of the Istari—naturally possesses some of this power. We see it manifest in a few places, most notably when he opposes evil beings of similar power, such as the winged Nazgûl attacking Faramir's retreating forces, or the Balrog of Moria at Khazad-dûm: "'You cannot pass,' [Gandalf] said. . . . 'I am a servant of the Secret Fire, wielder of the flame of Anor. You cannot pass. The dark fire will not avail you, flame of Udûn. Go back to the Shadow! You cannot pass'" (II/v). This passage is interesting to note with respect to Gandalf's power, because in it Tolkien (through Gandalf) gives his readers a hint of the source of this power. What is meant by "servant of the Secret Fire" and "wielder of the flame of Anor"? The flame of Anor may refer to Narya, the Ring of Fire, one of the three elven-rings. We learn at the end of the trilogy that Gandalf is the *wielder* of Narya, which had been given him earlier by Círdan. However, there is no explicit connection between Narya and Anor; the name *Anor* is just a derivative of *Anar*, the elven name for the sun. So if the flame of Anor refers to Narya, why is that particular name used for Narya here and nowhere else? Whether the flame of Anor refers to Narya or not, it is the Valar who put Anor (the sun) in the sky, and who govern its course (*Silm*, 98–102). This is also suggestive of the significance of the title Gandalf takes for himself, for the Valar originally set the sun above Middle-earth to help thwart Melkor's evil deeds done in darkness. Anor is drawn on its path by Arien, a "spirit of fire whom Melkor had not deceived nor drawn to his service" (*Silm*, 100). Melkor feared Arien and Anor "with a great fear, but dared not come nigh her" (*Silm*, 101). We also might simply note that the realm of the sun is in the heavens, and so the flame of Anor would seem to be a reference to the heavens, or to heaven, or to the supernatural power of heaven set against Melkor's own dark powers.

Of equal or greater interest is the reference to the "Secret Fire." Again, readers of *The Lord of the Rings* might guess that this also is a reference to Narya, which, as mentioned, is the Ring of Fire. Narya certainly gives Gandalf power. However, it doesn't quite make sense for Gandalf to claim that he is a servant of a ring; Narya would have been something he wielded rather than served. It is more likely that the Secret Fire is another name for the Flame Imperishable. In the fourth paragraph of the *Ainulindalë*, the tale of the creation and the Music of the Ainur, which is the opening part of *The Silmarillion*, there is a reference to the "secret fire" (though as here, with lower-case *s* and *f*); and again in the first paragraph of the *Valaquenta*, the second part of *The Silmarillion*, there is another reference to the "Secret Fire" (this time capitalized). In both cases it seems to be another name or description for the Flame Imperishable (which is also referred to in the *Ainulindalë* as the Imperishable Flame). But the Secret Fire, or Flame Imperishable, is with Ilúvatar (*Silm*, 16)—that is, in heaven. Thus, this is another reference to the power of heaven.

In fact, the imagery of the Secret Fire may be even more specific than this. Clyde Kilby, who spent the summer of 1966 working with Tolkien at Oxford, helping him prepare *The Silmarillion* for publication, wrote: "Professor Tolkien talked to me at some length about the use of the word 'holy' in *The Silmarillion*. Very specifically he told me that the 'Secret Fire sent to burn at the heart of the World' in the beginning was the Holy Spirit."[8] Thus, the creation passage in *The Silmarillion* with its reference to the "Secret Fire" is akin to Genesis 1:2: "And the earth was void and empty, and darkness was upon the face of the deep; and the spirit of God moved over the waters." This makes the words of Gandalf even more telling. They may mean, quite plainly: "I am a servant of the Holy Spirit."

Udûn, by contrast, is not only a region of Mordor but is more importantly a name that means the "un-west"[9] and is used by the elves as a synonym for hell. (See the index at the end of *The Lord of the Rings*.) Thus Gandalf makes it clear that the battle between himself and the Balrog is in reality a battle between heaven and hell—or specifically, between a servant of Ilúvatar and a servant of Morgoth, Ilúvatar's enemy. Furthermore, as Gandalf indicates, since Ilúvatar is the more powerful, he has the confidence to face this enemy. Readers of this passage who are familiar with the biblical narrative will recognize his words as not unlike those spoken by David to Goliath: "And David said to the Philistine: Thou comest to me with a sword, and with a spear, and with a shield: but I come to thee in the name of the Lord of hosts, the God of the armies of Israel, which thou hast defied" (1 Sam. 17:45). As with David, whose confidence comes from his trust in God, Gandalf's confidence, or hope, comes from his hope in Ilúvatar's power. In any case, from the letter we quoted earlier we see that the power given to Gandalf after his return is a supernatural power enhanced by Ilúvatar so that he can do the work that Ilúvatar sent him to do. This is a message of hope for Sauron's enemies: such a power is being used on their behalf against their enemy.

It is more surprising, perhaps, to see supernatural power at work not through a wizard but through the hobbit Sam, a lowly gardener from the Shire. Yet this seems to be what happens when he faces Shelob.

> "Galadriel!" he said faintly, and then he heard voices far off but clear: the crying of the Elves as they walked under the stars in the beloved shadows of the Shire, and the music of the Elves as it came through his sleep in the Hall of Fire in the house of Elrond.
>
> *Gilthoniel A Elbereth!*
>
> And then his tongue was loosed and his voice cried in a language which he did not know:

A Elbereth Gilthoniel!
o menel palan-diriel
le nallon sí di'nguruthos!
A tiro nin, Fanuilos! . . .

As if his indomitable spirit had set its potency in motion, the glass blazed suddenly like a white torch in his hand. It flamed like a star that leaping from the firmament sears the dark air with intolerable light. (IV/ix)

One might be tempted to see this display of power merely as Sam's unconscious memory recalling words he heard months earlier in the Shire, or as the potency of Galadriel herself at work through her star-glass, given as a gift to Frodo, or even as some latent power at work in Sam's "indomitable spirit." All these ideas are present in the passage, but there are two additional things suggesting this miraculous display of power is of a supernatural source, coming from a higher power—perhaps from Ilúvatar himself—at a time of great need. Some readers may recognize this passage as resonating with the New Testament narrative of the coming of the Holy Spirit on the apostles at the day of Pentecost (see Acts 2:1–4). When the Holy Spirit comes—not insignificantly, in the visible form of a flame—Jesus's apostles receive the supernatural power to speak in languages they do not know. Many other miraculous powers also follow in the coming days, including the power to heal, and even power to drive out evil spirits. This is precisely the manifestation of power we see in Sam. First he speaks words he does not understand in a language he does not know. They are, of course, words of great power! Then he drives out Shelob, the evil being. It is probably not coincidental that the passage speaks of Sam's indomitable *spirit* rather than his body or even his will, for with such a reference Tolkien leads the readers at least to be thinking about the spiritual reality rather than the physical.

Additionally, we must consider the name on which Sam now calls for help. It is not Galadriel, the powerful elven queen whom he has met and would have reason to recall but who is nonetheless a being of flesh more akin to him than to the Valar. Rather, it is the Vala Elbereth. Elbereth, which means "Star-Queen," is another name for Varda, the queen of the Valar and spouse of Manwë the king. Of her we read: "The light of Ilúvatar lives still in her face. . . . Elbereth [the Elves] name her . . . and they call upon her name out of the shadows of Middle-earth, and uplift it in song at the rising of the stars" (*Silm*, 26). She is also called Gilthoniel, meaning "Star-Kindler," a title of praise and adoration used only of Elbereth, who made the stars. When Frodo strikes the Black Rider at Weathertop, Aragorn comments, "More deadly to him was the name of Elbereth" (I/xii). Indeed, in the light of Tolkien's Catholicism, we cannot help but see in the honoring of Elbereth some reflection of the veneration of Mary. Thus, though he does not understand it himself, Sam is praising the Queen of Angels and calling on her for aid. So his vague memory, the potency of the star-glass, and his indomitable spirit are not *sources* of this power but rather *vehicles* through which the greater power is at work.

Thus, Tolkien lets his readers see both Gandalf and Sam as instruments through whom the Creator demonstrates his power in *The Lord of the Rings*. However, the most important demonstration of the power of Ilúvatar does not involve any physical being within Middle-earth at all. Rather, it is the battle of the winds that takes place high above Middle-earth in *The Return of the King*. This battle is the turning point in the siege of Minas Tirith, for the reversal of winds blows back the black clouds of Mordor and lets the sun shine once again. So important is it that it is noticed in all of the separate threads of the narrative going on at this point, and it is used to tie all the threads together. Merry notices it as he travels with Théoden and Éowyn: "Then suddenly Merry felt it at last, beyond doubt: a change. Wind was in his face! Light was glimmering. Far, far away, in the South the clouds could be dimly seen as remote grey shapes, rolling up, drifting: morning lay beyond them" (V/v). It is noticed by Pippin and Gandalf as they make their way back from Gandalf's confrontation at the gate: "They felt the wind blowing in their faces, and they caught the glimmer of morning far away, a light growing in the southern sky" (V/vii). Gimli recalls it as he and Legolas recount to Merry in the House of Healing something of their strange tale with Aragorn: "Hope was indeed born anew, . . . a change coming with a fresh wind from the Sea. . . . And so it was, as you know, that we came in the third hour of the morning with a fair wind and the Sun unveiled" (V/viii).

Perhaps the clearest expression of the spiritual significance of the wind change can be seen in Sam and Frodo's part of the story.

> There was battle far above in the high spaces of the air. The billowing clouds of Mordor were being driven back, their edges tattering as a wind out of the living world came up and swept the fumes and smokes towards the dark land of their home. Under the lifting skirts of the dreary canopy dim light leaked into Mordor like pale morning through the grimed window of a prison.
>
> "Look at it, Mr. Frodo!" said Sam. "Look at it! The wind's changed. Something's happening. He's not having it all his own way. His darkness is breaking up out in the world there. I wish I could see what is going on!" (VI/ii)

It is significant that Tolkien uses the word *battle* to describe what is happening. The first thing he shows us here is that the change in winds is not just a coincidence, or good luck, but yet another part of the great war going on in Middle-earth. The imagery that follows is equally significant. Though the winds certainly are a part of the physical universe, the phrase "far above in the high spaces of the air" carries the suggestion of heaven. That is, this is a war going on in heaven or in the spiritual realm. Certainly no physical being within Middle-earth accomplishes this; these are the winds of Manwë or of Ilúvatar himself. Ilúvatar's power is at work to rescue the people of Middle-earth. Sauron may be powerful, and his power brings terrible despair to his enemies, but there is one who is infinitely more powerful than Sauron. Thus, Sauron does not have it all his own way. His darkness does not go unopposed. Tolkien shows his reader that the power that is against Sauron is the power that controls the winds and the air. This, as is evident in Sam's words, is a source of tremendous hope to the people of Middle-earth.

Free Will and the Hand of Ilúvatar

That the hand of Ilúvatar intervenes in the affairs of Middle-earth on behalf of those who serve him—whether through Gandalf, through Galadriel's glass, through battles in the heavens, or through what appear to be lucky events—can be, as we saw, a source of hope.

Ilúvatar's intervention does not remove the significance of the choices made by the Children of Ilúvatar, but in many ways it can redeem those choices. Or, to put it another way, the characters are responsible only for their own choices and not for the outcome of those choices; they are responsible for the means, while the ends are in Ilúvatar's hands.

We see this principle at work in countless ways throughout *The Lord of the Rings*. Earlier in this book, we saw that many choices made by the wise and noble are not aimed at military victory. We now observe that by the power of Ilúvatar many of these choices result in a greater good than was imagined by those making the choices. Among these, one of the best examples is Aragorn's choice to pursue the orcs across Rohan to rescue Merry and Pippin. As we noted in chapter 4, of the three courses of action considered by Aragorn, this one makes the least sense from a strategic standpoint. The fate of Middle-earth lies with the actions unfolding to the east, as Frodo and Sam make their way toward Mordor. Gondor lies to the south, and there, it seems to Aragorn at the time, also lies the hope of Middle-earth as well as Aragorn's own heart. To the west are only two seemingly insignificant hobbits. Aragorn, however, feels a moral duty to go west and rescue the hobbits rather than let them suffer torture. In doing so, he guesses (wrongly, as it turns out) that he may be taking himself out of the battle for Middle-earth. Yet this choice proves pivotal, as Gandalf explains: "You chose amid doubts the path that seemed right: the choice was just, and it has been rewarded. For so we have met in time, who otherwise might have met too late. But the quest of your companions is over. Your next journey is marked by your given word" (III/v). Gandalf does not say that Aragorn's choice was strategic, or even wise, but rather that it was *right* and *just*—words in which the idea of moral goodness is implicit. Likewise, Aragorn's next choice is not determined by strategic planning or military foresight but is determined morally, by his "given word," meaning that holding to the virtue of faithfulness is more important than good strategy—a point made several times in the fourth chapter of this book. Yet Ilúvatar is able to take these choices and *reward* them, making them bear fruit that may be unintended but that is good. Indeed, had Aragorn not followed Merry and Pippin, his help might never have come to Rohan, in which case King Théoden might never have been healed. And had Rohan fallen, then its help would not have reached Minas Tirith but instead a whole new host of enemies. Nor would Aragorn have followed the Paths of the Dead. In short, it is likely that Gondor would have fallen had Aragorn chosen to go directly to Minas Tirith to try to rescue it. If Gondor had fallen, the diversionary assault on the Black Gates would never have taken place, and it is most likely that Frodo would also have failed.

The same may be said of the decision to include Merry and Pippin in the Fellowship—another decision made, at least on the surface of things, on the basis of friendship and not for any demonstrable strategic advantage or military wisdom. "I think, Elrond," Gandalf advises as they are planning the membership of the Fellowship, "that in this matter it would be well to trust rather to their *friendship* than to great *wisdom*" (II/iii, emphasis added). Yet as Gandalf discovers in hindsight, much later in the story: "It was not in vain that the young hobbits came with us, if only for Boromir's sake. But that is not the only part they have to play. They were brought to Fangorn, and their coming was like the falling of small stones that starts an avalanche in the mountains" (III/v). Of course, what looks like hindsight may well have been foresight on Gandalf's part, but if so, he was able to offer no concrete reasoning for that foresight other than the value of friendship. Yet as we see, even the downfall of Isengard is brought about because of the presence of the hobbits.

Indeed, even the work of the enemy can be used by Ilúvatar to accomplish something good. This is one of the central themes of *The Silmarillion*. Ilúvatar says to Melkor: "And thou, Melkor, shalt see that no theme may be played that hath not its uttermost source in me, nor can any alter the music in my despite. For he that attempteth this shall prove but mine instrument in the devising of things more wonderful, which he himself hath not imagined" (*Silm*, 17). Later he says of the race of men: "These too in their time shall find that all that they do redounds at the end only to the glory of my work" (*Silm*, 42). This theme might be seen as reflecting a Christian principle that the apostle Paul expresses in Romans 8:28: "And we know that to them that love God, all things work together unto good, to such as, according to his purpose, are called to be saints." It is a principle illustrated wonderfully in *The Lord of the Rings* in the story of Merry and Pippin, for it is important not only that these two hobbits are a part of the Quest—a decision of their own and of Elrond's—but that their enemies the orcs capture them. They do not go to Fangorn of their own will; they are *brought* there. Brought by whom? By the orcs, yes. But if we carry over our understanding from *The Silmarillion*, the hand of Ilúvatar is also involved. That is, Ilúvatar takes something that was intended for the harm of those who are doing good, namely the imprisonment and ill-treatment of Merry and Pippin, and uses it to accomplish good and to help those who seek good.

Now for most of the characters in the story, there is no indication of any knowledge of or faith in Ilúvatar. In the wisest of the wise, however—especially Gandalf, Elrond, and Galadriel, and at times Aragorn, Faramir, and a few others—there is often seen an explicit faith in a divine power. It is faith in the power and purpose of the Creator that enables them to do what is morally right rather than what appears to hold the most promise. It is faith that enables Gandalf to be full of joy even when all is dark. And from Gandalf, Elrond, and Galadriel, this vision of faith often passes to others, whether it is Gandalf (and later Aragorn) trying to comfort Frodo with the thought that he was *meant* to find the Ring, or Elrond telling the strangers at the council that they were *called*, or Galadriel speaking to the companions toward the end of their stay in Lothlórien: "Sleep in peace! Do not trouble your hearts overmuch with thought of the road tonight. Maybe the paths that you each shall tread are already laid before your feet, though you do not see them. Good night!" (II/viii). The message in each case is similar: there is a good and powerful hand at work in the world, guiding the events and preparing the paths so that his purposes are fulfilled. Those who follow him need concern themselves only with doing what is right and not with the results of those decisions. "It is not their part to master all the tides of the world," Gandalf tells them, "but to do what is in them for the succor of those years wherein they are set, uprooting the evil in the fields that they know, so that those who live after may have clean earth to till. What weather that will be is not theirs to rule."

What better example is there than the final success of Frodo's Quest? The list is long of those who, somewhere along the way, show mercy to Gollum and spare his life, doing what they think is right even though it seems to be a risky thing. And their mercy is rewarded, despite the failure of Frodo at the very end. One word for this is *grace*. Another—a word coined by Tolkien—is *eucatastrophe*: a "good catastrophe," a "sudden joyous 'turn,'" or "sudden and miraculous grace"; a "fleeting glimpse of Joy, Joy beyond the walls of the world, poignant as grief" ("Fairy," 62).

10

Ilúvatar's Theme
and the Real War

"Those who have dwelt in the Blessed Realm live at once in both worlds, and against both the Seen and the Unseen they have great power."

—Gandalf

In his essay "On Fairy-Stories," J. R. R. Tolkien makes several comments about the goals and purposes of the literature of Faery, a category that includes what we now call fantasy literature. Of the mythical and fairy-tale setting, he writes: "They open a door on Other Time, and if we pass through, though only for a moment, we stand outside our own time, outside Time itself, maybe" ("Fairy," 129). And a little later he adds, "The peculiar quality of the 'joy' in successful Fantasy can thus be explained as a sudden glimpse of the underlying reality or truth" ("Fairy," 155). Fantasy literature and its cousins, myth and fairy tale—at least the higher and better literatures of these kinds—transport us outside our own time and space. Or at least they open the door that we may travel there ourselves. And once there, we look at something that is timeless, and we are able to see truths that we might not see within the context and confines of our own limited perspective. If the fantasy is written well—if it is "successful," to use Tolkien's term—then it gives a glimpse of the "underlying reality or truth." And because that truth is seen apart from our own particular and peculiar time, we are able to see its universality rather than merely associating it with one cultural setting. For as we have seen illustrated in numerous ways in *The Lord of the Rings*, *The Hobbit*, and even in the essay "On Fairy-Stories," Tolkien did believe that there is an objective truth, just as there is an objective morality. It is a truth that underlies all truths. It is not relative to time or space. And furthermore, that underlying truth is one that we can (and ought to try to) see.

In his book *The Orphean Passages*, Walter Wangerin Jr. expresses in slightly different words something of what I think Tolkien is saying in his essay.

> In order to comprehend the experience one is living in, he must, by imagination and by intellect, be lifted out of it. He must be given to see it whole; but since he can never wholly gaze upon his own life while he lives it, he gazes upon the life that, in symbol, comprehends his own. Art presents such lives, such symbols. Myth especially—persisting as a mother of truth through countless generations and for many disparate cultures, coming therefore with the approval not of a single people but of *people*—myth presents, myth *is*, such a symbol, shorn and unadorned, refined and true. And when the one who gazes upon that myth suddenly, in dreadful recognition, cries out, "There I am! That is me!" then the marvelous translation has occurred: he is lifted out of himself to see himself wholly.[1]

Wangerin's "mother of truth" is Tolkien's "underlying reality or truth," which myth (and fairy tale and fantasy) is an ideal vehicle for revealing. It is not just some distant inapplicable truth that we see but a truth that speaks to our own situation. As Tolkien also writes, in describing the recovery that fairy stories can bring us: "We should meet the centaur and the dragon, and then perhaps suddenly behold, like the ancient shepherds, sheep, and dogs, and horses—and wolves. This recovery fairy-stories help us to make" ("Fairy," 146). The glimpses of the fantastic in the realm of Faery can help us see in a new light that which is common and part of our primary world. In fact, we even see ourselves more clearly in a way we might not otherwise see; we see the truth about ourselves in "dreadful recognition."

My goal in writing this book has been to suggest some of the underlying reality or truth into which Tolkien gives us so many glimpses. Of course one need not agree with Tolkien's understanding of what that truth is in order to enjoy and appreciate his work. Yet whether or not one agrees with Tolkien's views, it is tremendously helpful, and perhaps indispensable, to at least understand what those views are if one is to understand what Tolkien was seeking to accomplish.

Then again, it may just be—and this is my own view here—that part of the reason for the phenomenal success of *The Hobbit* and *The Lord of the Rings* is that the books really do speak truly. They have the ring of truth through all of their important particulars because they are drawn from deeper and more permanent, or fundamental, truths. Even readers who do not assent to those truth claims that are fundamental to Tolkien's work (when they are spelled out as they are in this book) may be subconsciously drawn to the work as being true.

Of course if Tolkien's theistic worldview is in any sense correct—if the Christian expression *is* the underlying truth about the world— then the most permanent and fundamental thing we might wish to talk about, even if the topic is uncomfortable to some, is Ilúvatar himself: Eru, the One, both the Author of Middle-earth and the Author*ity* over it. As Tolkien also wrote of myth and fairy, "Something really 'higher' is occasionally glimpsed in mythology: Divinity, the right to power (as distinct from its possession), the due of worship; in fact 'religion'" ("Fairy," 124). These words are certainly a true description of what may be found in Middle-earth. Amid the many glimpses of the corruption of the earthly (or Middle-earthly) desire for the power of domination are also numerous glimpses of real divinity, the right to power. If Tolkien is correct about the reality of divinity, then this existence and importance and power of the Creator, Ilúvatar, is a truth worth exploring if we wish to understand Tolkien's world. In particular, these strong theological underpinnings of Tolkien's work, especially with respect to salvation, raise one more question—a question that has been raised by many Tolkien scholars over the decades: Do *The Silmarillion*, *The Hobbit*, and *The Lord of the Rings* compose a Christian mythology?

My answer to this last question is a firm and unequivocal "no and yes."

I would feel guilty giving such an answer (or nonanswer) if it were not that Tolkien's own answer to this question would, I think, also be "no and yes," depending on how the question was meant and the context in which it was asked. Indeed, any easy answer to this question (whether "no" or "yes") is almost certain to be at least overly simplistic, if not altogether wrong, and would do injustice to Tolkien and his works.

Illustrating just how complex the question is, Paul Kerry devoted an entire book chapter to a historiographic analysis of how it has been answered over the past fifty years.[2] He illustrates that there have been not only different answers, but even entirely different frameworks or approaches to the question, including some framed by moral concerns, others by romanticism, some by the question of modernity, some by the question of free will, and some by the importance of Tolkien's sources. His essay contains well over two hundred footnotes! Kerry has done an excellent job, and I will not attempt to reproduce his work but will note only that the equivocation of my own answer gives credence to the complexity of the question. As with many such questions, perhaps the important starting point is understanding just what is meant by the asking.

Not a Christian Myth?

I will begin by answering, "No, *The Lord of the Rings* is not a Christian mythology." There are several reasons for giving this answer. A starting point, though by no means a convincing argument in and of itself, is what Tolkien wrote about his own works in his foreword to the second edition of *The Lord of the Rings*. Of the origins of *The Silmarillion*, he writes, "It was primarily linguistic in inspiration" (Foreword), and of *The Lord of the Rings*, he adds:

> The prime motive was the desire of a tale-teller to try his hand at a really long story that would hold the attention of readers, amuse them, delight them, and at times maybe excite them or deeply move them. . . .
> As for any inner meaning or "message," it has in the intention of the author none. It is neither allegorical nor topical. (Foreword)

In other words, if by saying that the *legendarium* was a Christian mythology one meant that the author had some hidden agenda leading him to write a cleverly disguised bit of Christian propaganda, or even a Christian allegory, then Tolkien offers a clear denial. The stories of Middle-earth are not written as Sunday school lessons or mere devotional guides (though I don't doubt that passages from the works have prompted important spiritual reflections among readers). In the stated intention of the author, they are, on the one hand, linguistic explorations and, on the other, stories intended to amuse, delight, and move the reader. Of course authors don't always know why they write something, and even when they do, they are not always fully forthcoming about those reasons. But given what I have read about Tolkien in various biographies and in other works exploring his academic career, and his relationships with the group of fellow writers known as the Inklings, I am strongly inclined to take his words at face value.

This is not to say that his goals of telling a good story, or his aversion to allegory, are somehow *un*-Christian. Christian theology says much about delight, and about the value of art and creativity, and about language. I merely observe that there is nothing *uniquely* Christian about either linguistic exploration or telling a good story. Remember that the question of this section is not whether the *legendarium* is an *anti*-Christian myth—it certainly is not—but simply whether it constitutes a Christian myth. And such a designation would seem to imply a much more religious motive than the motive given by the author.

Another reason to answer "no" (and a considerably more important one) is the sheer amount of source material that Tolkien drew upon that was pagan, or pre-Christian, especially Norse tales and mythologies. Tolkien was enamored by early Northern mythology, appreciating both its richness and depth. In "On Fairy-Stories" he writes: "I had no desire to have either dreams or adventures like Alice [in Wonderland], and the account of them merely amused me. I had very little desire to look for buried treasure or fight pirates, and Treasure Island left me cool. . . . But the land of Merlin and Arthur was better than these, and best of all the nameless North of Sigurd of the Völsungs, and the prince of all dragons" ("Fairy," 134–35). The nameless North of Sigurd is not a Christian world. Far from it.

And yet we see this inspiration of the nameless North in numerous places through Tolkien's Middle-earth writings. Even the names of the dwarves (and the wizard) in *The Hobbit* are borrowed from Snorri Sturluson's *Prose Edda*, an important piece of twelfth-century Icelandic writing. Recall also the tale of Éowyn, Théoden, and the people of Rohan discussed in chapter 2. As already noted, they are clearly modeled after the Anglo-Saxon people; their values, customs, and ceremonies are those of pagan Germanic peoples. We should also note that one of Tolkien's two elvish languages is modeled after Old Finnish, and the pagan Finnish work known as the *Kalevala* was important source material. In addition to the *Völsungasaga* and the *Kalevala*, other important pagan sources for Tolkien's work such as *The Saga of Hrolf Kraki* and other Eddic stories have been well documented, and we will not dwell on them here.

Even *The Silmarillion*, the most theological of Tolkien's Middle-earth writings, provides an example of pagan influence. Though Middle-earth is clearly a monotheistic world—Eru means "the One," and this Creator, also known as Ilúvatar, is a self-existent being upon whom all else depends for its existence—once we get beyond the short creation story of the *Ainulindalë*, we see much more of the Valar (the gods) than we do of Ilúvatar (the God). Thus despite the monotheistic beginnings, in many ways the remainder of the book reads more like Norse mythology than it does like the biblical book of Genesis. The point here is that the story—by which I now mean the plot, the characters, the setting, and the language of both *The Hobbit* and *The Lord of the Rings*—has far more *visible* elements that are identifiable with Norse and Germanic mythology than with the Christian myth.

One source worth exploring in a little detail is the poem *Beowulf* because it is so important to Tolkien and influences him considerably. While it would be very difficult to find in *The Hobbit* or *The Lord of the Rings* any overt traces of biblical characters or biblical narratives (such as one might expect to find in a "Christian myth"), it is nearly impossible *not* to see myriad traces of *Beowulf* throughout Tolkien's works. One of the most interesting aspects of this influence is the presence of the character Beowulf himself in Tolkien's Middle-earth—though his presence is not as obvious as finding Icelandic dwarf names borrowed from Eddic writings.

Tolkien scholar Michael Drout, in an essay titled "Tolkien and Beowulf: Medieval Materials for the Modern Audience," argues that, rather than inserting a simple and obvious Beowulf character in *The Lord of the Rings*, Tolkien instead gives a three-fold portrayal of Beowulf: "I think [Tolkien] took the attributes of Beowulf the character and spread them through Aragorn, Éomer and Théoden. Each character in *The Lord of the Rings* has some key similarities to Beowulf, but each is also different. Thus Tolkien can with a straight face deny the influence of Beowulf on *The Lord of the Rings* [and yet] at the same time make use of all his Anglo-Saxon source material—which includes *Beowulf*."[3] Why would Tolkien do this? One reason may have been that he felt he could "take the hints" from medieval sources but then "improve on them," as Tom Shippey argues Tolkien did with many other sources, especially the dragon Fafnir, slayed by the hero Sigurth, which (along with the *Beowulf* dragon) provides important inspiration for Smaug. Tolkien also thought, as Shippey argues, that he could rework and improve on many of the devices of Shakespeare's *Macbeth*, and thus he could at the same time both claim that he greatly disliked that particular play of Shakespeare and be "indebted" to it "again and again."[4] Mightn't this be what Tolkien was doing with the hero Beowulf?

But Drout gives another very plausible reason: "This technique of taking the attributes of medieval characters and dividing them among multiple *Lord of the Rings* characters is necessary, I believe, in order to make a modern audience accept the characters in *Lord of the Rings*. A true analog of Beowulf, with all of Beowulf's bravado, fearlessness, and legalistic perfection would be too scary to a Modern audience. We wouldn't trust him."[5] A different way to say this is that modern readers have a difficult time relating to an undiluted Beowulf as a hero. He is too foreign to the modern imagination, which is trained to be cynical, *especially* of its heroes. As Drout might have pointed out if he had written his essay in 2007 or later, when that modern cynicism is applied to Beowulf the hero, we get the Beowulf of the 2007 Robert Zemeckis film (played by Ray Winstone), who ends up being seduced by Grendel's mother (played by Angelina Jolie) and then conceives a child with her rather than slaying her. And, of course, he hides this little fact from everyone else. Unfortunately, the child turns out to be the dragon that returns to kill him. As Martha Monsson pointed out bluntly but astutely, the so-called heroes of Zemeckis's *Beowulf* "are lying scoundrels" while his "women are useless, helpless ornaments, unfit for anything except to be the property of a man." As a side note, she adds (also accurately), "It is safe to say there is very little in the movie a real Anglo-Saxon would recognize."[6] Tolkien, by contrast, though his heroes are by no means perfect, did not blindly apply cynicism to them all.[7] I think he did not want his readers to be cynical either—or, rather, did not want their cynicism to be born out. Yet he seemed to anticipate the ingrained cynicism of most of his readers, that they could not accept the Beowulf given to us by the medieval poem. Thus he instead gives us Beowulf in three smaller doses, in the persons of Aragorn, Éomer, and Théoden. That, I think, is Drout's point.

My own opinion is that Shippey and Drout are both correct about this; both of these motives were at work in Tolkien. Furthermore, I think that Tolkien had already done something with the hero Beowulf in *The Hobbit* similar to what Drout argues he did in *The Lord of the Rings*. In *The Hobbit*, three different characters each individually reveal one aspect of Beowulf in isolation from the other aspects. Beowulf's superhuman strength, his excessive pride, and his moral virtue—three traits Tolkien believed were centrally important traits of the medieval hero as represented in the poem that bears his name—are taken by Tolkien and given (one each) to three different characters in *The Hobbit*. In doing this, readers can see what that trait looks like in isolation from the other two. Yet Tolkien does this in a way that keeps each of the three characters still connected to the Beowulf of legend in some recognizable way.

The most obvious Beowulf character in *The Hobbit* is Beorn (though Beorn also draws inspiration from the Böthvarr Bjarki, or "Warlike Little-Bear," in the Old Norse *Saga of Hrolf Kraki*[8]). Beowulf possesses superhuman strength—the strength of thirty men, we are told by the poet—and is invincible in battle until he faces the dragon at the end of his life. Likewise, Beorn is a bear-man, whose superhuman strength and prowess are clearly visible at the Battle of Five Armies. "He came alone," the narrator tells us, "and in bear's shape; and he seemed to have grown almost to giant-size in his wrath. The roar of his voice was like drums and guns; and he tossed wolves and goblins from his path like straws and feathers

. . . so that nothing could withstand him, and no weapon seemed to bite upon him" (*Hobbit*, 349). We could add to this that Beorn's house closely resembles a medieval Germanic mead hall, down to the beverage served there; it is described as "a wide hall with a fire-place in the middle," where they "sat long at the table with their wooden drinking-bowls filled with mead" (*Hobbit*, 168, 177). Tolkien's sketch of Beorn's house (found in some editions of *The Hobbit*) could easily be a drawing of a mead hall and is highly similar to a mead-hall drawing in the 1927 book *Introduction to Old Norse* by Tolkien's colleague E.V. Gordon.⁹ Given Tolkien's philological interest, it is certainly significant that the name Beowulf is poetic for "bear"—though in a roundabout way: *Beowulf* is translated literally to "bee-wolf," but a wolf is another name for a thief, hence a bee-wolf is a bee-thief, or honey-thief, or bear. Now Beowulf is not actually a bear or even a were-bear, but his name at least gives that hint, possibly pointing to the source of his strength. Tolkien simply takes that a step further: Beorn, whose name also means "bear," really is a bear-man, or were-bear.

However Beorn is not by any means a complete Beowulf character. He has the superhuman were-bear character and strength of Beowulf, but he has neither Beowulf's concern for moral virtue nor his excessive pride. Consider first the issue of excessive pride. Tolkien's understanding of the work of the *Beowulf* poet is important in grasping his threefold portrayal of the Beowulf hero. In his essay "The Homecoming of Beorhtnoth Beorhtelm's Son," Tolkien explains that Beowulf, according to the poet who told the tale, is too concerned with his own glory. While this is excusable in his fight against Grendel, because at the time Beowulf has no people of his own to protect, it is not excusable in his fight against the dragon when at that time he is a king with responsibility to protect his people. His "excess persists," Tolkien argues. "He will not deign to lead a force against the dragon, as wisdom might direct even a hero to do; for, as he explains in a long 'vaunt,' his many victories have relieved him of fear." As a result, "the people lose their king disastrously." As Tolkien concludes, "In *Beowulf* we have only a legend of 'excess' in a chief" ("Homecoming," 23). Whether one agrees that Beowulf was guilty of excessive pride, the point here is that Tolkien thought so, and this is a significant aspect in his understanding of the poem and its hero. A complete Beowulf character or analog, as Tolkien understood him, would have this excessive pride.

Having said that, we must note that Beowulf also shows concern for moral virtue in many other instances, such as in his refusal to take unfair advantage in a fight over Grendel or in his refusal to usurp the throne of the Geats from his younger and weaker cousin Heardred after King Hygelac is killed in battle. In the hero Beorn, by contrast, neither the characteristic of excessive pride nor that of moral virtue is made evident—or at least they are not shown to be important traits in the story (unlike in the tale of *Beowulf*). Beorn doesn't appear at all concerned with what others think of him. (In fact, he doesn't have much contact with the human race at all.) He isn't concerned with receiving glory. He also isn't particularly concerned with rules for moral conduct. Although he is certainly brave and fierce, Beorn is something of a morally neutral character, neither good nor evil. His murder of a goblin prisoner whose head he then sticks on his gate is ruthless and gruesome. Shippey calls Beorn "insufficiently socialized," writing that he "comes from the heart of the ancient world that existed before fairy-tale, a merciless world without a Geneva Convention."[10]

And then we have Thorin Oakenshield, who by contrast seems to represent all of Beowulf's pride, without either his moral virtue or his superhuman strength. Thorin is perfectly willing to break his bargain with Bard and the elvenking and is certainly overcome at the end of the tale with excessive greed and pride, seemingly untempered by virtue. If, after considering Beorn, one thinks it a stretch to also associate Thorin with Beowulf, consider the numerous parallels between the characters and their tales. Like Beowulf, Thorin is the descendant of the great heroes of old and yet has been dispossessed of his kingdom. Of course both Beowulf and Thorin lead a group of fourteen companions (if you count Gandalf) on a quest in which they face several monsters, culminating with the dragon who is woken by a thief and enraged. After their respective dragons are slain, both Thorin and Beowulf die and are buried with their great swords and with treasures taken from the worm's hoard. Thus the similarity of plot elements between *The Hobbit* and *Beowulf* also ties together Thorin and Beowulf. Indeed, the plot at least would tie Beowulf more closely to Thorin than to Beorn.

Who, then, represents the third aspect of Beowulf in this three-fold portrayal, the moral virtue without either the excessive pride or the strength? None other than the hero: Bilbo Baggins the hobbit. Bilbo lacks Beowulf's superhuman strength (although he can be said to have gained, through the Ring, some measure of superhuman abilities). He certainly is not guilty (as Thorin is) of excessive pride. Yet he is clearly the hero who most displays moral virtue. Bilbo's virtue even includes the same sense of fairness that prevents Beowulf from using a sword to slay the unarmed Grendel, for Bilbo also decides that it would not be a fair fight for him to slay the unarmed Gollum. As for other explicit connections between Bilbo and Beowulf (in addition to the alliteration of their names), consider that at the end of the quest it is Bilbo, and not Thorin, who is the real leader of the company. It is also Bilbo, and not Thorin, who aids Bard in slaying the dragon. Most importantly though—and this may have been Tolkien's philological hint—Bilbo is himself a bee-thief like Beowulf, though with a little twist typical of many of Tolkien's philological jokes. Rather than being a thief *of* bees as Beowulf the bear is, Bilbo is a thief (a burglar to be exact) who *is* a bee (he carries a "Sting," which is the name of his sword). Tolkien seems to be drawing on this threefold portrayal of Beowulf in *The Hobbit* to suggest that real heroism is not demonstrated by strength or by pride, but by virtue. If this was his conscious intent, he accomplishes it by drawing on a fundamentally Germanic source.

The point here in looking at Tolkien's primary sources is not that the poem *Beowulf* is pagan (though many of the other important Norse, Finnish, and Germanic sources were) or anti-Christian. Indeed, the version of the poem that has survived for us today was told (or *re*told) by a poet who was likely a Christian. It was not even written in Old Norse but in Old English. But in its roots it is a pre-Christian tale rich in its Norse-ness, its heroes are Norse, and it was only vaguely Christianized by the English poet who passed it on to us. If it is at all a Christian poem, it is a Christian poem about a pre-Christian time. (We will return to this later in this chapter.) And it is certainly *not* the Bible. If Tolkien was giving us a Christian myth, why would *Beowulf* rather than the Bible provide such central source material?

This, in turn, raises another issue that may be even more important. In answering the question of whether the Middle-earth mythology is Christian, we also must recognize that there are almost no explicit references to religion anywhere in *The Lord of the Rings* or *The Hobbit*. Though these tales contain veiled references to a higher power—many of which have been discussed earlier—there are very few examples of anything resembling a religious practice and no references to Ilúvatar or any particular monotheistic divinity. (There are several scattered references to the Valar, but since they function in a literary way more like pagan gods, these references can be seen as strengthening the point that Tolkien's myth is not Christian.)

The only example of a recognizable religious practice in *The Hobbit* or *The Lord of the Rings* that I would consider obvious is when Faramir and his men face west in a moment of silence before their meals. Faramir explains the practice to Frodo, saying, "We look towards Númenor that was, and beyond to Elvenhome that is, and to that which is beyond Elvenhome and will ever be" (IV/v). This practice strongly echoes Christian prayer, especially the prayer known as the "Gloria Patri," which ends referencing God the Creator as the one "who was and who is and who ever shall be." But although Faramir's phrase "that which . . . will ever be" certainly brings to mind the divine with phrasing familiar to Christian prayer, there is no explanation beyond that. Only readers familiar with *The Silmarillion* would recognize this last phrase as a reference to Ilúvatar.

Other examples are even less obvious. One could certainly make many connections between the *lembas* of the elves and the bread of Holy Communion—a sacrament that Tolkien, as a Roman Catholic, celebrated his entire life. Bradley Birzer has noted, "Indeed, the Elven *lembas* arguably serves as Tolkien's most explicit symbol of Christianity."[11] But while Birzer and others have done an excellent job exploring this symbolism, and I have no doubt that it was intentional on Tolkien's part, it is nonetheless a symbol easy to miss, in large part because there is nothing resembling a religious ceremony each time the wafer is consumed.

We could also note that in his dialogue with Gandalf and Frodo, after he was discovered listening at the window, Sam says both "Lor bless you, Mr. Gandalf, sir!" and, a short time later, "Lor bless me" (I/ii). "Lor," of course, is short for "Lord," which is a reference to the divine, and the theistic form of blessing is certainly an example of religious practice. But it is difficult to make too much of such a minor practice that is not repeated elsewhere and has nothing else attached to it. Certainly these two offhand references to the "Lor[d]" don't suffice to turn the story into a Christian story.

Gandalf's chastising of Denethor when the Steward attempts to take his own life is more significant as a reference to religion: "Authority is not given to you, Steward of Gondor, to order the hour of your death. And only the heathen kings, under the domination of the Dark Power, did thus" (V/vii). Indeed, this example rightly belongs in a chapter defending a premise that *The Lord of the Rings* is a Christian work, or at least an explicitly theistic one. It is certainly a reference to the existence of a greater moral authority, and thus is another good example of Tolkien's portrayal of morality as being rooted in real objective standards and not just personal or cultural opinions. Gandalf believes that even the highest authority of a great kingdom must yield to objective moral standards. It is also a hint at one of the main topics of this chapter: there is a war with two opposing sides, one being Ilúvatar, the authority in whom is rooted objective moral standards, and the other being the Dark Lord, who is mentioned by Gandalf in this passage. (Interestingly, the Dark Lord is most likely a reference not to Sauron, but to Morgoth, whom Sauron serves.) Like the words of Gandalf to the Balrog discussed earlier, these words of Gandalf put the wars of Middle-earth—and more importantly, the decisions of individuals—into a decidedly religious context. But of course none of this is in any way overt or explicit. If it is religious and theistic, it is so only in a very veiled way.

The most important aspect of this passage to consider and explain may simply be Gandalf's use of the word *heathen*. The word is an explicitly religious term. The *Oxford English Dictionary* (OED) defines the noun *heathen* as "one who holds a religious belief which is neither Christian, Jewish, nor Muslim" and dates the earliest use of the term to an Old English Christian text from around AD 1000, where it would have had an even narrower meaning: "one who is not a Christian." Gandalf uses the adjectival form, which keeps the same meaning in the OED: "of an individual or people: holding religious beliefs of a sort that are considered unenlightened, now esp. ones of a primitive or polytheistic nature; spec. not of the Christian,

Jewish, or Muslim faiths." At face value, then, Gandalf is rebuking Denethor for not holding to Christian religious practice, which of course implies the norm of those practices (at least within Gondor). It is possible that Tolkien simply missed this one-time word usage when he sought to cut out of his work any references to religious practice (a point to which we shall soon return). It may also be that he was using the word with a different meaning that would draw more on its roots in Old English. The root of *heathen* is *heath*, and the accepted meaning of *heathen* (as given by the *OED*) is derived from a more literal meaning: one who is from the heath rather than from the city—that is, an uneducated peasant. But the reference to the Dark Lord probably suggests something nearer to the religious meaning. Yet even if the religious meaning was the one intended, and it was left in the text intentionally, it is still only a small and passing reference to religious practice.

The Missing Piece

The vague and passing references to religion mentioned above might—if there were more of them and if Tolkien had not drawn so heavily on pagan literary sources—be taken as evidence of the Christian nature of Tolkien's work. Tolkien himself, at one point, even acknowledges that his works contain more religious aspects and references to God than many readers seem to notice. Referring to invocations of the divine uttered by Sam and Frodo, he writes, "These and other references to religion in *The Lord of the Rings* are frequently overlooked."[12]

But one overarching reason to say "no" to categorizing the Middle-earth mythology as Christian still remains, and it would apply even if we included the far more theological work, *The Silmarillion*, along with *The Lord of the Rings* and the posthumously published Histories. This last reason is both the simplest and the most profound: there is no Christ in these stories! That is, there is no presence of the Creator, Eru Ilúvatar, as an incarnate being within his creation. Christianity rests fundamentally on a set of historical events: the birth, life, death, and especially the resurrection of the first-century Jew named Jesus, believed by Christians to be the eternal Creator

216

God having taken on physical human form as the Messiah long promised by the Jewish prophets. (The word *Christ*, used as a title for Jesus and from which we get the term *Christian*, is just the Greek translation for the Hebrew word *messiah*.) According to Tolkien's Christian faith, at a real moment in the earth's history, God the Son was incarnate; he became a man and lived on the earth. As is written about Jesus in the Gospel of John: "He was in the world, and the world was made by him, and the world knew him not. . . . And the Word was made flesh, and dwelt among us" (John 1:10, 14a).

Paul the apostle, the first international missionary of Christianity in its infancy, also understood clearly the significance of the historical incarnation and resurrection when he wrote:

> For I delivered unto you first of all, which I also received: how that Christ died for our sins, according to the scriptures: And that he was buried, and that he rose again the third day, according to the scriptures: And that he was seen by Cephas; and after that by the eleven. Then was he seen by more than five hundred brethren at once. . . .
>
> And if Christ be not risen again, then is our preaching vain, and your faith is also vain. . . . And if Christ be not risen again, your faith is vain, for you are yet in your sins. (1 Cor. 15:3–6a, 14, 17)

Paul's use of the phrase "first of all" suggests the primary importance of these events, and his appeal to eyewitnesses adds to his claim for their historical validity. His later argument about the vanity of Christian faith if the events of Christ's life—especially the historical resurrection—are not true drives home his point. In short, the story of Christ may be a beautiful story, but in the Christian understanding it won't bring salvation unless it really happened as a historical event: unless God the Creator entered his creation at a particular moment in its history. Faith in this story, if it is not historically true, is futile and worthless. According to Paul, this historicity is of *first importance* to Christianity.

Tolkien also understood the importance to Christianity of the incarnation as a real historical event, in addition to its status as a powerful myth. He writes, toward the end of "On Fairy-Stories":

> But this [gospel] story has entered History and the primary world; the desire and aspiration of sub-creation has been raised to the fulfillment

217

of Creation. The Birth of Christ is the eucatastrophe of Man's history. The Resurrection is the eucatastrophe of the story of the Incarnation. This story begins and ends in joy. It has pre-eminently the "inner consistency of reality." There is no tale ever told that men would rather find was true, and none which so many sceptical men have accepted as true on its own merits. ("Fairy," 156)

Emphasizing the reality of the incarnation, Tolkien uses the term *history* twice, and also twice uses the word *true* to refer to the actuality of the events of the gospel story within history. Even the term *eucatastrophe*, which Tolkien coined, implies a real event—that is to say, an event with a real, sudden, and dramatic impact: literally, a *good catastrophe*. Thus, the power of the gospel story, which Tolkien describes earlier in that paragraph as containing "a fairy-story of a larger kind which embraces all the essence of fairy-stories," goes beyond words to the underlying truth, which in this case is the reality of history. The story itself is beautiful, containing "many marvels— peculiarly artistic, beautiful, and moving: 'mythical' in their perfect self-contained significance" ("Fairy," 156). However, the chief part of the power and beauty of that story, the ultimate "fulfillment" of the creative art at work in story itself, comes from the fact that this story has entered the history of the primary world.

It is interesting to note here that Tolkien doesn't say the story originated in history, or that it describes history, but rather that it *entered* history, implying that the story preexisted history. As he writes in the next paragraph, "This story is supreme; and it is true. Legend and History have met and fused" ("Fairy," 157). If Tolkien is correct, then the gospel story is the truth by which all story truths are measured. But no such gospel is present in *The Lord of the Rings* or even in *The Silmarillion*: the story that Tolkien believes has entered the earth's history has not entered the history of his Middle-earth. Yet if the historical presence of that story is critical to the Christian mythology—as Tolkien believed it was—and if it doesn't exist in Tolkien's mythology, then in what sense can Tolkien's mythology be Christian?

Now, one might claim that in fact there are Christ-figures in Middle-earth. If by "Christ-figure" one is referring to characters who imitate Christ in significant ways—by living out the definition

218

of Christian charity; by embodying mercy, truth, wisdom, humility, and faith; and more specifically by giving their lives for the sake of others—then it is easy to agree with this statement: there are characters in Tolkien's writing who are Christlike. Indeed, there are numerous such figures. Gandalf is wise and merciful, committed to truth, and full of faith. At Khazad-dûm, he sacrifices his life for his companions. In this way he is a "Christ-figure." Of greatest importance, he not only dies but is resurrected, passing from death back into life. Aragorn also makes Christlike sacrifices; though his heart longs to go to Minas Tirith, where he might take up the throne of Gondor and earn the right to wed Arwen, he instead sacrifices his goals and ambitions for the sake of the hobbits Merry and Pippin. Like Christ, Aragorn also is a healer, calling back Éowyn even from death, and Faramir and Merry as well, and later on, Frodo and Sam. And he too experiences a sort of resurrection in entering the Paths of the Dead and coming out again into life. It is also interesting to compare what Aragorn accomplished at the Paths of the Dead with the apostle Paul's description of Christ; in Ephesians 4:8–10, Christ is desribed as descending from heaven into the depths of the earth and rescuing the captives there—usually understood to mean rescuing the spirits of the dead from their torment in hell.

Likewise, Frodo, when he takes upon himself the Quest to Mount Doom, is offering his life in Christlike sacrifice for the sake of all the free peoples of Middle-earth. Frodo could certainly be seen as fitting the prophet Isaiah's depiction of the promised Christ: "There is no beauty in him, nor comeliness: and we have seen him, and there was no sightliness, that we should be desirous of him" (Isa. 53:2). Which is to say that Frodo had no great physical stature that would have made him one of the great of Middle-earth. His experience at the Tower of Cirith Ungol furthers this image. Richard Purtill points out, "His physical sufferings parallel those of Christ: he is imprisoned, stripped of his garments, mocked, and whipped."[13] And though he does not actually die a physical death and return to life, he is thrice brought back from the *verge* of death: once from the blade of the Nazgûl when he was well on his way to becoming a wraith, once from the sting of Shelob when even Sam had given him up for dead, and once by Aragorn at the end of the Quest. In this last instance we read that he went "to the very brink of death ere

[Aragorn] recalled [him]" (VI/iv). At the conclusion of the trilogy, we see just how real his sacrifice is, for like Christ he always carries the scars of his death wounds (on his hand!) and is never able to really return to his life again.

Even Boromir, in the final moments of his life, is a sort of Christ-figure in that he gives up his life defending the hobbits. Yet not one of these characters is Christ, for not one of them is the incarnate God, and neither is any one of them perfect. Christ is the ultimate fulfill-ment and embodiment, in both the mythic sense and the primary historical sense, of the completeness of God's love, truth, wisdom, mercy, and, ultimately, self-sacrificial giving. He is the perfect sacrifice given for the sins of all mankind. That element is left out of Tolkien's Middle-earth. Gandalf comes the closest to this, but though he is a Maia (or "incarnate angel," as Tolkien ventured to write in a letter) who "passes the test, on a moral plane anyway (he makes mistakes of judgement)" (*Letters*, 202), he is not Ilúvatar incarnate. Though he loves words and takes on flesh, he is not the Word made flesh. And even on the moral plane, though he may pass the ultimate test of refusing the Ring—a test the wizard Saruman fails—Gandalf may have failed other, smaller moral tests, as we discussed in the first chapter. Certainly Gandalf shows hints of pride and self-satisfaction, as noted in *The Hobbit*: "The wizard, to tell the truth, never minded explaining his cleverness more than once" (*Hobbit*, 141). The Chris-tian understanding of the importance of the cross depends both on Jesus's divinity—that he is the Creator and not a created being, and in some mysterious way the fullness of his divinity continues to be in his fully human and incarnate form—and on his sinless perfection.

In fact, to deal with these sacrifices within Tolkien's story by labeling the characters involved as "Christ-figures," and then subse-quently dismissing them as if that "Christ-figure" label says all that needs to be said, diminishes both their sacrifices and the sacrifice of the real Christ. (Such a simplifying label also gets at why Tolkien disliked allegory and was wary of explicit religion in fairy tale and myth.) Jonathan Evans explained well one of the shortcomings of such oversimplifications.

> The idea of symbolic sacrificial death to save someone or everyone is too universally encountered to permit a narrow definition of one

of them as a pattern for all of them. Not that the pattern isn't there: but the way specific instances of this motif are related is probably not one of a simple transference of the pattern from one to another. Like triads, redemption through death and resurrection is a pattern of meaning so deeply inscribed into the nature of things that they will appear in many narratives otherwise unconnected in the literature and mythology of many cultures in many times and places.[14]

These examples of Christlikeness may point back to a Christ, but to find that Christ we must look into the primary world, and into Tolkien's Christian (and specifically Catholic) faith, for we will not find that Christ in Middle-earth.

So if we return to my discussion of salvation in chapter 8, we realize that something is missing there too. As I claimed, Tolkien certainly uses Christian *imagery* of salvation—though he does so by relying on words like *cured* rather than *saved*—and, like the Christian Gospel writers, even ties the spiritual notion of salvation to repentance, especially in the case of Boromir. But the *means* of salvation is never spelled out. In the Christian faith, one is saved through faith in Jesus Christ: faith that he died on a cross to pay the penalty for sin and that he was raised again from the dead. That is, salvation is not earned by anything the individual does, but rather it comes by God's grace, which is worked out through the death (a real, physical death, occurring within human history) and resurrection of the Christ; Jesus had to die a real death in order to pay for our sins, and in his rising from the dead, death itself is conquered. But this saving faith (or belief) in the Christ cannot be at work in the world of Middle-earth because there is no Christ in Middle-earth in which to have faith! And since this incarnation of the Creator within his creation is so important to Christianity, as is his sacrificial death to pay for our sins, it must be argued that any mythology that does not include the death and resurrection of a Christ is therefore not finally a "Christian mythology."

Sorrow and Loss

This last point connects to another aspect of Tolkien's Middle-earth that I have always found very curious. It is hard to read either *The*

Silmarillion or *The Lord of the Rings* and not come away with a profound sense of sorrow and loss. Galadriel captures this pathos early on in the trilogy when she welcomes the Fellowship to Lothlórien with the strangely solemn comment, "For ere the fall of Nargothrond or Gondolin I passed over the mountains, and together through ages of the world we have fought the long defeat" (II/viii). This sense of sorrow abounds wherever the reader turns. Consider, for example, our last encounter with the Ents when Treebeard speaks with Aragorn: "Treebeard's face became sad. 'Forests may grow,' he said. 'Woods may spread. But not Ents. There are no Entings.'" And a short time later, saying farewell to Celeborn and Galadriel, he adds: "It is sad that we should meet only thus at the ending. For the world is changing: I feel it in the water, I feel it in the earth, and I smell it in the air. I do not think we shall meet again" (VI/vi). This is a clear picture of loss: no Entwives, no Entings, no future. Tolkien leaves the reader with the knowledge that the Ents are doomed to disappear from Middle-earth, and with them something good and wonderful is forever lost.

Likewise, we also learn from Celeborn that his own doom is to be separated from Galadriel, while Galadriel's doom is to see—with the destruction of the One Ring—the subsequent loss of all that she has worked for in Lothlórien. Nor are these isolated examples. Rather, this tone pervades the story. There is also the grievous parting of Arwen from Elrond, her father: "None saw her last meeting with Elrond her father, for they went up into the hills and there spoke long together, and bitter was their parting that should endure beyond the ends of the world" (VI/vi). Galadriel, Elrond, and Gandalf also depart from Middle-earth forever, leaving it a lesser place. Théoden asks Gandalf, "For however the fortune of war shall go, may it not so end that much that was fair and wonderful shall pass for ever out of Middle-earth?" To which Gandalf replies: "The evil of Sauron cannot be wholly cured, nor made as if it had not been. But to such days we are doomed" (III/viii).

We might sum up much of this sadness simply by pointing out that *The Lord of the Rings* does not end with the victory celebration and wedding at the Field of Cormallen (though these joyous occasions are described in brief) but with the parting at the Grey Havens. Before we even reach that parting, we read that "Frodo dropped quietly out of all the doings of the Shire, and Sam was pained to notice how little honour he had in his own country" (VI/ix). For in the end, Frodo is "too deeply hurt"; he "tried to save the Shire," and it is saved, but not for him. He left "filled with a sadness that was yet blessed and without bitterness" (VI/ix).

It is not that *The Lord of the Rings* is all sadness. There are frequent glimpses of joy. But the joy is a distant, veiled joy, whose source we are not given to see clearly. It is like the passage, discussed earlier, when Sam sees the star from the Land of Shadow: "And hope returned to him. For like a shaft, clear and cold, the thought pierced him that in the end the Shadow was only a small and passing thing: there was light and high beauty for ever beyond its reach." And yet the next moment he is back in Mordor, and the suffering resumes, and light and high beauty are lost and never explained.

The Silmarillion is an even more deeply sorrowful piece. It is centered on the curse of Fëanor and the evil that arises because of it, yet all of Middle-earth is caught in that web of deceit and destruction. Every major elven kingdom fails and falls: Hithlum, Lothlann, Nargothrond, Doriath, and lastly, Gondolin. Likewise, nearly all of the great elven lords are killed: not only the sons of Fëanor but also Fingolfin, Finrod, Turgon, Thingol, and many others. The tales of Húrin and his son Túrin are especially tragic. In the version of the tale published in *The Silmarillion* and titled simply "Of Túrin Turambar," the narration notes, with profound understatement, "It is called the Tale of Grief, for it is sorrowful" (*Silm*, 199). To the extent that Tolkien's longer and fuller version of the tale, called *The Children of Húrin* and published in 2007, reveals more of the characters, including their strengths, and hopes, and joys, and their great love for each other, the result is that it also delves even more deeply into the sorrow and loss.

Even the victory of the Valar over Morgoth at the end of the *Quenta Silmarillion* brings little joy. Two of the three Silmarils are lost, and a dark shadow is cast by the last evil act of Fëanor's sons, who hold to their father's wicked oath and slay the guards in the camp of Eönwë, Manwë's herald, in a final effort to possess the jewels. Thus, of Manwë's victorious forces returning to Valinor, we read: "Their joy in victory was diminished, for they returned without the Silmarils from Morgoth's crown, and they knew that those jewels

223

could not be found or brought together again unless the world be broken and remade" (*Silm*, 254).

The depths of sorrow, even in victory, are expressed in the final lines of the *Quenta Silmarillion*: "Yet the lies that Melkor, the mighty and accursed, Morgoth Bauglir, the Power of Terror and of Hate, sowed in the hearts of Elves and Men are a seed that does not die and cannot be destroyed; and ever and anon it sprouts anew, and will bear dark fruit even unto the latest days" (*Silm*, 255). The sadness of this ending should not come as a surprise, though. That *The Silmarillion* (as well as *The Lord of the Rings*) will be so filled with sorrow is foretold early in the *Ainulindalë* in a description of the battle being waged between the Theme of Ilúvatar and that of Melkor. Ilúvatar's Theme, we are told, is "deep and wide and beautiful, but slow and *blended with an immeasurable sorrow*, from which its beauty chiefly came" (*Silm*, 16–17, emphasis added). The sorrow in these books truly is immeasurable!

And yet, as the author claims, there is beauty in it. There is tragedy in the tale of Húrin, but there is great joy also when Húrin finally comes before the throne of Melian and by her power is released from the lies of Morgoth and is his thrall no longer. There is great beauty in the forgiveness Fingon offers Maedhros, and in his memory of their former friendship, which prompts him to heal the feud that divides their people. There is beauty in the valor of Fingolfin, even when he falls crushed beneath the left foot of Morgoth. There is beauty in the self-sacrificing loyalty of Finrod to Beren. Indeed, the examples of beauty are made all the more poignant because they are surrounded by such tragedy. It is not idly that Tolkien begins the tale of Beren and Lúthien with these words: "Among the tales of *sorrow and of ruin* that come down to us from the darkness of those days there are yet some in which *amid weeping there is joy* and under the shadow of death light that endures" (*Silm*, 162, emphasis added).

As Tolkien suggests in the *Ainulindalë*, for many of his readers the beauty of the stories comes from their sorrow. But where does this sorrow come from? The sadness of *The Silmarillion* and *The Lord of the Rings*—and even of *The Hobbit*, which ends with the deaths of Thorin, Fili, and Kili—can be seen in part as echoing the sadness of Norse mythology that Tolkien found so moving. Here the gods themselves are doomed to disaster, and with them is doomed all the earth. Glory is not to be found in the hope of the hero, or in the hero's final victory, but rather in the hero's willingness to continue to fight the battle even though he knows he is fated to die in the end. There is something of this type of sorrow present.

There is perhaps even more of the sorrow of the Old Testament (at least as it is understood from a Christian perspective), full as it is of stories of betrayal, of broken families, and of ruin. Its primary subject is the people of Israel. The stories of Abraham, Isaac, and especially Jacob, the patriarchs of Israel, are stories of deception, loss, and unfilled promises. None of them makes a permanent home in the promised land. Brothers turn on their brothers seeking to kill them or sell them into captivity, uncles mistreat and exploit their nephews and daughters, and fathers curse their own sons.

And it doesn't get any happier in the days of the judges or the kings, especially in the days of the kings after David. Most of the heroes of faith of the Old Testament die without seeing their hope fulfilled. There is ever a sense that they are strangers in the world. As the author of the New Testament book of Hebrews writes of these heroes: "All these died according to faith, not having received the promises, but beholding them afar off, and saluting them, and confessing that they are pilgrims and strangers on the earth. . . . And all these, being approved by the testimony of faith, received not the promise" (Heb. 11:13, 39). As for the nation of Israel itself, it goes from captivity to captivity: from slavery in Egypt to slavery in Babylon, with numerous captivities in between, such as the frequent periods of subjugation to the Philistines during the time of the judges and the reign of King Saul. In all of the centuries of Israel's history recounted in the Old Testament books of Judges, Samuel, Kings, and Chronicles, there are only a few brief lifetimes of glory and victory, such as during the reigns of King David and King Solomon. Even the years of David's reign have significant tragedies, including the rebellion and subsequent death of David's own son Absalom. The Old Testament is full of sorrow that is not unlike the sorrow of many Norse and Germanic legends, such as the poem *Beowulf*, which ends with its hero dead and his nation destined to come to an end.

Or perhaps the two sorrows go hand in hand. In both cases it may be the case that the pervasive sadness comes from the absence of Christ and thus an absence of a means for redemption and salvation;

there is, in the body of Tolkien's Middle-earth writing, the knowledge that such redemption is necessary—that is, there is an understanding that the Christian hope lies in a historical incarnation of the Creator—but no such Christ has come to Middle-earth.

Shippey has mentioned this pervasive sense of sadness both in his writings on Tolkien and in lectures. I asked him what he made of it. His reply is very interesting and it illuminates some of what I have just written. His sense is that both Tolkien and his good friend C. S. Lewis were drawn to the stark beauty of early Germanic paganism but were also concerned with the way that England was "slumping back" toward this paganism. They saw England moving away from the specifics of Christianity toward a vague deism, and as devout Christians they worried about that move. What they desired, according to Shippey, was a sort of mediation. They wanted to show the beauty and the splinter of truth in paganism and its literature, without adopting its beliefs. They wanted to present the people of the pagan Germanic North as doing the best they could under the circumstances, but also to show that without the revelation of Christianity they couldn't help but be sad. Thus, these people were not to be blamed but rather to be pitied; there is no happy ending without divine intervention. "A point I would make at length if I ever had to comment on the subject is how horrible paganism was in reality," Shippey adds, before concluding: "Tolkien occasionally showed signs of impatience with sentimental neo-paganism of the kind now thoroughly familiar. I think he wondered what it would have been like for a decent honest sort of man, an Englishman in fact, indeed someone like him, living in a pagan world before Christ. Sad, that's the word!"[15]

Returning to the pre-Christian sorrow of the Old Testament, we see that the Old Testament holds the *promise* of the coming Messiah, but none of these promises are yet fulfilled; they are still centuries away when the Old Testament ends. What separates the New Testament from the Old? In the Christian understanding, it is fundamentally this: the coming of the Messiah; the incarnation of God the Son; the entering of the Creator into his creation; the fulfillment of the plan of salvation, so that salvation is not merely a word or idea or plan but an actuality. That is also what separates a Christian understanding from the mythology of Middle-earth. To quote once again from Richard Purtill: "If *The Silmarillion* seems to

226

end on a somewhat dark and despairing note, it is because Tolkien has not allowed himself to introduce any hint of the true Hope of the World. Partly, this is his personal reticence; partly it is his artistic purpose. But the Christian hope is in Tolkien's own heart and is hidden in the heart of his work."[16]

A Christian Myth?

To some it might seem odd, after the declarations of the past few paragraphs, to turn around and suggest that Tolkien's Middle-earth mythology is, after all, a Christian mythology. And yet, just as there are important reasons for arguing that it is not, there are other significant ways in which the *legendarium* most certainly is a Christian myth and should be viewed as such. It could be argued that even its most hobbicentric parts, *The Hobbit* and *The Lord of the Rings*, are best seen in the light of a distinctly Christian outlook.

To understand this answer, we should again begin with Tolkien's own words, once more from a letter written in 1953.

> *The Lord of the Rings* is of course a fundamentally religious and Catholic work; unconsciously so at first, but consciously in the revision. That is why I have not put in, or have cut out, practically all references to anything like "religion," to cults or practices, in the imaginary world. For the religious element is absorbed into the story and the symbolism. However that is very clumsily put, and sounds more self-important than I feel. For as a matter of fact, I have consciously planned very little; and should chiefly be grateful for having been brought up (since I was eight) in a Faith that has nourished me and taught me all the little that I know. (*Letters*, 172)

Tolkien is very clear in this letter regarding his own opinion of his works: his trilogy is not merely peripherally Christian but *fundamentally* so. Not only fundamentally so but *consciously* so. Indeed, this seems so obvious to the author that he can only say "of course" to the suggestion. All that he knows—and thus all that he is able to put into his stories—has been nourished by his Christian faith.

In explaining this, Tolkien also answers a question we posed earlier: Why are the references to the divine so vague and veiled in *The*

Lord of the Rings? We now see part of the answer. It is not, according to Tolkien, because the work is not Christian but rather because the work is so *thoroughly* Christian. Tolkien would rather have readers moved by the deep and profound Christian nature of his writing than distracted by the trappings of religious practices, especially if those practices come with negative connotations or are simply associated with one narrow cultural expression of Christianity. Furthermore, having visible elements of the religious *practices* of our world appear in Middle-earth would provide too great a temptation to view the work as allegory. Many readers start chasing exact parallels: *this* equals *this*, and *that* equals *that*. They proceed in an allegory as if the story can be reduced to mathematical equations rather than appreciating what is actually there. And then there are other readers—and I include myself in this second category—who, like Tolkien, are suspicious of overt allegory. It makes a work feel more like a sermon than a story, more like a secret code to be deciphered than a work of art. If I sniff any sort of clumsy and obvious allegory, I usually quit reading. In either case, allegory would interfere with the deeper and more profound Christian themes by trivializing them.

By contrast, the fabric of reality is far more complex, far richer and more wonderful than a formulaic representation of one idea by a single neatly packaged, analogous narrative symbol. Tolkien, therefore, instead of letting the Christian *element* remain on the surface, where it might easily be dismissed with little thought—by those who agree with it as well as by those who disagree—lets his faith be *absorbed* into the story and the symbolism, largely unconsciously. It is there to be pondered, thought about, and reflected on, to bring new insights with each subsequent reading. In fact, the most conscious thing he does is to remove the explicit religion. But he does this, it is very important to note, not because he wants to make the work less Christian, but rather (according to his letter) because he wants it to be fundamentally more Christian.

It is also worth noting that, while Tolkien's use of pagan and pre-Christian literary source material is undeniable, it is a mistake to *over*emphasize the importance and influence of that material to the exclusion of other sources. For example, we have already mentioned ways that Tolkien drew upon themes and events in various Shakespearean plays, especially *Macbeth*. Even more significant perhaps,

228

but often overlooked, are ways that Tolkien was inspired by and drew upon (consciously or not) nineteenth- and early twentieth-century romance and fantasy literature, especially that of Samuel Crockett and George Macdonald (whose Christian faith played an important role in his fairy tales and fantasy novels). Douglas Anderson, in his notes in *The Annotated Hobbit*, provides an example of a clear connection between a scene in Crockett's 1899 novel *The Black Douglas* and a passage in the chapter "Out of the Frying-Pan into the Fire" in *The Hobbit*.[17] Jared Lobdell's treatment of this topic in his book *The Rise of Tolkienian Fantasy* provides an intriguing look into these and other sources, arguing that Tolkien was as much or more inspired, at least in narrative structure, by these works as by pagan myths.[18]

We will return shortly to both the presence of pagan influences and the (apparent) lack of overt religion in the stories of the Third Age of Middle-earth, but since Tolkien himself spoke of his Catholic Christianity as being "absorbed into the story," we should first explore in what ways it was absorbed and just what that means. One explanation of what is meant by "absorbed" is simple and can be seen in all the ways we have been discussing in this book: in the Christian understanding of objective morality and moral responsibility (which is certainly present in other religions but not in secular modernism); in the Christian importance of hope; in ideas of human worth, nobility, and purpose having their source in a divine Creator; in Christian notions of stewardship; in the understanding of human creativity as also having its source in a Creator (another uniquely Judeo-Christian idea in sharp contrast with modern naturalism that views humans as complex biochemical computers);[19] in Christian notions of salvation (as a spiritual and not merely physical state or event); in the acknowledgment of the reality of the spiritual plane as well as the physical; and especially in the ever-present hand of the Creator—"Ilúvatar" as he is called by the elves, "God" as he is called by Christians—at work within his creation.

In a letter written in 1958, Tolkien suggests that most of the biographical information one might learn about him would not significantly aid one in understanding his writing (including *The Lord of the Rings*). Most facts about him would be completely useless. Some pieces of information, such as his tastes in languages, might have some relation to his writings but would require significant unraveling to figure out exactly what that relationship was. However, a few facts about him are actually quite significant in understanding his work. Of these he mentions only three, of which the "more important" is his Christian faith: "And there are a few basic facts [about myself], which however drily expressed, are really significant. . . . I am a Christian (which can be deduced from my stories), and in fact a Roman Catholic" (*Letters*, 288). There are two important points to be made here. The first is Tolkien's claim that knowing the "fact" of his Christian faith is "really significant" and "important" in explaining his works. The second is his belief that his Christianity is evident in his writings, or *deducible from his stories*, as he puts it. But if the Christian faith of the author is evident in the stories, that seems to be reasonable evidence that the work itself is a Christian work. And if that work is a myth, then it is a Christian myth. Of course Tolkien may be mistaken about the deducibility of his beliefs; many fans of his writing seem to be oblivious to his Christianity (though my own guess is that this is largely due to a lack of knowledge of just what the tenets of the Christian faith are). As to the former point, I think Tolkien is absolutely correct that an understanding of his Christian beliefs is tremendously helpful to understanding his works. A significant part of this book has been to explain how those beliefs are manifest in various ways in the Middle-earth mythology. But isn't that an argument that the mythology can and ought to be understood, at some level, as being Christian?

If we turn our attention from *The Hobbit* and *The Lord of the Rings* to *The Silmarillion*, we see even more clearly Tolkien's Christian faith woven through the fabric of the tale, or *absorbed into its symbolism*. Whereas references to Ilúvatar are veiled in *The Lord of the Rings*, and religious practices are almost completely expunged, *The Silmarillion* is fully and overtly theistic. Ilúvatar is explicitly present, personally and directly, as well as through his angelic servants, the Valar. It is Ilúvatar himself who throws down Númenor and sunders the seas.

> Then Manwë upon the Mountain called upon Ilúvatar, and for that time the Valar laid down their government of Arda. But Ilúvatar showed forth his power, and he changed the fashion of the world; and a great chasm opened in the sea between Númenor and the Deathless

Lands, and the waters flowed down into it, and the noise and smoke of the cataracts went up to heaven, and the world was shaken. And all the fleets of the Númenóreans were drawn down into the abyss, and they were drowned and swallowed up for ever. (*Silm*, 278–79)

A full exploration of *The Silmarillion* would be beyond the scope of this book. (This book, like *The Hobbit* and *The Lord of the Rings*, is intended to be *hobbicentric*, which is really anthropocentric since hobbits belong to the race of men, while *The Silmarillion* is *elvicentric*.) However, there are three aspects of that work that must be discussed in the context of this book, for they suggest a profoundly Christian understanding of the mythology of Middle-earth and relate to comments made in the previous section. These three aspects will be discussed at length.

The first aspect is that while nearly all references to religious practices were cut from *The Lord of the Rings*, they play a central role in the *Akallabêth: The Downfall of Númenor*, which is part 4 of the published version of *The Silmarillion*. The worship of Ilúvatar is the central element of the *Akallabêth* (which mirrors the history of Israel from the kingdom of David onward, as told in the Old Testament books of Kings and Chronicles, ending with the fall of Israel to Babylon). At the start of the great kingdom of Númenor, we read: "But in the midst of the land was a mountain tall and steep, and it was named the Meneltarma, the Pillar of Heaven, and upon it was a high place that was hallowed to Eru Ilúvatar, and it was open and unroofed, and no other temple or fane was there in the land of the Númenóreans" (*Silm*, 261). The decline of the kingdom is then intimately linked to the loss of faith in Ilúvatar, to the cessation of his due worship, and to the persecution of those faithful to him.

Tolkien chronicles this downfall by coming back at key times to the state of this temple. We later read that "after the days of Tar-Ancalimon the offering of the first fruits to Eru was neglected, and men went seldom any more to the Hallow upon the heights of Meneltarma in the midst of the land" (*Silm*, 266). This is the first major step in the decline of Númenor. Under the kingship of Tar-Palantír, there is a brief period of restoration, but then the kingdom grows even worse, until by the end we read that "the Meneltarma was utterly deserted in those days; and though not even Sauron dared to defile the high place, yet the King would let no man, upon pain of death, ascend to it, not even those of the Faithful who kept Ilúvatar in their hearts" (*Silm*, 272). Instead, a temple is built to Morgoth, and people begin to worship the Dark Lord. Then the downfall is complete: "And men took weapons in those days and slew one another for little cause" (*Silm*, 274). Though the military might of Númenor actually reaches a peak in these days, the internal state of the kingdom is abysmal, and its final end approaches quickly. Thus the fate of Númenor parallels the state of Ilúvatar's temple and of the faithful who worship him. When Ilúvatar is worshiped properly, Númenor prospers in the way it ought to prosper. When worship of Ilúvatar ceases and his people are persecuted, Númenor declines and becomes like the worst of the heathen kingdoms of Middle-earth. It is difficult, then, to see Tolkien's *Akallabêth* as anything other than a deeply religious work. In many ways it mirrors the Bible's narrative of the downfall of Israel under the kings who succeed David and Solomon, leading up to the fall of Israel into captivity to Babylon. Of course it may also reflect Tolkien's view of the West and in particular of England in his own time, as it moved away from a significant Christian influence to a post-Christian culture with only a remnant still worshiping the Christian God. If the *Akallabêth* is not a Christian mythology, then at the very least it is a profoundly Christian understanding of a pre-Christian or possibly a non-Christian time.

But what, then, do we make of the influence of Northern mythologies that has led some scholars to wrongly associate Tolkien's work with paganism?[20] There is at least one explicitly Christian reason, or biblical model, for Tolkien to have made so much of pagan sources even in a work he wanted to be deeply Christian. The most clear biblical defense of this approach can be found in Acts 17. Beginning in verse 16, the passage describes the apostle Paul's first missionary visit to Athens. It takes place in the middle of the first century when Athens was a polytheistic culture full of idols and temples to numerous gods, including the goddess Athena (after whom the city gets its name) and the god Ares, known to the Romans as Mars (whose hill, the Areios Pagos or "Rock of Ares," or "Mars' Hill," Paul preached on). The Athens of this time was certainly what Christians would call a pagan city.

Now up to this point, Paul's preaching had been primarily in synagogues among Jews and God-fearing gentiles. In order to defend his points he had relied (often successfully) on the Hebrew Scriptures, which would have been accepted by these audiences. In Athens, however, Paul ventures into the marketplace where, as the Douay-Rheims translates, "He disputed . . . every day with them that were there," and the Jerusalem Bible[21] translates, "He debated every day with anyone whom he met" (Acts 17:17). These were not Jews, or even monotheists. Among his audience and those who disputed with Paul were philosophers from Epicurean and Stoic traditions. And the problem Paul seems to encounter is that his previous approach of reasoning from Hebrew Scriptures doesn't work with this new and different crowd. Not only do they have no reason to accept the Hebrew Scriptures as true, but Paul's words don't even make sense to them. The Greek word *anastasis* that he uses for "resurrection" sounds to them like just the name of another goddess. So they refer to Paul with a derogatory term that might be translated as "seed spitter," meaning a bird that indiscriminately picks up random seeds from the ground and spits them out without any discernment or understanding.[22] The Douay-Rheims translates the insult as "word sower," but the Jerusalem Bible renders it more poetically as "parrot," to capture the idea of one who repeats words without understanding. Paul's response to these philosophers is revolutionary in the Christian church, though the significance of what he did is often forgotten today. Rather than forcing the Greeks to first understand the Hebrew Scriptures and learn a whole new set of stories and poems from Jewish culture before being taught Christianity, Paul takes a brand new approach to proclaiming the Christian gospel: he searches out their own pagan myths and poetry and finds the glimmers of truth there, and then he speaks to the Greeks using the language and imagery of *those* myths.

Now Paul certainly didn't believe that those myths were true in the full or complete sense (or historical sense) that he understood the Christian gospel to be true. Indeed, as the book of Acts has just finished explaining, "His spirit was stirred within him, seeing the city wholly given to idolatry" (Acts 17:16). Or, to refer again to the Jerusalem Bible, "His whole soul was revolted at the sight of a city given over to idolatry." Paul certainly could have stirred up considerable additional animosity by telling the Athenians that they had everything completely wrong in worshiping Athena and other gods, or that there was no worth in their religions. Instead, however, he actually praises them for being "extremely scrupulous . . . in all religious matters" (Acts 17:22 JB). He then preaches a sermon that draws on their own myths and poets and suggests that those myths have in them the seed of truth that points to the deeper truth of the gospel: "What therefore you worship, without knowing it, that I preach to you" (Acts 17:23).

Paul's sermon can be read starting in Acts 17:22. It is fascinating how, in order to speak of a God who through his incarnate Son, Jesus Christ, both reveals his name and shows mercy, Paul uses the pagan myth of the *unknown god* who also, in his mercy, stops a plague from wiping out the city of Athens. Paul uses the truth and beauty in pagan myths and puts them in the service of a higher truth. This use of a pagan myth as the central piece of his sermon must be seen, then, as a Christian approach, modeled by the greatest Christian missionary of the first century. It is neither pagan nor un-Christian.

In this myth of the unknown god, when the plagues are advancing on their city, the Athenians send for advice to a prophet and poet named Epimenides. It is Epimenides who tells the Athenians to make a sacrifice of sheep to the unknown god. This sacrifice moves the god to end the plague, and the people of Athens are saved. Paul's Greek audience would have known the myth well, and so he didn't recount all of this detail in his sermon in Athens, nor did he mention Epimenides by name—or if he did, the summary of his sermon provided by the author of Acts leaves it out. But Paul does quote from this prophet-poet, saying, "For in him we live, and move, and are; as some also of your own poets said: For we are also his offspring" (Acts 17:28). In fact, a larger section of the poem from which Paul quotes is still preserved among the surviving works of Epimenides.

> They fashioned a tomb for thee, O holy and high one—
> The Cretans, always liars, evil beasts, idle bellies!
> But thou art not dead: thou livest and abidest forever,
>   For in thee we live and move and have our being.[23]

Pagan poet that Epimenides was, Paul nevertheless almost certainly recognized in this poem, especially in the first and third lines above, a prophetic reference to the death and resurrection of Christ. Likewise, the fourth line—which is quoted by Paul in his sermon—also conveys a truth to which Christians can give full assent. Whatever Épimenides thought he was writing about, Paul saw a deeper truth, and he likely believed that God was the one who inspired these words in this pagan Greek prophet.

What Paul did with the pagan myths of the Greeks, showing in them a truth pointing to the deeper truth of his Christian gospel, Tolkien believed could be done with the pagan myths of the Norse. Tolkien's use of those myths does not come from a hidden pagan impulse but from a deeply Christian impulse—one he shared with the apostle Paul. And we needn't read between any lines to attribute this reasoning to Tolkien, for he was explicit about it. The argument for the possibility of pagan myths and stories of Faery being capable of revealing Christian truth is not only central to his essay "On Fairy-Stories" (cited in many passages already) but was also an argument that he made to his friend C. S. Lewis, one that helped lead Lewis into the Christian faith. Tolkien's poem *Mythopoeia*, indirectly addressed to Lewis, contains some of the argument as well. In his essay "Beowulf: The Monsters and the Critics," Tolkien also speaks of the Christian *Beowulf* poet making use of pagan material to convey Christian thought, even suggesting in his long appendix B that "the language of *Beowulf* is in fact partly 're-paganized' by the author with a special purpose, rather than Christianized (by him or later) without consistent purpose" ("Monsters," 41). The re-paganization of the *language* of the poem in certain places serves to make it truer and more beautiful, and in its core ideology more Christian and less pagan.

Tolkien does the same thing as the *Beowulf* poet. And so in Tolkien's work we see the presence and influence of many pagan Germanic values, as we noted earlier, but we also see the author understanding, presenting, and ultimately judging those values from a Christian perspective. In *The Hobbit*, we see both the values of the mead hall—"food and cheer and song," or simply friendship and fellowship—and the code of the warrior, whose glory comes from amassing treasure and defeating and subjecting enemies in war. What we see is reminiscent of how the *Beowulf* poet starts his poem.

Yes, we have heard of the glory of the Spear-Danes' kings in the old days—how the princes of that people did brave deeds.

Often Scyld Scefing took mead-benches away from enemy bands, from many tribes, terrified their nobles. . . . He lived in comfort for that, became great under the skies, prospered in honors until every one of those who lived about him, across the whale-road, had to obey him, pay him tribute. That was a good king.[24]

However, the perspective Tolkien brings to these values is that of the Christian: the perspective that there is an objective morality and a spiritual reality that make moral victory more important than military victory. It is a worldview that includes, among other things, a belief in life after death, a belief in a day of judgment, and a belief that reality includes both a spiritual plane and a material plane, an unseen and a seen. This perspective leads one to view the world with eternal rather than temporal values. As we saw in the previous chapter, Tolkien uses the words of Thorin on his deathbed to present that perspective. In the face of the eternal, Thorin is able to see in a new light what he previously valued. Gold and silver have temporal worth. Friendship has eternal worth. And so Thorin repents of his earlier words and deeds. So while Tolkien's writing upholds from the Christian worldview the mead-hall values of "food and cheer and song," it shows the vanity of the warrior's pursuit of glory and riches. Likewise, in chapter 2 we saw the Anglo-Saxon warrior's glory epitomized in Théoden, especially at his death, and yet even as Tolkien presents this glory he also lets us see it from another perspective, which in that case is through the eyes of Merry.

The Absence and the Presence of the Incarnation

In fact, the reasons for labeling even *The Lord of the Rings* a "Christian work" are plentiful enough that we must return to the final and most important reason for answering "no" to the question at the start of this chapter. The last and most significant reason for saying that Tolkien's mythology is not a Christian mythology was that there is no incarnation—there is no Messiah, no divine Savior—in Middle-earth. Tolkien himself acknowledges in a draft of a letter written in 1956 that "there is no 'embodiment' of the Creator anywhere in this story or mythology." Why not? He gives one answer in the same letter draft: "The Incarnation of God is an *infinitely* greater thing than anything I would dare to write" (*Letters*, 237). Again, it is the importance of the incarnation, not its lack of importance, that Tolkien claims as one motivation for not including it. This answer is, I think, a thoroughly honest one and is consistent with a humility Tolkien always shows with respect to the gospel story.

Another part of the answer is that there would be no real way to present the actual incarnation in Middle-earth without it becoming allegory. Unless, of course, Tolkien were to fully connect Middle-earth to our world. But while that might in some way be possible,[25] the moment that final step was made, not only would Middle-earth cease being Middle-earth (as we know it in the stories), but the incarnation itself would simply be the event in our world as it has already been described in the Gospels; it would not be an incarnation in Middle-earth.

There is, however, another answer to this question of why no incarnation, if indeed Tolkien's myth was so deeply Christian. It may be the same as the answer Michael Drout astutely gives to the question of whether the hero Beowulf was present in *The Lord of the Rings*. As we noted, Drout argues that while Beowulf was not present in a single obvious or allegorical way, he was present in a more subtle way in Tolkien's threefold division of Beowulf into Aragorn, Éomer, and Théoden, with each of the Middle-earth characters taking a different set of the medieval hero's important characteristics. In this sense, Beowulf was present, allowing Tolkien to make a significant commentary on a hero he thought very important without actually admitting to including that hero. He seemed to have done the same thing with Beowulf in *The Hobbit*, neatly dividing his great strength and fearlessness, his excessive pride, and his moral virtue amongst Beorn, Thorin, and Bilbo respectively. Again, he reveals the importance of Beowulf.

But if Christ was even more important to Tolkien, might he not have done the same thing with him? Yes, and we pointed out earlier in this chapter exactly how: by using the same threefold portrayal in the characters of Aragorn, Frodo, and Gandalf. None of these three alone are Christ allegories, but together they form a prophetic picture of the hero of the Christian faith. Tolkien takes the characteristics of Christ as king and healer and descendant of David, who releases from captivity not only human slaves but even the captive dead, and gives those characteristics to Aragorn the descendant of Elros. He takes the characteristics of Christ the suffering servant, who endures the passion and the shame of being stripped and tortured as he sacrifices his life to save those he loves, and gives those characteristics to Frodo, even down to the wounds on his hands and the stripes on his back. And he takes Christ as an incarnate spiritual being, who casts out demons and is raised from the dead, and gives those to Gandalf, who both defeats the demonic Balrog and rescues Faramir by driving off demonic Ringwraiths. These are not allegories, and we would miss the complexity and beauty of Tolkien's portrayal if we sought to turn them into allegories. But an argument every bit as strong or stronger could be made for the threefold portrayal of the incarnate Christ in *The Lord of the Rings* as for the threefold portrayal of Beowulf in either *The Hobbit* or *The Lord of the Rings*.

But there is another answer to the question that may be even stronger, though it is somewhat different. And here I must address a second aspect of *The Silmarillion*—or rather, *The Silmarillion* as it might have been. There is a very interesting dialogue scene buried in *Morgoth's Ring: The Later Silmarillion, Part One*, which is the tenth volume of the History of Middle-earth, written by Tolkien and edited posthumously by his son Christopher. According to Christopher's notes, there is a strong indication that his father viewed this particular dialogue (which is now called "Athrabeth Finrod Ah Andreth"), as well as an essay discussing the dialogue, as *finished* and as a part of the canon he intended for publication in *The Silmarillion*. According to these notes, the story itself was to have been included in *The Silmarillion* proper, and the essay included in an appendix. (Tolkien often placed his most important material in appendixes. He claimed that the tale of Aragorn and Arwen told in appendix A, subsection I.v, was very important to understanding Middle-earth.) So what is this scene? In "Athrabeth Finrod Ah Andreth," the great King Finrod Felagund, lord of the realm of Nargothrond (and the brother of Galadriel), is having a conversation with a wise woman named Andreth. Finrod, who is of the race of elves, and Andreth, of the race of men, are trying to understand the differences between their races and what hope each race has separately or together. Andreth mentions an old belief that one day Ilúvatar himself will enter into his creation: "They say that the One will himself enter into Arda, and heal Men and all the Marring from the beginning to the end" (*Morgoth*, 321). Finrod and Andreth then have a discussion about this ancient belief, during which Finrod comments that it seems right to him for an artist to enter his creation, and that if any artist could and would do it, it would be Ilúvatar. Moreover, Finrod believes that such an incarnation is actually the only hope that elves and men have for the healing of the hurts of Morgoth. Thus Finrod concludes:

> If Eru wished to do this, I do not doubt that he would find a way, though I cannot foresee it. For, as it seems to me, even if He in Himself were to enter in, He must still remain also as He is: the Author without. And yet, Andreth, to speak with humility, I cannot conceive how else this healing could be achieved. Since Eru will surely not suffer Melkor to turn the world to his own will and to triumph in the end. Yet there is no power conceivable greater than Melkor save Eru only. Therefore Eru, if He will not relinquish His work to Melkor, who must else proceed to mastery, then Eru must come in to conquer him. . . . If any remedy for [Melkor's evil] is to be found, ere all is ended, any new light to oppose the shadow, or any medicine for the wounds: then it must, I deem, come from without. (*Morgoth*, 322)

Reading this passage reveals one thing at least: Tolkien viewed the incarnation of God, coming to earth as Messiah, as somehow inevitable in Middle-earth. Through the voice of Finrod, he describes the incarnation as necessary: as the only hope for Middle-earth, the only way "healing could be achieved," the only way to prevent Melkor from "triumph[ing] in the end," the only possible "remedy" for Melkor's evil. No other solution to the fundamental problem of evil is conceivable—none except for the incarnation of the Creator, Ilúvatar. "Surely" Eru will do it, Finrod reasons; he "must."

That Tolkien wrote such a scene, describing the incarnation of the Creator within his creation, illustrates both how thoroughly Tolkien's Christian faith is ingrained in his mythology and also that he realized just what would need to happen in his world for it to fully reflect his deep and profound Christian joy. Shippey even suggests that a dialogue between Gimli and Legolas at the start of "The Last Debate" might actually be about the "Incarnation, the

Coming of *the Son of Man.*"[26] The conversation concerns the hope of men and the seed of men. Shippey examines Gimli's pessimistic response that all that men do will "come to naught in the end but might-have-beens" (V/ix), and Shippey notes that Gimli's comment "would be entirely true without qualification, in the Christian view, if fallen humanity had not been rescued by a Power from outside, a Power beyond humanity which nevertheless became human."[27] As Finrod tells Andreth, the coming of Ilúvatar into his creation is the *only* hope. Since that hope has not yet been fulfilled, and indeed is not even widely known among the peoples of Middle-earth, it is not surprising that the stories are so full of sorrow and sadness; Melkor's evil is still without a cure.

To return to the question, we might now answer that Tolkien's Middle-earth mythology is certainly not un-Christian nor in any way pagan, but neither is it fully Christian; rather, it is a Christian understanding of a pre-Christian time. It is undeniably a work coming from a fully Christian mind, and yet it does not describe a fully Christian world. In that way it is very much like the poem *Beowulf*. But the Christian understanding of truth and reality seems (at least to me) to be far more deeply woven into the fabric of the Middle-earth *legendarium* than it is in the poem *Beowulf*.

The Theme of Ilúvatar

The third aspect of *The Silmarillion* that reflects its Christian underpinnings brings us to the conclusion of this book, for it gets at a root issue in understanding *The Lord of the Rings* and indeed all of Tolkien's Middle-earth mythology. In Tolkien's mythology, the original fall (the rebellion of some of the created order against the Creator) begins before the physical earth is even made, affecting the earth before any of the Children even appear. In the *Ainulindalë*, the account of the creation of Middle-earth (*Silm*, 15–22), Ilúvatar begins a great Theme of Music that his first created beings, the Ainur, are to take part in, "each with his own thoughts and devices." However, Melkor, to whom "had been given the greatest gifts," in seeking "to increase the power and glory of the part assigned to himself" begins to weave into his music an aspect of discord that is

240

seemingly in opposition to the Theme of Ilúvatar in which the other Ainur are partaking. The result is discord, and before long some of the Ainur begin to follow Melkor rather than Ilúvatar. There is, as it were, a rebellion in heaven. Here, rather than stopping Melkor's music altogether or expelling him, Ilúvatar begins a second Theme. Against this second Theme, Melkor also rebels with discord. So Ilúvatar begins yet a third Theme. Here we get to one of the most important moments in the creation, around which all of the events in the coming history of Middle-earth revolve.

> And it seemed at last that there were two musics progressing at one time before the seat of Ilúvatar, and they were utterly at variance. The one was deep and wide and beautiful, but slow and blended with an immeasurable sorrow, from which its beauty chiefly came. The other had now achieved a unity of its own; but it was loud, and vain, and endlessly repeated; and it had little harmony, but rather a clamorous unison as of many trumpets braying upon a few notes. And it essayed to drown the other music by the violence of its voice, but it seemed that its most triumphant notes were taken by the other and woven into its own solemn pattern. (*Silm*, 16–17)

In this imagery, Tolkien gives us a history of Middle-earth. Indeed, the Music *is* the history of Middle-earth, as Ilúvatar tells the Ainur. This imagery is at the heart of all the tales in *The Silmarillion*, *The Hobbit*, and *The Lord of the Rings*—or, we might say, of the one long tale that weaves through them all. These tales are about the rebellion of Melkor, and his desire to destroy the works of Ilúvatar. More importantly, however, they are about how Ilúvatar responds, taking the most triumphant notes of his enemy and weaving them into his own solemn pattern. In other words, Ilúvatar's plans are not thwarted by Melkor's evil. The Creator is able to foresee everything that Melkor is going to do in opposition to him and to work his own plans so that they encompass even the actions done by his enemy in rebellion.

In his use of this metaphor of music and his portrayal of the war of sound, Tolkien is working out in his writing a great principle of Christianity. The apostle Paul, whom I have already quoted, is one of the most important figures in understanding Christianity. In a letter Paul writes to the first-century Christian church in Rome, he encourages its recipients by telling them that God is able to take all things—even those things intended for evil—and work them out so that they result in good (Rom. 8:28). This is at the heart of the Christian understanding of history. What was the greatest triumph of Satan, the devil, in all of history? It was having Jesus, the Christ who was sent to save the world, nailed to a cross by the very people he had come to save. Yet God takes that most triumphant note of his enemy and makes of it his own greatest victory, for in Christ's death on the cross and his ensuing resurrection, God works out his plan of salvation: the solemn pattern that has been at work since God promised to Abraham that through his offspring all the nations of the earth would be blessed. Satan, in working to have Jesus put to death, ends up aiding in the fulfillment of the prophecy made to Adam and Eve when evil first entered into the world, that a descendant of Eve would one day deal Satan the crushing blow. That crushing blow is dealt by Jesus on the cross, when he dies for the sins of the world and then rises again from death and conquers both sin and death. This story, more than any other, is at the heart of the Christian faith that is woven into the fabric of Middle-earth. As Ilúvatar says to Melkor, none can alter the Music in his despite: "For he that attempteth this shall prove but mine instrument in the devising of things more wonderful, which he himself hath not imagined" (*Silm*, 17). And later he says of men, "These too in their time shall find that all that they do redounds at the end only to the glory of my work" (*Silm*, 42).

One of the most moving examples of this principle illustrated in *The Silmarillion*—at least in terms of the beauty of the imagery—comes very shortly after Ilúvatar makes this proclamation. Ulmo, one of Ilúvatar's chief servants, and one of the most wise and powerful of the Valar, laments the destruction that Melkor is causing in the new creation.

> And Ilúvatar spoke to Ulmo, and said: "Seest thou not how here in this little realm in the Deeps of Time Melkor hath made war upon thy province? He hath bethought him of bitter cold immoderate, and yet hath not destroyed the beauty of thy fountains, nor of thy clear pools. Behold the snow, and the cunning work of frost! Melkor hath devised heats and fire without restraint, and hath not dried up

thy desire nor utterly quelled the music of the sea. Behold rather the height and glory of the clouds, and the everchanging mists; and listen to the fall of rain upon the Earth! And in these clouds thou art drawn nearer to Manwë, thy friend, whom thou lovest." (*Silm*, 19)

Ilúvatar doesn't merely proclaim empty words of hope to the Ainur, that the deeds of his enemies will prove but his instrument in the devising of things more wonderful; he immediately shows Ulmo how he works it out. Bitter cold, intended to destroy the works of Ilúvatar and his servants the Valar, instead becomes a vehicle through which the beauty of snow and frost is brought to life. Heat also, intended by Melkor to dry up the waters of Ulmo, instead results in the height and glory of clouds and ever-changing mists and rain. We see this principle at work time and again in Middle-earth, in *The Lord of the Rings*, and elsewhere. We see it in the plans of Saruman: the orcs capture Merry and Pippin to bring them to Isengard, and yet Ilúvatar uses Saruman's betrayal as a means both of waking the Ents and of bringing Aragorn to Rohan to arouse Théoden, Éomer, and the latent strength of the Rohirrim. Eventually, we see it even in Gollum's wickedness, for he becomes the instrument by which the Ring is destroyed when Frodo becomes unable to complete his task.

Indeed, it is in understanding the Theme of Ilúvatar that much is tied together, including the importance of moral victory over military victory, and even the nature of Gandalf's power and actions. If Ilúvatar is capable of taking the most evil acts of Melkor, the most powerful of all created beings, and bringing good out of them—even while the acts themselves remain evil—surely he can bring good from the efforts of his servants. The outcome of the war is in Eru's hands; what he desires from his servants is their love and obedience—that they do what is right—and not that they win the war for him. In that sense, the story is not so much about Melkor's rebellion, nor even about Ilúvatar's work to bring his good purposes to pass despite the rebellion of Melkor, though of course both of these are incorporated into the story. Rather, it is about the choices of all the beings with free will created by Ilúvatar, and whether they choose to do what is good and right (and thus serve Ilúvatar), using their time and gifts and talents as good stewards. It is about a choice that every free being must make: On which side of the war will they fight? To draw on the language spoken by Aragorn to Théoden, "Open war lies before [us all], with Sauron or against him." But it might better have been said, had Tolkien desired for religious aspects to be more overt, "Open war lies before us all, with Ilúvatar or against him."

The Real War and the Happy Ending

And now we have come full circle, for we are once again speaking of war. In the first chapter of this book I explored the ethics of war, and especially the question of torture, and in the second chapter I asked whether Tolkien glorified war and violence. My conclusion was that, in Tolkien's writing, something we might call *moral* victory is much more important than *military* victory. Put another way, war is not what *The Lord of the Rings* is really about. That is, the physical conflict between the armies of Sauron and those of the West, even if that battle takes narrative center stage, isn't the deepest concern. For Ilúvatar has the power, at any time, to destroy entire kingdoms if he so desires. He does so with Númenor. What, then, is the power of Sauron to him? Nothing.

But at another level, war is exactly what the story is about. Not the wars fought with sword, spear, and bow against orc, troll, and warg, but the war that Melkor is waging upon Eru Ilúvatar: "About his throne there was a raging storm, as of dark waters that made war one upon another in an endless wrath." It is the conflict in which "the discord of Melkor rose in uproar and contended with [the Theme of Ilúvatar], and again there was a war of sound more violent than before" (*Silm*, 16). It is not ultimately a war over land or territory but a war over the hearts of the Children of Ilúvatar. It is, as we saw in the confrontation between Gandalf and the Balrog, a war between heaven and hell, between the Secret Fire (the realm of Anor) and the realm of Udûn. It is, in short, a spiritual war rather than a physical one. *The Lord of the Rings* is, in fact, a working out of another great Christian principle, expressed again by the apostle Paul: "For our wrestling is not against flesh and blood; but against principalities and powers, against the rulers of the world of this darkness, against the spirits of wickedness in the high places" (Eph. 6:12). The real battle is not against physical armies but against spiritual enemies.

The goal of these spiritual enemies is not to destroy the body but to destroy the spirit.

This is why this enemy cannot be defeated using weapons of evil. This is why, as Paul explains, the Christian's real armor is truth, righteousness, peace, faith, and ultimately salvation and prayer. Frodo has a mithril coat, but he also is defended by his own mercy. Sam wears loyalty and hope. Aragorn and Faramir have the armor of truthfulness. Interestingly enough, Tolkien visualizes this spiritual battle in the physical realm in a handful of places, in order to give the readers an imaginative glimpse of it. We saw it in the battle of Gandalf and the Balrog, as well as in the confrontation between Gandalf and the Nazgûl in front of Minas Tirith. We even see it in the confrontation between Glorfindel and the Nine outside Rivendell. Gandalf explains to Frodo: "Those who have dwelt in the Blessed Realm live at once in both worlds, and against both the Seen and the Unseen they have great power. . . . Yes, you saw [Glorfindel] for a moment as he is upon the other side" (II/i).

Many of the separate elements of the story come together in this understanding. What is at stake is the salvation of the Children of Ilúvatar, and therefore the moral choices of those Children are what matters. This is why Faramir would not snare even an orc with a falsehood. The physical battle might be won in such a way, but a battle in the real war—the spiritual war—would be lost. This, of course, relates directly to the moral landscape of Middle-earth, and to the heroism of Tolkien's characters, and to the potential for heroism in his readers and the war we all fight. Jared Lobdell comments on what Tolkien brought to our modern world and hints also at how it not only comes together but comes together *for us*: "The past, and this includes the heroic past, *is* alive in the present; the Great Days *do* live on inside us, no matter how unheroic and Hobbit-like we may be, or seem; the green and pleasant land *must* outlast the dark Satanic mills, and we can call upon our hidden heroism to help; there is Right and there is Wrong, and we can know the difference between the two—and fight for the right—that is indeed a message of hope."[28] Not everyone in Middle-earth understands this, of course, but the wise do. In the dialogues between Gandalf and Denethor, it becomes clear that Gandalf understands the spiritual nature of the war, while Denethor sees only military victory or defeat. Consider that Gandalf, himself a spiritual being who took the form of flesh in order to aid the people of Middle-earth, almost never takes up arms against a fleshly foe but reserves the full demonstration of his powers for other foes of like spiritual nature: the Balrog (itself a spirit of flame and shadow in service of Melkor, who is renamed Morgoth by Fëanor), Saruman (another of the Istari), and the Nazgûl (once a man but now a wraith who has entered the spirit world). As Gandalf tells Frodo shortly before the Council of Elrond: "There are many powers in the world, for good or for evil. Some are greater than I am. Against some I have not yet been measured. But my time is coming" (II/i). This is also why Gandalf is so concerned with the "cure" of the characters of Middle-earth (Gollum, Saruman, and Wormtongue, as well as Bilbo and Frodo); why he always wants to give people the chance to repent; why he would rather encourage people to fight the battle themselves (that is, to choose well) than to fight the battle for them. As we saw in chapter 8 on salvation, the outcome of the spiritual war has eternal consequences: salvation or damnation.

In this battle, the unity of those who oppose Sauron (and his master, Morgoth) is vitally important, but this is true as much because unity itself is a good thing as because unity will bring about a great military force. Unity is the goal, not just the means to a goal. Or, to put it another way, the music of Morgoth (if it may be called music) is the sound of "discord" or disunity. For Morgoth, it is not that the disunity of his foes is merely a means to some other end; rather, the disunity of his foes is itself an end. "Indeed in nothing is the power of the Dark Lord more clearly shown than in the estrangement that divides all those who still oppose him," the elf Haldir acknowledges to the Fellowship when he must blindfold them upon their entry into Lothlórien (II/vi). And a short time later, Galadriel also tells the Fellowship: "Your Quest stands upon the edge of a knife. Stray but a little and it will fail, to the ruin of all. Yet hope remains while all the Company is true" (II/vii). It is not by chance that Galadriel mentions hope in the same breath that she speaks of the values of faithfulness and unity within the Fellowship. Hope too is part of the battle. Hope and despair are not simply means to some other end but are the ends themselves. For Ilúvatar, the desire is for his Children to have hope; for Morgoth and his servant Sauron, they have already won a battle the moment they have brought about despair.

But here, again, we must pause. As I noted before, whenever someone speaks of the importance of a spiritual reality, there is (and
should be) a certain wariness of gnostic tendencies. When I argue
that, in Tolkien's Christian understanding of the world, there is an
underlying spiritual battle that is more important than the physical
confrontation of opposing armies, am I saying that the physical world
is not important? Not at all.[29] As I explored at the end of chapter 8,
salvation is won neither by freeing an immaterial soul from a physical body nor by trying to deny the body and becoming somehow
more spiritual. Though at certain times the heroes must be willing
to suffer great bodily hardship, as Frodo and Sam do in crossing
Mordor and climbing Mount Doom, and though their willingness
to (in a sense) deny their bodies is certainly part of their heroism,
the denial of the body is not in any way an end or a goal. These
moments of denying the body are merely means—and short-term
ones at that—toward some other greater end.

The war in Tolkien's mythology, even if it can rightly be called
a spiritual one, is still fought by embodied creatures in a physical
world. And, moreover, it is fought precisely in the way those physical
beings use their bodies. As I argued earlier, battles are won in small
acts of kindness, meeting the physical needs of other beings: building houses for dispossessed hobbits, feeding strangers who appear in
your forest, showing mercy even to enemies who seek to harm you,
planting trees and cleaning fouled rivers (whether in the Shire or in
Isengard). Bilbo wins a battle by choosing the "duty" of feeding the
dwarves who unexpectedly appear at his door (at the start of *The
Hobbit*), even if it means he gets less food himself. And his practice of
that duty helps prepare him to be the sort of hobbit who also accepts
the more heroic duty of being willing to reenter a goblin-infested
mountain to help rescue the same dwarves. (As it turns out, he is not
required to do this, but he understands his *duty* and is *willing* to.)
Butterbur never picks up a sword, and yet he takes part in the battle.

> "I am [still willing to help]," said Mr. Butterbur. "More than ever.
> Though I don't know what the likes of me can do against, against—"
> he faltered.
> "Against the Shadow in the East," said Strider quietly. "Not much,
> Barliman, but every little helps." (I/x)

Most simply put, those in Tolkien's world who most deeply understand the spiritual reality also care most profoundly about the physical reality, about every single tree that might flower or bear fruit. Even the willingness of physical beings to take up the sword and give their lives for the sake of others is, as Théoden learns, also a way to fight the good fight, the spiritual fight.

Every chapter in this book has had this war behind it: the reality of the spiritual as well as physical realms, the importance of the eternal as opposed to the temporal. So we end with a final question. What is the applicability of this understanding to our lives today? Or, to phrase it another way, drawing on Tolkien's own view of fantasy literature, what is the underlying reality or truth that Tolkien would have us see? I return again to two passages from the end of Tolkien's essay "On Fairy-Stories." The first paragraph comes from the section immediately before the essay's epilogue, and the rest from the epilogue itself.

> The consolation of fairy-stories, the joy of the happy ending: or more correctly of the good catastrophe, the sudden joyous "turn" (for there is no true end to any fairy-tale): this joy, which is one of the things which fairy-stories can produce supremely well, is not essentially "escapist," nor "fugitive." In its fairy-tale—or otherworld—setting, it is a sudden and miraculous grace: never to be counted on to recur. It does not deny the existence of *dyscatastrophe*, of sorrow and failure: the possibility of these is necessary to the joy of deliverance; it denies (in the face of much evidence, if you will) universal final defeat and in so far is *evangelium*, giving a fleeting glimpse of Joy, Joy beyond the walls of the world, poignant as grief. ("Fairy," 153)

> It has long been my feeling (a joyous feeling) that God redeemed . . . men, in a way fitting to this aspect . . . of their strange nature. The Gospels contain a fairy-story, or a story of a larger kind which embraces all the essence of fairy-stories. They contain many marvels—peculiarly artistic, beautiful, and moving: "mythical" in their perfect, self-contained significance; and among the marvels is the greatest and most complete conceivable eucatastrophe [consolation]. But this story has entered History and the primary world; the desire and aspiration of sub-creation has been raised to the fulfilment of Creation. The Birth of Christ is the eucatastrophe of Man's history. The Resurrection is the eucatastrophe of the story of the Incarnation.

248

This story begins and ends in joy. . . . There is no tale ever told that men would rather find was true, and none which so many sceptical men have accepted as true on its own merits. . . . To reject it leads either to sadness or to wrath.

. . . The Christian joy, the *Gloria*, is of the same kind; but it is pre-eminently . . . high and joyous. Because this story is supreme; and it is true. Art has been verified. God is the Lord, of angels, and of men and of elves. Legend and History have met and fused.

. . . The Christian has still to work, with mind as well as body, to suffer, hope, and die; but he may now perceive that all his bents and faculties have a purpose, which can be redeemed. ("Fairy," 155–56)

What Tolkien is saying here is that we fight the same battle in our primary world. It is not fought with swords and spears against physical foes, the armies of Sauron. Rather, it is fought with our truth, righteousness, peace, faith, and prayer. It is fought as we "work, with mind as well as body." It is fought as we "suffer, hope, and die." Barliman Butterbur fights the battle as much in his Prancing Pony Inn at Bree as soldiers fight it on the front lines of Gondor. The hobbits must fight this battle in the Shire as much as the men of Rohan fight it on their borders. Indeed, the "Scouring of the Shire" is not an appendix tacked on to the end of the story, but it is the real story; it is what the entire book is about. Gandalf is training the hobbits so that they are prepared to do in the Shire what they have seen him and Aragorn do in Rohan and Gondor. That training succeeds. They don't need Gandalf anymore. The hobbits are all grown up. Frodo shows to Saruman the same mercy that Gandalf does.

Of course it is not just Gandalf training the hobbits to fight this battle; it is also Tolkien training his readers. But if Tolkien is right—if the Christian story is true, as he and "so many sceptical men" have come to believe—then the victory of salvation is possible. And if sadness and wrath come from rejecting that story, then salvation comes in the opposite way: from believing it. What is exciting to Tolkien is not only that the Children themselves may be redeemed but that all of their efforts, their working as well as their suffering, and even their art, may have redemptive value and may be redeemed.

Fortunately, the war is not destined to continue through eternity. Eventually the war will come to an end. At the end of Tolkien's story "Leaf by Niggle," which I mentioned in chapter 9 in the context of

Tolkien's tree, the painter Niggle has gone on a Journey and finally meets the Shepherd, who leads him into the Mountains. All of the imagery of the book leads us to believe that this Journey is Niggle's death—or the life that follows his death—and that the Shepherd is none other than the Great Shepherd of Christian faith—namely, Jesus. Niggle follows the Shepherd into the Mountains. (If one discerns the more obvious imagery of the Shepherd, then understanding the Mountain imagery is not difficult either.) Niggle's final surviving painting—a single leaf that had hung in a museum—is lost: "For a long while 'Leaf: by Niggle' hung there in a recess, and was noticed by a few eyes. But eventually the museum was burnt down, and the leaf, and Niggle, were entirely forgotten in his old country" ("Niggle," 95). Nonetheless, Niggle's creative art is ultimately vindicated in the most profound and fitting of ways. His tree is given the gift of reality; his "desire and aspiration of sub-creation has been raised to the fulfillment of Creation."

I have no doubt that Tolkien had his own story, his own art, and his own hopes in his mind when he wrote the ending to his story "Leaf by Niggle." Throughout the tale we have come to understand that the mysterious person known only as the Second Voice is a Divine being, both wise and merciful: a member of a trinity that includes the First Voice, the Second Voice, and a Doctor. Niggle's painting of a tree has become a real tree, with a surrounding land and in the distance behind it a few of the Mountains—understood to be a sort of heavenly realm, or a final destination of reward. As the tale ends, we hear the First Voice say of Niggle's now-living painting: "It is proving very useful indeed. As a holiday, and a refreshment. It is splendid for convalescence; and not only that, for many it is the best introduction to the Mountains" ("Niggle," 95). For countless people, *The Lord of the Rings* has provided splendid refreshment. For that, the author would be glad. But his deeper desire is that for some it would be an introduction to the Mountains.

Notes

Introduction

1. It is only partly true that the publication of *The Lord of the Rings* can be called the "fruition" of Tolkien's labors. One reason for the delay in publication was that the author earnestly sought the publication of *The Silmarillion* in conjunction with *The Lord of the Rings*. Sadly, because of the combined lengths of the books, he was ultimately unable to find a willing publisher, and *The Silmarillion* was not published in his lifetime. He was, however, able to convince Allen & Unwin to publish *The Lord of the Rings* in its entirety, including appendixes.

2. The Diamond Jubilee refers to the year 1897, the sixtieth anniversary of the reign of Queen Victoria. Warwickshire is a county in England's West Midlands.

3. In a footnote to appendix F.II, "On Translation," Tolkien acknowledges the similarity between the relationship of Rohan with Gondor and that of medieval England with Rome, describing both as "a simpler and more primitive people living in contact with a higher and more venerable culture, and occupying lands that had once been part of its domain."

4. Peter Kreeft, *The Philosophy of Tolkien: The Worldview behind "The Lord of the Rings"* (San Francisco: Ignatius Press, 2005), 23.

5. C. S. Lewis, "Time in Tide," cited in ibid., 16.

6. The author goes on to add, with equal insight, "and much study wearies the body." Though it must be noted, with perhaps a touch of irony, that the author of Ecclesiastes was himself writing a book.

7. Alan Jacobs, *The Narnian* (New York: HarperCollins, 2005), x.

8. Because Tolkien did not (as Lewis did) write numerous books and essays, or give regular BBC radio talks, in which he explicitly addressed philosophy and theology, readers are left to discover Tolkien's ideas as they are incarnate in his fantasy. Although—as I will argue in this book and as many others have argued—those fantasy novels are deeply philosophical and at times theological, they are neither didactic nor consciously allegorical, and thus are far more open to interpretation than, say, Lewis's *Miracles*, *The Abolition of Man*, or *Mere Christianity*, or even than *The Chronicles of Narnia*.

9. See also Matthew Dickerson and Jonathan Evans, *Ents, Elves, and Eriador: The Environmental Vision of J. R. R. Tolkien* (Lexington: University Press of Kentucky, 2006); and Matthew Dickerson and David O'Hara, *From Homer to Harry Potter: A Handbook*

of Myth and Fantasy (Grand Rapids: Brazos, 2006)—which, despite the title, is primarily about the ideas of J. R. R. Tolkien and C. S. Lewis rather than those of J. K. Rowling or the Greek mythopoet Homer.

10. "'Don't the great tales never end?' [said Sam]. 'No, they never end as tales,' said Frodo" (IV/viii).

11. See especially the *Letters* collection, edited by Humphrey Carpenter.

12. I could also take many more trips to the Tolkien archives at the Raynor Memorial Library and continue to examine original material that was available prior to 2004 but that I simply had not yet explored in depth.

13. Peter Kreeft, "Afterword: The Wonder of *The Silmarillion*," in *Shadows of Imagination: The Fantasies of C. S. Lewis, J. R. R. Tolkien, and Charles Williams*, ed. Mark R. Hillegas (Carbondale: Southern Illinois University Press, 1979), 161.

14. Spencer Ackerman, "'Some Will Call Me a Torturer': CIA Man Reveals Secret Jail," *Wired*, July 1, 2011, www.wired.com/dangerroom/2011/07/am-i-a-torturer/.

15. For a more complete treatment by the author, see Dickerson and O'Hara, *From Homer to Harry Potter*.

16. See, for example, the draft of a 1959 letter declining an invitation to speak at a symposium on writing for children: "I write things that might be classified as fairy-stories . . . because I wish to write this kind of story and no other. I do this because if I do not apply too grandiloquent a title to it I find that my comment on the world is most easily and naturally expressed in this way. . . . Since large numbers of adults seem to enjoy what I write—quite enough to keep me happy—I have no need to seek escape to another and (possibly) less exigent audience" (*Letters*, 297). He goes on in that letter to add, "But long narratives cannot be made out of nothing; and one cannot rearrange the primary matter in secondary patterns without indicating feelings and opinions about one's material" (*Letters*, 298).

Chapter 1: On Hobbits, the Treatment of Prisoners, and the Ethics of War

1. T. A. Shippey, *J. R. R. Tolkien: Author of the Century* (Boston: Houghton Mifflin, 2000), xxiv.

2. Ibid., xx–xxi.

3. Jared Lobdell, *The Rise of Tolkienian Fantasy* (Chicago: Open Court Publishing, 2005), 146.

4. John Elder, *Reading the Mountains of Home* (Cambridge, MA: Harvard University Press, 1998), 53.

5. A related question that arose from the treatment of prisoners in World War II, especially in German concentration camps but also in Japanese prisoner-of-war camps, was whether it was ethical to use prisoners in scientific experiments that might help win the war, or even might help the human race. This is also an important question, but while the principles explored in this book would certainly have direct implications for that question, it is not one we will explicitly explore.

6. As I provide evidence of and exploration into this principle numerous times and in a variety of ways in this book, I do not defend it here.

7. Stratford Caldecott, *Secret Fire: The Spiritual Vision of J. R. R. Tolkien* (London: Darton, Longman and Todd, 2003), 186.

8. A footnote at this point in the text reads: "Few Orcs ever did so in the Elder Days, and at no time would any Orc treat with any Elf. For one thing Morgoth had achieved was to convince the Orcs beyond refutation that the Elves were crueler than themselves, taking captives only for 'amusement,' or to eat them (as the Orcs would do at need)."

Chapter 2: Epic Battles

1. In a footnote to appendix F.II, "On Translation," Tolkien acknowledges using the Old English language to translate the names of the Rohirrim, but he otherwise denies any other direct connection: "This linguistic procedure [of translating the names of Rohan into Old English] does not imply that the Rohirrim closely resembled the ancient English otherwise, in culture or art, in weapons or modes of warfare." What we may be seeing here is more evidence of Tolkien's distaste for conscious intentional allegory. Despite his disavowal of any intentional inference, however, the examples in the following paragraphs are just a few of many that show a very strong connection—in culture, art, and weapons, though not, at least as far as horses are concerned, in "modes of warfare"—between the Anglo-Saxons (or ancient English people) and the people of Rohan. Several other scholars have made similar observations. See, for example, T. A. Shippey, *J. R. R. Tolkien: Author of the Century* (Boston: Houghton Mifflin, 2000), 90–97. Still, Tolkien's connection of the Rohirrim with the Anglo-Saxons has at least one ironic twist: the real Anglo-Saxons that inhabited England were not, in any sense, lovers of horses.

2. *Beowulf*, ed. J. F. Tuso, trans. E. T. Donaldson, Norton Critical Edition (New York: W. W. Norton, 1975), 5.

3. Sandra Miesel, "Life-Giving Ladies," in *Light Beyond All Shadow: Religious Experience in Tolkien's Work*, ed. Paul E. Kerry and Sandra Miesel (Madison, NJ: Fairleigh Dickinson University Press, 2011), 139.

4. Ibid., 143.

Chapter 3: Frodo and the Wisdom of the Wise

1. "'A Fund of Wise Sayings': Proverbiality in Tolkien" has since been presented elsewhere and was published in *Roots and Branches: Selected Papers on Tolkien by Tom Shippey*, ed. Thomas Honegger (Zollikofen, Switzerland: Walking Tree, 2007), 306–19.

2. Ibid., 306.

3. Ibid., 309.

4. Ibid. Shippey's primary example of a speaker of either worthless or false proverbs is Barliman Butterbur, whose proverbs are "a string of utter clichés" (309). The proverbs of Sam Gamgee and his father the Gaffer sometimes fit this description as well (309–10), and one proverb spoken by an orc is also proven completely false (318).

5. Of course Gandalf does act; he doesn't merely sit around knowing. The point, however, is that much of his doing has to do with either the gathering of knowledge—for example, tracking Gollum around Middle-earth in order to discover what he can about the Ring—or with the passing on of knowledge (that is, teaching): arousing the minds of those threatened by Sauron. The rest of his doing focuses on arousing the hearts of those threatened by Sauron. This is a role we shall consider in chapter 7, exploring Gandalf and stewardship.

6. T. A. Shippey, *J. R. R. Tolkien: Author of the Century* (Boston: Houghton Mifflin, 2000), 9.

7. Ibid., 10.

Chapter 4: Military Victory or Moral Victory?

1. T. A. Shippey, *J. R. R. Tolkien: Author of the Century* (Boston: Houghton Mifflin, 2000), 115.

2. Ibid. A few pages later, Shippey summarizes the impact on Tolkien of life experiences that would have made him more sympathetic to this view than a medieval writer: "The major

disillusionment of the twentieth century has been over political good intentions, which have led only to gulags and killing fields" (117).

3. Ibid., 119.

Chapter 5: Human Freedom and Creativity

1. Matthew Dickerson, *The Mind and the Machine: What It Means to Be Human and Why It Matters* (Grand Rapids: Brazos, 2011). Chapter 5 explores the importance of free choice, creativity, and heroism in Tolkien's writings, in contrast with the free-choice-denying philosophy of physicalism espoused by Richard Dawkins, B. F. Skinner, and others.

2. B. F. Skinner, *Beyond Freedom and Dignity* (New York: Alfred A. Knopf, 1971), 30.

3. T. A. Shippey, *J. R. R. Tolkien: Author of the Century* (Boston: Houghton Mifflin, 2000), 194.

Chapter 6: The Gift of Ilúvatar and the Power of the Ring

1. For a more thorough treatment of magic, see chapter 10 of Matthew Dickerson and David O'Hara, *From Homer to Harry Potter: A Handbook of Myth and Fantasy* (Grand Rapids: Brazos, 2006).

2. T. A. Shippey, *J. R. R. Tolkien: Author of the Century* (Boston: Houghton Mifflin, 2000), 128–43.

3. Ibid., 142.

4. Ibid., 141.

5. Sandra Miesel, "Introduction: Exploring Tolkien's Universe," in *Light beyond All Shadow: Religious Experience in Tolkien's Work*, ed. Paul E. Kerry and Sandra Miesel (Madison, NJ: Fairleigh Dickinson University Press, 2011), 1.

6. In a personal conversation with Clyde Kilby, Tolkien suggested that the *Secret Fire*, a term used interchangeably with the *Flame Imperishable*, is meant to represent the Holy Spirit, the third person of the Trinity in the Christian understanding of God. Rather than contradicting the assertion that the Flame Imperishable is associated with our free will, this strengthens the assertion. The Greek New Testament word for "spirit," used in the title "Holy Spirit" (see Acts 2:4, for example), is *pneuma*, which comes from the word for "breath." But the Genesis 2:7 account of the creation of man in the Septuagint—the Greek translation of the Old Testament—also uses the same word *pneuma* to describe the breath of life given to man as a being with free will made in the image of God: "And the Lord God formed man of the slime of the earth: and breathed into his face the breath of life, and man became a living soul." The word *pneuma* may also be used to mean "life," "mind," or "reason," all concepts associated with free will. Even in ancient Hebrew, the same word used in Genesis 1:2 to refer to the "spirit of God" is also used in Genesis 6:17, seemingly in reference to the *life of man*. It is the life-giving spirit of Genesis 6:3.

7. Dwarves, when they are created, will also be given stature as Children of Ilúvatar, but they will be known as children by adoption. Hobbits are a subrace of men and thus also are among the Children.

Chapter 7: Moral Responsibility and Stewardship

1. Bertrand Russell, "Has Religion Made Useful Contributions to Civilization?," in *Why I Am Not a Christian, and Other Essays on Religion and Related Subjects* (New York: Allen & Unwin, 1957), 37.

2. Ruth Benedict, "Anthropology and the Abnormal," in *An Anthropologist at Work*, edited with an introduction by Margaret Mead (Cambridge: Riverside Press, 2011), 276. The article first appeared in *Journal of General Psychology* 10, no. 2 (1934): 59–80.

3. T. A. Shippey, *J. R. R. Tolkien: Author of the Century* (Boston: Houghton Mifflin, 2000), 132.

4. Ibid., 133.

Chapter 8: The Seen and the Unseen

1. Toward the end of this essay, Tolkien addresses the "Christian Story" contained in the "Gospels." Before doing so, he comments: "It is a serious and dangerous matter. It is presumptuous of me to touch upon such a theme; but if by grace what I say has in any respect any validity, it is, of course, only one facet of a truth incalculably rich" ("Fairy," 155).

2. The absence of this section in my earlier publication, *Following Gandalf*, is my primary regret regarding that book. Along with the new introduction and chapter 1, it is the main addition to this new and revised (and renamed) edition. Though shorter than the other new additions, it is nonetheless at least as important.

3. This is such an important point, and is so central to Tolkien's writing, that it far exceeds the scope of this book. Another of my previous books, *Ents, Elves, and Eriador: The Environmental Vision of J. R. R. Tolkien* (Lexington: University Press of Kentucky, 2006), coauthored with Jonathan Evans, explores this topic in great depth.

4. Sandra Miesel, "Introduction: Exploring Tolkien's Universe," in *Light beyond All Shadow: Religious Experience in Tolkien's Work*, ed. Paul E. Kerry and Sandra Miesel (Madison, NJ: Fairleigh Dickinson University Press, 2011), 3. Miesel also addresses another aspect of gnosticism that I have not touched on in this book. Gnosticism, especially as associated with Manichaean dualism, sees the world as existing in a state of constant battle between two equal and opposite forces, one good and the other evil. If Tolkien had given his readers only the Valar in opposition to Melkor, his writings might well have fallen under an overarching Manichaean form of gnostic dualism. But, as Miesel also points out, Tolkien likewise "avoids Gnosticism by having the One alone originate and realize the themes elaborated by his creature. . . . The Creator is wholly distinct from Creation and retains complete freedom to change matters as he wills" (ibid.).

5. This aspect of the spiritual as well as physical reality, and of the important interconnectedness of the two, is explored in far greater depth in Dickerson and Evans, *Ents, Elves, and Eriador*.

Chapter 9: A Shift in Tone

1. Some of the ideas in this and the next two paragraphs were influenced by a lecture by Keith Kelly: "Beneath the Shadow: Heroism and Despair in *The Lord of the Rings*" (Middlebury College, Middlebury, VT, January 9, 2003).

2. I use the term *monsters* in keeping with Tolkien's own use of the term (from his seminal essay "Beowulf: The Monsters and the Critics") to describe Grendel, Grendel's mother, and the dragon—the collection of evil creatures faced by the hero Beowulf in the poem *Beowulf*. (There is also reference to Beowulf's past battles with various sea creatures, but these creatures are not described in detail, and the encounters happened before the tale begins.) Note that both Grendel and his mother, like the goblins, the trolls, and Gollum, are roughly human in shape and are not wholly unrelated to the human race. A significant difference, however, is that Tolkien gives to all his "monsters" in *The Hobbit* the capacity for rational speech.

3. An argument could be made to add the wolves to this list. Certainly the *wargs* of *The Lord of the Rings* could qualify as "monsters." But for this discussion, I will categorize the wolves as animals rather than treating them as a sixth category of monster.

4. For a further treatment of the anachronism of hobbits, see T. A. Shippey, *J. R. R. Tolkien: Author of the Century* (Boston: Houghton Mifflin, 2000), especially 6–11.

5. In a 1938 letter, after the publication of *The Hobbit* but well before *The Lord of the Rings*, Tolkien acknowledges that George MacDonald is the one Victorian author from whom he derives any aspects of "epic, mythology, and fairy-story" (*Letters*, 31). In a long letter to a fan in 1954, Tolkien is more specific about one element of MacDonald's writing that he draws on, the goblins: "[I] owe, I suppose, a good deal to the goblin tradition (*goblin* is used as a translation in *The Hobbit*, where *orc* only appears once, I think), especially as it appears in George MacDonald, except for the soft feet which I never believed in" (*Letters*, 178). And later the same year, he explains in another letter his shift from *goblin* to *orc*, distancing himself further (though not completely) from MacDonald: "Personally I prefer Orcs (since these creatures are not 'goblins,' not even the goblins of George MacDonald, which they do to some extent resemble" (*Letters*, 185).

6. Gandalf himself must certainly be considered a hero, and he does offer them his time and aid on the quest. However, we must note that even Gandalf leaves the company at a critical moment to take care of more important "pressing business" of his own (*Hobbit*, 187). It is also the case that Gandalf was not motivated by revenge or treasure; the aid he gave to Thorin seemed to come rather from old friendship to Thorin's father and from promises made long before. And I think a strong case could be made that Gandalf's real motivation for the quest was both to help the dwarves grow, from being exposed to Bilbo's values, and to help Bilbo grow by freeing him from the constraints of his small world. In other words, Gandalf was concerned with the character development of all parties that would result from the *process* of the quest rather than any stated *goal* of the quest.

7. This particular wording comes from a personal phone conversation with T. A. Shippey on February 2, 2003. However, similar ideas are suggested in his books.

8. Clyde Kilby, *Tolkien and "The Silmarillion"* (Wheaton: Harold Shaw Publishers, 1976), 59.

9. The meaning of *dûn* also appears in the name *Dûnaden*, meaning "men of the west."

Chapter 10: Ilúvatar's Theme and the Real War

1. Walter Wangerin Jr., *The Orphean Passages* (Grand Rapids: Zondervan, 1986), 14–15.

2. Paul Kerry, "Introduction: A Historiography of Christian Approaches to Tolkien's *The Lord of the Rings*," In *The Ring and the Cross: Christianity and "The Lord of the Rings,"* ed. by Paul E. Kerry (Madison, NJ: Fairleigh Dickinson University Press, 2011), 17–53.

3. Michael Drout, "Tolkien and *Beowulf*: Medieval Materials for the Modern Audience" (lecture presented at the colloquium "J. R. R. Tolkien: Fantasist and Medievalist," University of Vermont, Burlington, VT, March 6, 2003).

4. T. A. Shippey, *J. R. R. Tolkien: Author of the Century* (Boston: Houghton Mifflin, 2000), 37, 192–94.

5. Drout, "Tolkien and *Beowulf*."

6. Martha Monsson, "Craftswomen and Imitation Men: Women in *The Lord of the Rings*" (lecture presented at the annual Tolkien Conference at the University of Vermont, Burlington, VT, April 9, 2011).

7. Boromir fails at some level. Saruman fails miserably. So does Denethor in the end. But Aragorn, Gandalf, Faramir, Legolas, Gimli, and the four hobbits, along with Éomer,

Théoden, and many others who appear on the edges of the story, really are the heroes they appear to be.

8. Shippey, *Author of the Century*, 31.

9. E.V. Gordon, *An Introduction to Old Norse* (Oxford: Clarendon Press, 1927). The similarity between Tolkien's drawing and Gordon's illustration was pointed out to me in person by Professor Jonathan Evans of the University of Georgia.

10. Shippey, *Author of the Century*, 32.

11. Bradley J. Birzer, *J. R. R. Tolkien's Sanctifying Myth: Understanding Middle-earth* (Wilmington, DE: ISI Books, 2002), 63.

12. J. R. R. Tolkien, *The Road Goes Ever On*, quoted in Paul Kerry, "Introduction: A Historiography of Christian Approaches to Tolkien's *The Lord of the Rings*," in *The Ring and the Cross: Christianity and "The Lord of the Rings,"* ed. Paul E. Kerry (Madison, NJ: Fairleigh Dickinson University Press, 2011), 19.

13. Richard Purtill, *J. R. R. Tolkien: Myth, Morality, and Religion* (New York: Harper & Row, 1984), 57.

14. Jonathan Evans, untitled lecture notes for a visiting lecture in a class on "Beowulf and the Lord of the Rings" (Middlebury College, Middlebury, VT, January 20, 2003).

15. T. A. Shippey, personal communication and correspondence, 2003.

16. Purtill, *Myth, Morality, and Religion*, 101.

17. Douglas Anderson, *The Annotated Hobbit* (Boston: Houghton Mifflin, 2002), 151.

18. Jared Lobdell, *The Rise of Tolkienian Fantasy* (Chicago: Open Court Publishing, 2005).

19. For more on this contrast, see Matthew Dickerson, *The Mind and the Machine: What It Means to Be Human and Why It Matters* (Grand Rapids: Brazos, 2011), especially chapters 2 and 5, which contrast a physicalist understanding of humans as biochemical computers with Tolkien's understanding of humans as creative beings made in the image of a creative God.

20. There are numerous examples. Ronald Hutton is a good and recent example, when he concludes an essay as follows: "If [the theology of Tolkien's imagined cosmos] was Christian, then it was a Christianity so unorthodox, and diluted, as to merit the term heretical. . . . That is why I characterize the non-Christian elements in his mythology . . . as 'pagan.' As they represented about two-thirds of the ingredients that made up his imagined universe, they are not an incidental, or mischievous, part of it" ("The Pagan Tolkien," in Kerry, *The Ring and the Cross*, 69). Though Hutton is a thoughtful scholar and his work worth careful consideration, I think his labeling of Tolkien's work as "unorthodox" and "heretical" is fundamentally misguided. Most of my book can be considered evidence to the contrary, with my following paragraphs explicitly addressing the issue of paganism. Where I do agree with Hutton, however, is in his final sentence of the passage just cited—the presence of pagan mythologies was not incidental. But I believe they are deeply rooted in Tolkien's Christian vision and well-supported by a biblical understanding.

21. Although the Jerusalem Bible, a Catholic translation into English, was not published until 1966, it is worth citing from in addition to the Douay-Rheims, as Tolkien contributed to it his translation of the book of Jonah.

22. Thanks to David O'Hara for this translation and for some of the ideas of this paragraph, inspired by a talk presented at Augustana College (Sioux Falls, SD, March 15, 2006). See also Matthew Dickerson and David O'Hara, *From Homer to Harry Potter: A Handbook of Myth and Fantasy* (Grand Rapids: Brazos, 2006), especially 65–92.

23. Again I am indebted to David O'Hara, professor of philosophy at Augustana College in Sioux Falls, South Dakota. This translation and several ideas in the previous three paragraphs were suggested by a lecture he gave at the Augustana College Chapel on March 15, 2006.

24. *Beowulf*, ed. J. F. Tuso, trans. E. T. Donaldson, Norton Critical Edition (New York: W. W. Norton, 1975), 1.

25. The introduction to this book suggests the strong connection in Tolkien's mind between Middle-earth and our world, despite the inconsistencies in geology and the fact that the history of Middle-earth does not connect with any one particular moment in our own real history.

26. Shippey, *Author of the Century*, 218–19.

27. Ibid., 219.

28. Lobdell, *Tolkienian Fantasy*, 149.

29. While forms of gnosticism have proven tempting to post-Enlightenment Protestants, the temptation is far less significant to Roman Catholic Christians such as Tolkien.

Sources

Anderson, Douglas. Annotations in *The Annotated Hobbit*. Boston: Houghton Mifflin, 2002.

Benedict, Ruth. "Anthropology and the Abnormal." *Journal of General Psychology* 10, no. 2 (1934): 59–80.

Beowulf. Edited by J. F. Tuso. Translated by E. T. Donaldson. Norton Critical Edition. New York: W. W. Norton, 1975.

Birzer, Bradley J. *J. R. R. Tolkien's Sanctifying Myth: Understanding Middle-earth*. Wilmington, DE: ISI Books, 2002.

Caldecott, Stratford. *Secret Fire: The Spiritual Vision of J. R. R. Tolkien*. London: Darton, Longman and Todd, 2003.

Carpenter, Humphrey. *J. R. R. Tolkien: A Biography*. Boston: Houghton Mifflin, 1977.

Dickerson, Matthew. *The Mind and the Machine: What It Means to Be Human and Why It Matters*. Grand Rapids: Brazos, 2011.

Dickerson, Matthew, and Jonathan Evans. *Ents, Elves, and Eriador: The Environmental Vision of J. R. R. Tolkien*. Lexington: University Press of Kentucky, 2006.

Dickerson, Matthew, and David O'Hara. *From Homer to Harry Potter: A Handbook of Myth and Fantasy*. Grand Rapids: Brazos, 2006.

Elder, John. *Reading the Mountains of Home*. Cambridge, MA: Harvard University Press, 1998.

Hutton, Ron. "The Pagan Tolkien." In *The Ring and the Cross: Christianity and "The Lord of the Rings,"* edited by Paul E. Kerry, 57–70. Madison, NJ: Fairleigh Dickinson University Press, 2011.

Jacobs, Alan. *The Narnian*. New York: HarperCollins, 2005.

Kerry, Paul. "Introduction: A Historiography of Christian Approaches to Tolkien's *The Lord of the Rings*." In *The Ring and the Cross: Christianity and "The Lord of the Rings,"* edited by Paul E. Kerry, 17–53. Madison, NJ: Fairleigh Dickinson University Press, 2011.

Kilby, Clyde. *Tolkien and "The Silmarillion."* Wheaton: Harold Shaw Publishers, 1976.

Kreeft, Peter. "Afterword: The Wonder of *The Silmarillion.*" In *Shadows of Imagination: The Fantasies of C. S. Lewis, J. R. R. Tolkien, and Charles Williams*, edited by Mark R. Hillegas, 161–78. Carbondale: Southern Illinois University Press, 1979.

———. *The Philosophy of Tolkien: The Worldview behind "The Lord of the Rings."* San Francisco: Ignatius Press, 2005.

Lobdell, Jared. *The Rise of Tolkienian Fantasy.* Chicago: Open Court Publishing, 2005.

Miesel, Sandra. "Introduction: Exploring Tolkien's Universe." In *Light Beyond All Shadow: Religious Experience in Tolkien's Work*, edited by Paul E. Kerry and Sandra Miesel, 1–14. Madison, NJ: Fairleigh Dickinson University Press, 2011.

———. "Life-Giving Ladies: Women in the Writings of J. R. R. Tolkien." In *Light Beyond All Shadow: Religious Experience in Tolkien's Work*, edited by Paul E. Kerry and Sandra Miesel, 139–52. Madison, NJ: Fairleigh Dickinson University Press, 2011.

Purtill, Richard. *J. R. R. Tolkien: Myth, Morality, and Religion.* New York: Harper & Row, 1984.

Russell, Bertrand. "Has Religion Made Useful Contributions to Civilization?" In *Why I Am Not a Christian, and Other Essays on Religion and Related Subjects*, 24–47. New York: Allen & Unwin, 1957.

Shippey, T. A. "'A Fund of Wise Sayings': Proverbiality in Tolkien." In *Roots and Branches: Selected Papers on Tolkien by Tom Shippey*, edited by Thomas Honegger, 308–19. Zollikofen, Switzerland: Walking Tree, 2007.

———. *J. R. R. Tolkien: Author of the Century.* Boston: Houghton Mifflin, 2000.

Skinner, B. F. *Beyond Freedom and Dignity.* New York: Alfred A. Knopf, 1971.

Wangerin, Walter, Jr. *The Orphean Passages.* Grand Rapids: Zondervan, 1986.